"The author acquired a vast amount of insider knowledge that he boldly reveals in this provocative and historically informative book. It will be a fascinating read not only for all Pitt alumni, retired and current faculty, but also for anyone who grew up in Pittsburgh after World War II and followed the growth and development of Pitt from a "street car stop" university into a top level nationally acclaimed institution of higher learning."

–CYRIL H. WECHT, FORENSIC PATHOLOGIST,
PITT '52, '56, '62

"These 70 years of memories vary from the strictly professional and the collegially gossipy to sweet and sour revelations of the conduct of admirable and reprehensible administrators, faculty members, students and friends. The result is an unforgettable bubbling brew of facts and wit."

–ROBERT L. GALE, EMERITUS PROFESSOR OF
ENGLISH, UNIVERSITY OF PITTSBURGH

"The volume did what nostalgia should do. Some parts brought back warm memories, some parts informed, others stirred up pride. The writing is clear, focused and witty. Never paid attention to the inner workings of the University faculty and staff while I was there. I was glad to have that gap in my college experience filled in."

–ROSEMARY RAY, PITT '57

"These critical but fair analyses provide a rare inside, oftentimes humorous, assessment of the sixties up to the nineties. With elegant and precise detail the book zeroed in on what one faculty member experienced during his long tenure."

–JOHN W. HUSTON, MAJOR GENERAL, USAF (RET),
PROFESSOR EMERITUS, US NAVAL ACADEMY (RET), PITT' 57

"As an alumnus and as a journalist for 40 years, I thought I knew a lot about Pitt athletics. But Jim Kehl's book took me behind the scenes, opened doors and answered questions. The information on the Ed Bozik era, and the downfall of Pitt football that came with it, was particularly enlightening."

–BOB SMIZIK, SPORTS EDITOR,
POST-GAZETTE (RET), PITT '65

"I thought that the volume was wonderfully well written, beautifully researched, and held my interest from the beginning to end.... Any reader who has the pleasure of meeting the author through his book will come away from it with the same conclusion—that he is a class act and a man of complete integrity, with high standards that we, as his readers, hope that we ourselves can meet.

The Posvar material is the strongest and most deeply felt part of the memoir.... The folksy quality of the preceding narrative is replaced by a tone of high dudgeon and outrage. I like this section best of all."

–JOHN SCHULMAN, OWNER OF CALIBAN
BOOK SHOP, PITT '87

THE
UNIVERSITY
REMEMBERED

PERSONAL REFLECTIONS ON PITT
AND A FEW OF ITS PEOPLE

THE
UNIVERSITY
REMEMBERED

PERSONAL REFLECTIONS ON PITT
AND A FEW OF ITS PEOPLE

JAMES A. KEHL

WORD ASSOCIATION PUBLISHERS
www.wordassociation.com
1.800.827.7903

ISBN: 978-1-59571-786-3

Library of Congress Control Number: 2012936401

Designed and published by

Word Association Publishers
205 Fifth Avenue
Tarentum, Pennsylvania 15084

www.wordassociation.com
1.800.827.7903

CONTENTS

ACKNOWLEDGMENTS

One glance at the title page will suggest the question: Why isn't this book being published by the University of Pittsburgh? The answer is relatively simple. When an earlier draft of the manuscript was completed, I called Vice Chancellor Robert Hill of the Public Affairs Department to inquire about possible publication.

At first he was interested because, as he volunteered, his office contemplated publishing an in-house update of University developments over the last 25 years. Such a project would have overlapped a significant part of my study—thus the basis for his curiosity.

Dr. Hill confided that his proposed work hit a stone wall almost immediately. He discovered that, if his document analyzed the Posvar years in detail, the Posvar family would be upset. But, if it glossed over those years, the study would understandably be panned for its superficiality.

From my perspective, Dr. Hill had created a paper tiger. Family embarrassment does not equate with legitimate coverage of University events and incidents. I understand that he may not want an analysis of those years to appear under a University imprint, but ultimately the details will emerge somewhere. Why not here!!

Other parts of my volume are perhaps too specialized, too informal, or too mundane to carry an official University label, but throughout the manuscript I consciously focused on portraying the University in a positive manner. Although unique to Pitt, this work is intended as an informative, humorous, and retrospective account of my personal experiences. I sincerely hope that you, the reader, will appreciate that this is only one man's view from inside the University and peruse it in that spirit.

I am indebted to all of the unnamed individuals whose deeds are remembered in these pages. Some have requested anonymity; some were assigned pseudonyms; and still others are nameless because I could not recall their names—only the incidents in which they were involved. In the same spirit that I omitted names, I also ignored academic rivalries, alcoholism, and personal scandals, which I regard as beyond the scope of this work.

I would be remiss if I did not identify those who contributed to the publication process. The late Liz Race flawlessly translated my scribbling to a computer printout; Marianne Kasica and David R. Grinnell at the Archives Service Center of the University of Pittsburgh located and graciously assisted in the selection of all photographs; and Word Association Publishers' Julie Csizmadia was an untiring graphic designer who patiently answered all queries and skillfully brought all parts of this publication together.

My final words of appreciation are reserved for my editors: my wife Barbara and Professor Bob Gale, an emeritus member of the Department of English at the University of Pittsburgh. More than 50 years ago, Bob had been Barbara's mentor in that department, but over the years they evolved different editing styles. They weren't in competition with each other, but after 25 years of retirement, Bob was proving that he is a master; and Barbara was demonstrating that, in a half-century, she has learned a few editorial skills of her own. Unfortunately for my pride, my manuscript was caught between their red pencils. Despite their efforts to prevail, I rejected their sage advice on numerous occasions and stand guilty of all errors that remain.

REFERENCE KEYS

KEYS	REFERENCES
Alberts	Robert C. Alberts, *Pitt: The Story of the University of Pittsburgh, 1787-1987, 1986.*
P-G	*Pittsburgh Post-Gazette*
Press	*The Pittsburgh Press*
Times	*University Times*
Weingartner	Rudolph H. Weingartner, *Mostly about Me: A Path through Different Worlds, 2003.*

INTRODUCTION

A university is forever. Its culture, on the other hand, changes from generation to generation, but not all such changes can be captured in official documents and periodic histories. Some are too minute or too specialized or fail to conform to the theme of a particular writer.

This does not mean that a second formal history, written about the same general period, will greatly expand the knowledge about that institution. All actions that motivate a university in a particular era can never be recovered, but a greater sense of its mythos can be achieved by a less formal approach.

Personal reflections, memoirs, autobiographies, and other remembrances can present a university from the inside practitioner to the outside public. Even while adhering to accuracy in utilizing the same factual materials as an official history, such writers can make an institution more human because they enjoy the freedom to express their thoughts with any combination of humor, sarcasm, burlesque, and innuendo that befits their styles. If the same individuals were writing an official history, they would adhere to more traditional phrasing in defining and enlarging a university's image.

The University of Pittsburgh has been well served by Robert C. Alberts' history entitled *Pitt: The Story of the University of Pittsburgh, 1787-1987*. When Alberts was researching this work, he and I talked on several occasions about specific subjects to be included. In the published version some of these topics were fully covered, others were relegated to a few phrases, and still others were omitted. Such omissions do not suggest a need for another history, but I regard this volume as a supplement to Alberts' work with my reflections on the University's role during the monumental period between World War II and the turn of the 21st Century.

For more than 65 years Pitt has occupied a significant place in my life, particularly the 46 years (1946-1992) that I served as a member of the faculty. During that time I moonlighted as a collector of odd facts and an observer of abnormal behavior, roles that should arouse a chuckle in every reader.

Eccentric personalities and bizarre incidents are no strangers to the college campus or to this volume. After all, both students and faculty are recruited, in part, because of their potential to think "outside the box." That capability is diligently pursued in the expectation that both groups will contribute solutions to society's myriad problems. Most succeed, but a few lose all contact with the box and fail, temporarily at least, with a flair. My reflections focus on out-of-box experiences that can be readily identified by those who have ever stepped into a classroom as student or teacher.

My saga, both inside and outside the classroom, is part of the history of the University community. Divided into three parts, the first examines the University under the inescapable influence of World War II and its aftermath. The second section covers my brief role in administration, plus insights into the careers of chancellors Edward H. Litchfield and Wesley W. Posvar. The third part examines humorous accounts from my teaching career. Appearing in varying lengths, these incidents offer implausible, true-to-life portrayals of the University scene. The subjects range from an instructor who believed that all administrators were enemies of society to an egocentric administrator who was. These two are supplemented by out-of-step students whose indiscretions or momentary lapses were part of the maturing process—quickly modified and generally forgotten.

College students are typical of young people everywhere. Like all of us as we approached adulthood, they resemble so many square pegs seeking to identify with one or more of the many round holes that constitute the mosaic of society. Most plug in naturally; some require a little time and experience to scrape away the rough edges before finding a comfortable round hole; others struggle valiantly before discovering their niche in society; and unfortunately a few are committed to remain square pegs forever in search of a gratifying life.

Straining to find a satisfactory slot was first called to my attention by a ninth grader who taught me a valued lesson in student ingenuity, one that revealed youthful creativity. When assigned as a substitute teacher at the outset of my career, I was presented with an opportunity to test my idealism, and this young man tossed it back at me. Fully convinced that, if humor and enthusiasm were injected into every class period, I was confident that study and learning would follow in due course without specific daily assignments.

After ten days I realized how bankrupt my theory was for students at that age. Disappointed, I promptly turned to daily assignments and sternly requested that the next chapter be outlined in detail. Providing a full week's notice before it was due, I warned the class: "The only excuse that I will accept for failure to complete the outline on time is death on your part!" That seemed clear enough and demanding enough even to ninth graders. I awaited the result without anticipating how Bob would lampoon it.

On the designated Monday this ingenious student was not prepared. Instead of admitting the fact, he dramatized his failure to produce an outline. Remaining outside the classroom with two of his friends until I had called the class to order, he directed his henchmen to carry him into the room, up the side aisle, and deposit him prostrate beside my desk. Like me, most students were clueless concerning the caper.

The class was abuzz as I smiled at the prone form before me. Bob had poured Mercurochrome on his forehead and down one cheek. Amid this substitute blood a black dot, an imitation hole, was penciled on his temple. Befitting a suicide victim, a pistol, cap-gun variety, lay in his hand across his chest, with a sheet of paper tucked into his shirt. On the paper he had scribbled a note liberally sprinkled with blots of fake blood. I picked up the note and read the contents to the class. His supposed last words exclaimed: "It's all your fault, Mr. Kehl; I didn't have my outline finished, so I committed suicide. Tearfully yours, Bob."

My demand had been cleverly and humorously twisted. The class reveled in laughter while waiting for my response to his note. I asked Bob to take his seat; he bounded up sprightly and followed the order. I then explained that creativity was a cherished quality that should always be encouraged, but that the fulfillment of assignments such as the outline was equally essential in order to acquire greater creativity through more extensive learning.

Thus I rewarded this unique effort by giving Bob an extension of three days in which to complete the assignment. The class applauded, and Bob provided the outline on the adjusted schedule. Because of this experience I came to my university career with an open, alert mind for instances of aberrant student behavior such as those presented here.

In the process of selecting the misguided student incidents to be chronicled in this work, I also uncovered a faculty spouse and a Tom Sawyer show-off parent; they added to campus life in my time and soothed the frustrations caused by those who strayed from traditional paths without providing a redeeming clue to their conduct.

Collectively these incidents and their perpetrators represent a by-product of higher education's mission. The focus of the vast majority of those on college and university campuses has consistently concentrated on imparting knowledge, acquiring knowledge, discovering new knowledge, utilizing new knowledge, and the administration of programs designed to achieve these goals. In contrast, the deviant few have caused the campus compass to gyrate sporadically, subsequently returning to a normal heading and charting a steady, positive course.

PART ONE

A WAR-DOMINATED GENERATION

(1940-1955)

By its nature the organization of a college or university includes teaching and administration. Aside from my student role, these functions provided focus for my career at the University of Pittsburgh.

The first part of that experience (1940-1955), however, was controlled by an external force: World War II and its aftermath. Formally that conflict began in September 1939 when the Germans invaded Poland. Never neutral toward the projected outcome, America definitely wanted to see Hitler defeated but expected someone else, France supported by Britain, to deliver the *coup de grace.*

Unfortunately history did not script the result that way. By the end of summer in 1940, the disturbing reality was evident on all fronts. In addition to Poland, Hitler's blitzkrieg had stormed across Czechoslovakia, Norway, Denmark, Holland, Belgium, and France. As a consequence, the United States was forced to undertake numerous "precautionary" measures, including the first peacetime draft in American history. Signed in September 1940, this legislation required all males between the ages of 21 and 35 to register for military service.

That same month I enrolled as a freshman at Pitt. Not old enough for the draft and like most Americans still clinging to the idea that Europe alone could muzzle Hitler, I proceeded with my education. Pitt's enrollment, like that of other institutions of higher learning, suffered a shock from the peacetime draft. After the Pearl Harbor attack, that shock was magnified; the loss of students, prospective students, and some faculty members to the military disrupted the University's ability to function normally.

At war's end the influx of veterans armed with the GI Bill of Rights, plus a surge of high school graduates into higher education, reversed the imbalance; the new conditions turned a paucity of students into a superabundance, with an understaffed faculty on hand to greet them. This combination dictated University strategy in the postwar years and thereby provides the theme for the chapters in the first part of this volume.

Certainly my undergraduate education and my initial teaching assignments were determined by the war, which also proved to the University that the Cathedral of Learning had outlived its ability to sustain expanding enrollments. The third and fourth chapters represent space and personnel problems, respectively, that were mandated by the war.

CHAPTER 1

A Career Takes Form

With more than a little trepidation, I cast a career ballot to continue my education. In September 1940 I enrolled as a freshman at the University of Pittsburgh. A wide-eyed kid, impressed by everything on the campus, particularly the Commons Room of the Cathedral of Learning, I often wondered if I belonged. Could I compete? Could I meet the requirements? My only positive feeling grew from the thought that many—although no member of my own family—had preceded me and were successful.

Inspired by many challenging teachers during my four years at Brentwood High School, I wanted to follow their footsteps into the classroom and become a teacher at the secondary level. Having not experienced any college instructors, I couldn't even aspire to teaching at that level. Fortunately my Pitt professors were superior. Their professionalism crystallized my desire to pursue a teaching career.

My freshman year was uneventful. Aside from above-average grades that appeared on the transcript, there was no significant comment on my progress until early in my sophomore year. In returning a history research paper, Professor John Geise complimented me by saying that he and Professor Ralph Turner, a colleague at Yale University, were planning a volume on the history of world civilizations and that I had shown the potential to join their team as an assistant after graduation.

To me, that was a huge slap on the back, a salutary boost to my non-existent morale. For the first time my thoughts turned toward a college position of any kind. I didn't think to question the meaning of the position he was dangling before me. Was I to be a "gofer"? A glorified footnote checker? A copy editor? As it turned out, I had little time to bask in the prospect of fulfilling any such ill-defined role. The Japanese rained their bombs on Pearl Harbor a few weeks later; the future of a Geise-Turner volume and of my budding career, like the plans of many Americans, was placed on hold and sometimes completely dislodged from the realm of future possibility.

The minds of all Americans were suddenly jolted into the reality of a war that they had hoped would never come. I can still recall my exact location when I first heard the startling reports from the Pacific battle zone. Some of the key words in the news flashes were strange to my ear. Pearl Harbor, Ford Island, and Oahu are terms I was hearing for the first time, but Hawaiian Islands and Honolulu, on the other hand, were already a part of my lexicon. As the war escalated, my vocabulary was enlarged when many other dots on the map acquired significance.

My movements on Monday, December 8, 1941, are still vivid. I attended all three of my morning classes, and each instructor deviated from the day's assignment to reflect on the ramifications of the Japanese attack. Some discussed the possible duration of the conflict, and others talked about the changes of lifestyles that were inevitable. Professor Ford Curtis closed his remarks by poetically reminding us, via Ernest Hemingway, that, no matter what our station in life, "The bell tolls for thee."

As usual I carried my brown bag lunch that day and ate it in the all-male cafeteria on the eighth floor of the Cathedral. I purchased a bottle of Royal Crown Cola and found a seat on a green leather couch alongside a young man I didn't know; all in the room listened to President Franklin Roosevelt's "Day that will live in Infamy" speech on the radio. Never was the room so silent and attentive.

Later that week the student newspaper published an article pertaining to professors' opinions concerning the duration of the war. All projections fell within the range of one to eight years, except that of Professor Carroll J. Amundson of the History Department. He foresaw the struggle lasting a hundred years. Even though it seemed like a wild assertion to me, I interpreted it personally and realized that, if it were accurate, my whole generation of American men would spend the rest of their active lives in the military. That possibility lingered long in my mind.

Many did not take Professor Amundson's comment seriously, because he did not elaborate, at least in the article. Years later, with his 1941 statement still in my memory, I asked him about it and received a cogent response. With Japan, Nazi Germany, USSR, and the US-British alliance all in the war, he knew that not all could be content with the initial result. Thus he anticipated that additional skirmishes would follow.

In part, that scenario was dramatically played out in the Cold War and other conflicts that followed World War II.

As a specialist on Britain and the British Empire, Amundson also understood that the world crisis would be exacerbated by the fact that the empire was already strained to the breaking point: Dissolution did follow gradually after the war. Predicting that the loss of British power in Africa, the Mideast, and other parts of Asia would expose regional hatreds, he forecast only dire consequences. This was his rationale for one hundred years of conflict. As he reminded me when we discussed his "hundred years" remark a decade later, the fighting wasn't continuous in the famous Hundred Years War that bridged the 14th and 15th centuries.

Although not as well known as some of his colleagues, Amundson was well respected by his students. He had come to the University as a graduate student from Oregon and earned a doctorate at Pitt. Tall, broad-shouldered, with short, blond, curly hair and a thin mustache, he was every inch a Scandinavian. Known for his extensive collection of tweed jackets, he was recognized by everyone who possessed the slightest sense of fashion.

When Amundson arrived at one of his classes with a 4" x 6" card, students knew that a superb lecture was about to be delivered. Unfortunately he didn't always carry such a card bearing the outline of his remarks. In my opinion he possessed perhaps the finest mind in the department, but often, personal issues eclipsed his abilities. Although he was my superior in the department and 15 years older, I was always pulling for his sustained genius to appear; I wanted his talents to reach a broader academic audience. With only encouragement and no disrespect intended, I once said to him: "Carroll, you have the greatest mind in the laziest body I have ever seen." He gave me a subtle smile, a shrug of the shoulder, and then walked away.

Immediately following December 8, the University assumed a wartime posture and developed a Civil Defense program. Professor Geise was named air raid warden for the Cathedral of Learning, and elaborate signs were posted in every corridor on every level listing specific precautions to be observed in an emergency. These instructions were intended as guides that would provide order in case of an enemy attack in the Pittsburgh area.

Dr. Geise propounded the theory that under no conditions would enemy bombers attack the Cathedral. He reasoned that, if planes came once, they intended to return and needed a beacon for further strikes at industrial targets, and no more obvious landmark than the Cathedral existed. Ergo, it would always be left standing because future targets could always be identified on coordinates in terms of this prominent reference point. Fortunately, Pittsburgh was never so threatened, and the theory was never tested.

As the weeks and months passed, both the University and the community grasped the war in realistic terms. Like so many others, I was forced to view the war from a personal standpoint. On September 6, 1942, I volunteered for the Naval Reserve's V-7 Program. This required that I stay in school at my own expense, pursue the degree of my choice, study spherical trigonometry and celestial navigation, speed up my program by attending summer school, earn a degree, and await a call from the Navy.

My last remaining requirement in September 1943 was practice teaching. Through the joint cooperation of the local superintendent of schools and the University, I was able to fulfill this assignment in my home school district. I assumed full time, independent responsibility for the schedule of a teacher who resigned to accompany her husband, who had been called to military duty. This placed me in the role of a substitute teacher and entitled me to the grandiose sum of $200.00 per month; I was extremely grateful, because I knew of no one else who was ever paid to complete practice teaching.

My inherited schedule included two classes in Problems of Democracy (seniors) and four sections of Civics (ninth graders). I fully enjoyed the classroom and believed that the students related favorably to me, not because I was a particularly good purveyor of information, but because I was young and enthusiastic. (One specific bit of this student-teacher relationship that prevailed has been described in the Introduction.)

Practice teaching was a rigorous, instructive four months, especially because I was enrolled in two night courses at the same time. The experience convinced me beyond all doubt that I wanted to become a teacher. I graduated during the last days of January 1944 and reported to Navy midshipmen school the following week.

My final undergraduate years had moved smoothly, but the war was an omnipresent force. During those months I had taken a course in the history of American Political Parties from Professor Russell Ferguson. That was the capstone of my undergraduate years. I thoroughly appreciated the course, and Professor Ferguson advised me that I had the proper grasp of that subject matter to pursue a doctoral program. He recommended seeking a PhD elsewhere to broaden my insights, and he provided me with the names of the most prominent professors in the field of political parties: William B. Hesseltine at the University of Wisconsin and Roy F. Nichols at the University of Pennsylvania. Unable to act upon this advice immediately because the Navy was calling, I kept both names in mind throughout the 30 months of my active Navy service.

The midshipman training was demanding and highly informative. I learned more in a short time than I had thought possible. The experience offered proof of what organized study in 12-hour working days could produce. At the end of that training period, I was commissioned an Ensign and immediately assigned to sea duty aboard a newly minted amphibious Landing Ship Medium (LSM) with a complement of 54 enlisted men and 5 officers. Without much fanfare, our LSM 144 was assigned to the Asiatic-Pacific Theater where we participated in the invasions of Lingayen Gulf (Luzon) and Okinawa before preparing to invade Japan. The atomic bomb relieved us from facing that ordeal.

My Navy experience included considerable time as an executive officer of our LSM before being elevated to Captain at the end of the war. These promotions, plus a few harrowing skirmishes, engendered a true sense of accomplishment in me, with perhaps even a little smugness or arrogance.

A demonstration of this attitude came when I exhibited annoyance at a simple Navy rule and its irrelevance at that time. Every three months, fitness reports had to be completed by each junior officer and signed by his commanding officer. One of the questions required the officer to respond to: What would you like as your next shore duty assignment? For the first three or four reports, I requested a billet to teach navigation at a midshipman school. My request was never fulfilled, so I concluded, wisely or unwisely, that no healthy amphibious officer was leaving the Pacific until the end of the war was in sight. To me, the report had become a formality without meaning, so I decided to burlesque the situation by answering the next shore duty question by proposing to recruit WAVES (women) in the Fourth Naval District, which included Pittsburgh.

At first the captain refused to sign my fitness form, arguing that my answer was frivolous. I countered by contending that it was no more frivolous than the question itself. Because someone had to recruit women, I offered to make the sacrifice. Furthermore, I argued that there was as much chance of having someone act on my request as having the Japanese Navy come over the horizon flying the surrender flag. The captain finally agreed, and as long as he remained in command, my reports were submitted as written.

After the war was over, the Navy acceded to my request to teach. Even then it was by accident, not the result of a fitness report. Following a brief hospital stay on Guam, I was temporarily without an assignment. Fortuitously for me, the Island Commander at the time was furious when he learned that sailors were operating their boats so recklessly that a boat a day was being sunk in Guam's Apra harbor. The commander ordered that, after January 1, 1946, no boat could be operated in the harbor without a special license issued by his command. I was enlisted to organize such a training facility, set up a teaching schedule, and inform all offices on the island of the process. All bases were eager to participate and enrolled their coxswains. I taught the rules of the road, tested the students, and issued licenses to those who qualified. After that, punishments for boat accidents were much more severe.

This was my first opportunity since commissioning not only to see the inside of a classroom but also to do what I thought I could do best. The Navy authorities on Guam were so impressed by the results of the boat-handling school that I was asked to establish schools for yeomen and storekeepers.

The Navy was required to discharge reservists according to a point system, and in this hectic time of discharging men and closing bases, yeomen and storekeepers were in high demand, particularly in forward areas such as Guam. I liked the challenge, organized a staff, and found many eager recruits for the program. All went well.

For my schools' project, I was awarded a letter of meritorious service to accompany the ribbons and stars earned during the final months of the war. By May 1946 I found myself in the Philadelphia Navy Yard about to be discharged.

Remembering Professor Ferguson's counsel, that one of the great political historians was at the University of Pennsylvania, I seized the moment to capitalize on that opportunity and establish contact. Lugging my clothes bag and still in uniform, I transferred from trolley to trolley from the Navy Yard to the Penn campus, where I met Professor Nichols in his office. I told him about my desire to work under him, and he shot a battery of questions at me. After an hour of conversation, it was agreed that we might enjoy a constructive relationship. On reflection, I think that he was as impressed by my arrival directly after being discharged that morning as by my qualifications. I had certainly demonstrated eagerness.

Wanting to be at home for at least a short time, I enrolled in summer courses at Pitt in June 1946 on the assumption that they could be transferred to Penn at a later date. During that summer the chairman of Pitt's History Department asked if I would like to teach several sections of the American History survey course beginning in the Fall. Because of my strong desire to teach, I concluded that my Penn venture could be delayed and gleefully accepted the offer to teach college-level courses with independent responsibility.

Several days later the chairman called me back to his office to inform me that the History Department at Carnegie Institute of Technology (CIT and now CMU) faced a crisis; a history staff member had announced his immediate resignation the day classes began. Pitt was asked to recommend a one-year temporary replacement, and the chairman nominated me. I accepted the challenge with the proviso that I could retain one course at Pitt, because I did not want to lose that connection for the future.

The 1946-1947 academic year was difficult, exciting, and highly instructive. I loved every minute of it. At CIT, I met numerous individuals with whom I remained friendly through most of my career. At the same time I developed a good relationship with members of the Pitt department.

In the following year, Pitt was so overwhelmed with an influx of students that it was forced to open a temporary campus in Shadyside, known as Ellsworth Center. I was asked to be the historian at Ellsworth, a position that I accepted and held for three years (1947-1950) before resigning to become a student at the University of Pennsylvania.

Although long delayed, this was obviously the proper decision, but my conservative nature brought a little doubt to mind. I was reluctant to surrender a regular salary check with no proof that there would be a vacancy upon my return.

I, therefore, asked Dean Stanton Crawford to grant me an official leave of absence. His response was negative, because it was University policy not to extend leaves to instructors. I accepted that, but surprisingly several weeks after I arrived at Penn, I received a letter from Dean Crawford apprising me that he had discussed the matter of leave with the chancellor. He was now writing to inform me that the chancellor wanted me to know that there would be a position for me in the History Department upon my return.

To me, that letter was as positive as any official leave of absence. My career was definitely beginning to unfold with broader horizons than I could possibly have envisioned ten years before when I stood at the University door as a freshman.

**1930, The Cathedral, like the University
Itself, a Work in Progress**

Photo courtesy of Archives Service Center, University of Pittsburgh

CHAPTER 2

Skyscraper U

Tall buildings do not grace the skylines of most college and university campuses. The University of Pittsburgh is a notable exception. Its Cathedral of Learning, the most photographed structure in the city, is recognizable worldwide. As a result it suggests the first image that comes to mind when the University is mentioned. No chancellor, no distinguished scientist/scholar, no logo, no discovery, no marching band, and no athletic record flashes across one's mental screen as quickly as one or more of the many views of the Cathedral.

Ever since its "declared" completion in 1937, the Cathedral of Learning has towered over the city's Oakland section. Groundbreaking had occurred in 1926, and only six years later, under primitive conditions, the first classes were held in the partially completed structure. Heat to individual classrooms was provided by electric or kerosene stoves vented out the sides of the building. Years later my senior colleagues who taught under those austere distractions pointed to the darkened stones on the sides of the Cathedral that marked the spots where the exhausts had stained the walls.

In those forbidding years, a student's knowledge wasn't enough to assure success in a course; with the nearest rest rooms across the street in the Schenley Hotel (now the William Pitt Union), good bladder control eased the anxiety of class attendance. It would be difficult to find more demonstrable evidence of the University's pressing need for added classroom space.

From the first projection of the Cathedral of Learning idea, stern opposition both from the community and within the Board of Trustees was evident. Critics questioned whether or not a Gothic skyscraper answered the school's educational needs. At times their hostility was vicious; some scoffed at the Cathedral as "an inverted mine shaft"; those less discreet dubbed it "Bowman's last erection" or "the height of ignorance."

By 1935 the one-upmanship competition in epithets had assumed a national dimension. In a *Time Magazine* article (July 15), the widely acclaimed American architect, Frank Lloyd Wright, described the Cathedral as "the most stupendous 'Keep off the Grass' sign I've ever seen." About the same time rumor persisted that the Cathedral's expertly manicured lawn was more heavily endowed than any of the University's academic programs. An incident from my freshman year of 1940 might contribute a small piece of evidence to tie this wealthy lawn theory to the architect's infelicitous slur.

In need of exercise, a friend and I proposed to catch ball on the lawn between the Cathedral and Heinz Chapel, a site clearly visible from the chancellor's office window. Unknown to us, the chancellor was watching. At the time this was a signal occasion for me, the only time during my undergraduate career that he acknowledged my presence. Within ten minutes after we two ballplayers stepped onto the green stuff, a marshal, with the chancellor's urging, ordered us to cease and desist and in the future remember to "keep off the grass." Since it was a beautiful, sun-filled afternoon and since we were the only ones engaged in any lawn activity at the time, perhaps most students had interpreted Wright's "sign" as he had so quaintly characterized it.

In the early stages of the structure's development, a significant minority of prominent locals, that at first included financier-philanthropist Andrew W. Mellon, expressed only skeptical endorsement of the Cathedral idea, but Chancellor John G. Bowman aggressively pushed construction. The progress he anticipated was unfortunately stymied when the national depression deepened. Funds for this grandiose project were drying up, and in 1932 the chancellor called a halt to work on his would-be edifice.

The same year those disgruntled with Dr. Bowman personally and/or with his Cathedral plan discovered an incident through which they might rebuke him. The occasion was graduation, and the chancellor had invited General Douglas MacArthur, the retiring Army Chief-of-Staff, to deliver the commencement address. At the time the nation was shrouded in a dense fog of isolationism, and the chancellor's adversaries decided to emphasize this prevailing sentiment in their attempt at embarrassment.

They challenged the idea of bringing a "militarist" to campus because his message would undoubtedly sway the minds of the young graduates in the wrong directions. Their publicly declared intentions to picket commencement, always a prominent date on any university calendar, captured the chancellor's immediate attention. Add to this the fact that the chancellor disdained all negative publicity, and a confrontation was in the making.

Dr. Bowman decided that, if threat became reality, he would be prepared to squelch any disruption of the solemn exercises scheduled for Pitt Stadium. With the Director of Athletics in charge, the strategy was designed to prevent any picketing. A Pitt faculty member, accompanied by a Pittsburgh police officer, was stationed at every entrance to the stadium. When the well-dressed, well-mannered pickets arrived in taxis, they alighted with placards in hand. Before they could raise these standards in protest, a Pitt professor stepped forward at each gate to ask his police escort to arrest the would-be pickets, who were thus prevented from ruining Bowman's day.

The savvy pickets asked to be taken before a judge, not a justice of the peace or an alderman. Fortunately or unfortunately they appeared in the courtroom of Judge Michael A. Musmanno, who seized the opportunity to ally himself with the Cathedral critics.

When he asked the officers what offense had been committed, the police explained that the defendants were about to picket. The judge keyed on the phrase "about to picket" and blistered the policemen for bringing these individuals to court for an offense that had not yet taken place. Regarding this as an illegal action, he dismissed all charges and released the pickets.

Musmanno then turned to the Pitt officials and lectured them on their role in this miscarriage of justice. His concluding remark was a biting indictment: "Higher buildings do not necessarily make for higher learning." [This version represents the lore handed down by my predecessors.]

During the Cathedral's early construction period, Pitt sponsored a student theatrical troupe known as Cap & Gown. Annually it wrote and produced a musical/comedy revue that displayed its artistry to the public at the posh downtown Nixon Theater and used the stage to lampoon the building problems of this sometime controversial structure. Over the years the show's most distinguished student performer was Gene Kelly of "Singin' in the Rain" fame, and one of its most memorable skits poked fun at the University for failure to complete the Cathedral's interior. A straight man asked: "How is the Cathedral like a drunk?" The comedian's response, "It's kinda high, but not completely plastered," brought rousing applause from audiences.

By the time I reached the campus as a freshman in 1940, the building's physical condition had been updated. Classroom décor still featured unplastered walls of red tile and mortar, but a central heating system had been installed. Although distracting in appearance, some radiator pipes conducting the heat were totally exposed, obviously installed after the concrete floors had been poured. This was apparent from the oddly shaped holes cut through the floors to permit the extension of piping from one level to another.

I cannot vouch for the cause of this unsightly appearance, but according to Cathedral lore the engineers/architects temporarily overlooked the need for a heating system until after the first floors had been constructed. To support this claim, I can recall a room on the third floor where an observer could peer through an inch and a half hole around the heating pipe and have a limited view of a desk and a student's arm in the room below.

I imagined a small piece of chalk falling through the opening, passing the nose of the student listening to a lecture, and landing on the desk. Although tempted, I never dropped the chalk, probably because I knew that genuine pleasure would come only from seeing the stunned face below, but every time I think about the potential of such an incident, a smile brightens my mind.

The completion of all classrooms, lavatories, and hallway ceilings wasn't realized until the Litchfield era (1955-1964). A regularly scheduled visit from the Middle States Association of Colleges and Universities prompted this final burst of activity. My most vivid example of this last push was the completion of the Ladies Room on the 29th floor, the floor assigned to the History Department. With its roughly poured cement floor and no fixtures, despite the lettering on the door, it had served as the storage room for the department's office supplies.

My personal awareness of the Cathedral of Learning's semi-complete status even predates its official opening in 1937 by a few years. Between 1931 and 1934 my sister and I accompanied our parents to occasional Sunday evening musical/religious programs at Syria Mosque. Since my father disliked driving in Pittsburgh traffic, we drove the family car to the Carrick streetcar terminal, parked, and boarded the Galloping Fraction (77/54) trolley that dropped us at the intersection of Forbes and Bigelow. To reach the Mosque (now razed), we had to walk a block up Bigelow past the imposing Cathedral construction.

As a ten-year old, I was unimpressed by the sprawling network of steel beams with wings jutting out in various directions; I didn't think of it as being steel or iron and didn't know the difference. I can't recall that my parents commented about the project as we walked by; even if they had used the term *college* or *university*, neither would have had meaning for me; certainly I had no thought that within eight years I would be enrolling as a freshman.

On subsequent Sunday evening jaunts to the Mosque, the steel framework still appeared undeveloped to my eye, but at the core of the construction, a building was taking form. I noted that the partial structure was loosely surrounded by a huge canvas or other cloth that flapped eerily in the night wind. It remained for history to let me know that the project had been shut down due to a lack of funds.

Even when the construction was restarted, Chancellor Bowman was aware that another financial crisis could occur. If such a critical juncture were reached, he feared that the University trustees would advise him to put a roof on whatever was completed at that moment, a confrontation he wanted to avoid. According to the lore, stonework on the lower floors was deliberately left undone while construction continued skyward. The chancellor knew that, if a scarcity of money did become a factor, the trustees could not demand that he put a floor under it. Thus his architectural dream was realized and ultimately reached a full 525 feet in height without further disruption.

Today it's difficult to imagine that the chancellor understood the ramifications of his cathedral. He had literally built a vertical campus. Aside from the health complex, the School of Engineering and Mines, the departments of Chemistry and Physics, and the Physical Education facilities, it was a university jammed into 42 stories.

This was home to four professional schools (Business including Economics, Education, Law, and Social Work) and 15 departments of the College of Arts and Sciences (Biology, Classics, English, Fine Arts, Geography, History, Mathematics, Military Science, Modern Languages (French, German, and Spanish), Music, Philosophy, Political Science, Psychology, Sociology, and Speech). In addition, the Cathedral housed such essential support offices as the Bookstore, Chancellor's Office, College Office, Dean of Men's Office, Dean of Women's Office, Evening Division, Faculty Club, Mail Room, Men's Health facility, Provost's Office, Registrar & Admissions, Treasurer's Office, Tuck Shop, University Library, University Press, Women's Health facility, and 87 classrooms.

VERTICAL TRAMS

Key to the functional success of this configuration was the elevator system. With four elevators designated as local (traveling between the Ground Floor and the 18th, but stopping only at 1, 5, 8, 10, 12, 14, 16, 17, and 18), and four more called express elevators stopping only at 1, 17, 18, 21, 24, 27, 30, 33, and 36, the system for many years was denounced as inadequate before it was ultimately updated. (These numbers are meaningless except to all those who depended on elevators to convey them to classes, libraries, and faculty appointments for four years.)

The floors above 36 are occupied mostly by elevator machinery, except for the Babcock Room, a penthouse conference area (40th floor) that is reserved for special meetings. It can be accessed via a special elevator from 36, but the key to that lofty retreat is retained in the Chancellor's Office and issued only to those with VIP status.

Faculty, staff, and students were all at the mercy of the elevator system until the campus spread over various parts of Oakland. The elevator crunch was most acute in the mornings and in the brief ten-minute periods between classes. Frustrating delays, class tardiness, missed appointments, and general exasperation were all attributed to elevator overloads. Such rationales were generally true, but the unwritten rules of elevator etiquette made the system tolerable. On the Ground Floor at the busy times of the day, an accidental brush or bump of another, with the appropriate *mea culpa*s, was an inevitable part of the routine.

As a junior member of the faculty in the late '40s and early '50s, I was unsure of the proper conduct when boarding an elevator. If I were standing next to an elevator door that opened, was I expected to enter the car or stand back and allow women to precede me? If I deferred to women on a busy morning, the elevator could be filled with me still waiting at the gate. That didn't seem equitable. On the other hand, it appeared impolite if I entered first, so I compromised. I would allow a few women to enter to show that I did possess at least a modicum of good manners; then I would break into a rush for the elevator and be aboard before the operator declared a full complement.

Once in, the male riders traditionally doffed their hats in deference to the women present, a practice that has become passé with the trend toward social informality. Riders tended to greet those around them, whether known or unknown. I endeavored surreptitiously to learn the names of the frequent riders at my arrival times so that I could greet them by name. Many were those with whom I had no contact other than the morning elevator commutes.

One such person was a nationally recognized social activist whose attitude was expressed wholly through her teaching and professional writings—never verbally in an elevator. A stately woman with a slight morning smile and tailored suits, she was known to me only by reputation.

A second regular rider was also a social scientist of about the same age (40-ish), but his demeanor was the opposite. Loud, jovial, with tousled hair, his appearance suggested that he regularly dressed in the dark. I was unaware that these two were any better acquainted than the woman and I were, but one day in early 1948, I learned that they had just been married. Because I knew the man, a popular instructor with underutilized talent, quite well, I could conjure up no scenario to explain how they were compatible; they seemed potentially combative.

The presidential election that year may not have contributed to the downfall of their marriage, but it did provide a humorous clue to their basic differences. In keeping with her social orientation, the wife expressed her commitment to George Wallace, who was seeking the presidency on the Progressive (third party) ticket. Displaying an 8½" x 11" photo of Wallace prominently on the living room piano, she gave visual evidence of her preference to her husband who, as a supporter of Thomas E. Dewey, was at the opposite end of the current political spectrum.

Every time he passed the Wallace photo, he turned it face down without uttering a word. In response the wife returned George to an upright position when she detected that he had been banned from view. In a semi-serious tone, the husband, an Air Force veteran, remarked to me in mid-August: "One day I had to turn that damned smiling face down seven times."

As election day approached and the political campaign heated up, the struggle to determine whether George was destined to stand on his own two feet or lie face down in the dust of the piano intensified. If only the couple had possessed two photos of the Iowa chicken-farmer-turned politician, they could both have claimed victory. Minus that reality, plus a few other salient details, the two divorced shortly after the November election, an announcement that surprised no one. I can't say that they met in a Cathedral elevator, but if they did, that would add luster to existing elevator lore.

Throughout the early decades of the Cathedral's existence, experienced but disgruntled riders attempted to "out-think" the elevator system. At peak hours of service, if they were on floors 5 or 8 particularly and wished to descend, these elevator jockeys would signal for an elevator to take them both up and down. If the Down-car arrived first, all was well. If the Up-car was first on the scene, the rider stepped aboard, believing that the quickest route to the ground was achieved by going up. This was based on the assumption that the other local elevators going down would be loaded to capacity before reaching floors 5 or 8. By going up to 18, the rider was assured that that elevator would take him to his destination.

This technique often proved to be most expeditious for the rider, but at the same time frustrated the operators because they were forced to carry the passenger in opposite directions to achieve one result. Occasionally an elevator reached the 18th floor fully loaded with riders who had no intention of getting off although it was the end of the "line." They all wished to be returned down past the floor where they boarded. Thus no new riders could be accommodated.

This percentage game was also played on the express elevators. Potential riders headed for the Ground Floor who were starting from floors 21 or 24 often opted to ride to 36 to assure their downward passage. Of course, individuals never knew for certain whether or not their circuitous route beat the established system. But when an elevator stopped at 21 or 24 going down because an operator failed to push the bypass key, the rider frequently identified those still waiting to board as those who were there when he elected to go up; he beat the system, at least for the day. Riders were confronted with this version of roulette three or more times a day. Those on 5 especially enjoyed a viable alternative; they could walk down, an option I exercised regularly in both my student and teaching days.

Frustrated by long elevator delays, one graduate student lamented that, when Chancellor Bowman dreamed about a Cathedral of Learning, he was dreaming vertically rather than horizontally. The student concluded that, if the Cathedral were lying on its side, there would be no need for elevators, thus no need for elevator lobbies and elevator shafts. That configuration, he argued, would have alleviated another major problem: the paucity of classrooms. With the Cathedral on its side, those 36 elevator lobbies, complemented by the eight elevator shafts, would have created 36 spacious classrooms, satisfied spatial needs, and prevented all the aggravation caused by elevator delays. [For this practical solution the student was awarded an "F" in aesthetics.]

At times the wait for an elevator seemed interminable, particularly to individuals stalled somewhere between the Ground Floor and either the 18th or 36th. An elevator might stop at a specific floor when ascending while the individual waiting there wanted to go down. The next time that the would-be rider saw that same elevator, it was again going up; it had bypassed that floor going down because it was already loaded to capacity. An individual with a sense of humor who understood the problem might say: "I guess it went down on the outside of the building." After a more extended wait, another might quip: "It looks as though we missed the 4:30 and must be content with the 4:45." One truly agitated rider yelled: "Elevator! Elevator! We got the shaft."

During one memorable week in this era, the concept of elevators operating on a time schedule became "serious business." In early September 1946 the employees of the Duquesne Light Company went on strike, and no electricity was supplied to the University; that severely crippled elevator service. With classes about to begin in several days, it was imperative that faculty, staff, and administrators reach their offices in the Cathedral to make final preparations.

Although the University owned an emergency auxiliary generator for such crises, it provided only enough power to service one elevator on a limited basis. Operation was confined to several trips in the morning, likewise at noon, and a few in the late afternoon. No trips took place during the intervening hours; those determined to reach any floor were shown the stairwells.

Under this in-house generated power, the elevator ran so slowly that I could run down from the 29th floor as fast as the elevator, making its many stops, could descend. At that speed, if a rider missed the 4:30 run, he was fortunate if the next opportunity to ride came by 4:45. If he failed to make the 5:15, he was doomed; the options were few: to walk down or remain overnight; I know of no one who took the latter alternative.

Just as the vertical campus depended on the elevators to whisk individuals to their destinations, the operators, in turn, had the task of doing so with dispatch. All elevators were manually controlled in the early years, and those at the helm were generally men retired from other occupations. Eligible for social security, they were not beneficiaries because the act granting retirement benefits had not been passed until 1935; not all details had been resolved immediately and that left men seeking employment in such capacities as elevator operators.

Being elderly, the operators' reflexes were slow and deliberate; several also wore hearing devices, often ineffective amid the din of the Ground Floor noises. This was a distinct disadvantage to affected operators because they alone had access to the control panel. When a rider called out his floor, the hearing-impaired at times pushed the wrong button or no button at all.

On occasions when there were few riders, I spoke with one particular operator during our many ups and downs. In those conversations I learned that he had served as a street-car motorman, like several of his colleagues, for more than 30 years. That explanation helped me to understand why he had a surprised look on his face at times when he turned the lever that propelled the car upward. After having reflexively felt the motion of a trolley with a similar lever for so long, he subconsciously expected the car to move horizontally—thus the momentary surprised facial expression when the elevator did not head for Forbes Avenue or Fifth Avenue.

Gradually the core of operators changed. Younger men took charge, none more debonair than George. In his late twenties, George exhibited pride not only in his clothes, but also in his shoes, always polished to a high shine. More provocative than his dress, however, was his monologue about his riders, again a sharp contrast to his mute fellow operators. George seemed compelled to comment on riders' apparel, particularly men's neckties, and he treated a college freshman and a college dean as though he didn't know the difference.

George and I were part of an incident that I can vividly recall. The express elevator did not stop at the History floor (29); that meant that riders like me were forced to walk down one or up two.

On numerous evenings during George's tenure, Bob Duncan and I, two young history instructors, went to dinner and returned to our 29th floor office for a few hours of study. If we were the only riders as the elevator neared our stop in those off-hours, we would prevail on George to let us off at 29 instead of the stipulated 30. We argued that it was not an extra stop and inconvenienced no one, a logic that George accepted.

After some weeks of this special treatment, George reminded us of his kind gesture and asked that we reciprocate by buying a one-dollar chance on $500.00 being raffled off by his church. We now saw George's logic; Bob handed George a dollar, filled out the stub, and I promptly handed Bob a 50-cent piece. (They were actually in circulation in those halcyon days.) Bob and I temporarily forgot about our purchase, but by the luck of the draw we won the money. George paid off in 500 one-dollar bills.

Bob received our loot when I was in class. When I returned, he shut the office door and asked me to sit at my desk with my eyes closed. He proceeded to drop the 500 ones over my head. As they cascaded across my desk and onto the floor, he yelled: "We're rich!" and told me about our good fortune. We scooped up the cash, paid George ten percent, went to dinner, and split our winnings. That was a tidy sum in those days, especially since neither of us earned that much in a month.

After 6:00 PM the elevators had a changing of the guard. Some were shut down, and the others were operated by part-time student employees with a member of the regular crew in charge. When that supervisor stepped out for a snack or cigarette, the window for high jinks was opened, particularly during the hours of least rider activity. A common practice found two part-timers racing each other to the 36th floor and back to the Ground or an operator "lending" his elevator to a friend for a personal round trip spin. [Is there any among us from that early elevator era who at some moment didn't have the urge to seize the "joy stick" and take off just for the thrill?]

Once when the night crew wasn't vigilant, a student admittedly "stole" an elevator for his late evening pleasure. After setting off for a carefree ride to the 36th floor, he started to descend before his mental processes kicked in. He began to wonder what reception awaited him when he opened the gate on the Ground Floor. Would he be lectured? Would he be banished from the building? Would the elevator police be on hand to escort him to jail? With these possibilities flashing before him as the elevator seemed to be plunging rapidly downward to his destiny, he immediately pushed the Stop button; it happened to be at the 8th floor; he jumped out, ran down the steps and out of the building.

ELEVATOR PRELIMS

The elevators were an unforgettable part of campus life. Thousands of people utilized the elevator system every weekday, with the peak hours being from 8:00-10:00 AM. In those two hours alone, hundreds converged in the Cathedral's Ground Floor lobby in an effort to reach their classrooms, libraries, and offices. They came from far and near by varied modes of transportation.

Pitt was accurately labeled a streetcar college obviously because each day a vast majority of students arrived by trolley. In the '40s and '50s, some came from McKeesport and Beaver via a combination of train and trolley. A few came by bus, and others were dropped off by parents or neighbors en route to downtown employment. Still others walked, and particularly after World War II, more and more arrived by auto, not only from Allegheny County, but also from surrounding counties.

Those electing to travel by car faced an arduous task in finding suitable parking. Oakland possessed few parking lots in those years, and the streets and free parking spaces in Schenley Plaza were inadequate for the demand. Although car-pooling was definitely in vogue, the problem remained acute. Some parked in Shadyside or Schenley Park and walked as much as a mile after their arrival. Those who competed for the close-in parking spots were forced to adopt creative measures, partly because parking meters were not yet widespread in Oakland. Since the Schenley Plaza spots were free, they naturally filled by 7:45 AM. Pitt faculty and students were challenged for them by downtown workers who drove in from the suburbs, parked free in the plaza, and boarded a trolley into the city.

A friend of mine was trapped in an incident that demonstrated how selfishly drivers vied for position. Bill spied a girl attempting to extricate her car from a choice space in the plaza that he hoped to occupy. The girl was in the one row of slots perpendicular to Forbes Avenue that permitted traffic to flow both behind and in front of the spaces. The car in the slot next to the inexperienced young lady was parked at an acute angle that made her unparking difficult.

Bill wanted the space so badly that he hopped out of his car to direct her maneuvering from the space. Before he could reenter his car, another driver from the back side slipped into it. Although he witnessed the incident unfold, the greedy little wiseacre nevertheless occupied Bill's space. An argument ensued, but Bill had been aced out; the other driver slammed his door and walked nonchalantly to class.

Bill left and managed to locate a vacant space near Phipps Conservatory where Pitt personnel had to contend with Carnegie Institute of Technology staff and students. When Bill walked back past the spot that was rightfully his, he let the air out of two of the "clever" driver's tires. If I had gone to that much trouble, I would also have thrown away the valve stems to prevent a hasty pumping up of the tires.

In another phase of the parking crisis, one student received dubious assistance from his uncle, an officer assigned to traffic detail in Oakland. Although head-in parking was permitted on the Bigelow side of the Cathedral, there was a specific point near Fifth Avenue where parking spaces ended and the taxi stand began. The uncle assured his nephew that, if he parked in one spot beyond the legal ones, he would not be ticketed. That illegitimate practice worked well until other students observed the nephew's daily parking pattern without receiving a ticket. They were unaware of a sympathetic uncle, gambled, and parked there. This converted the nephew's one-time certainty to an uncertainty. An added problem occurred when the uncle was off duty and his replacement didn't honor the special privilege; with several tickets on the windshield, the nephew had to reappraise the value of his original parking advantage.

I participated in a more sophisticated strategy. A group of us discovered that the janitors at Mellon Institute began work at midnight, at an hour when they faced no competition for choice parking spaces along Bellefield Avenue. As a result their shift ended promptly at eight in the morning when parking was at a premium in that area.

Our idea was to drive up Bellefield from Forbes precisely on the hour and hope that one of the ten or so "janitor" spaces would open up. In time our technique was honed to perfection; we would identify specific cars as those belonging to janitors and, at the top of the hour, double-park alongside one of them until the owner appeared; if someone beat me to a particular car, it was necessary to resort to Plan B and double-park by another "janitor" car.

This practice created a traffic jam in the Bellefield block between Forbes and Fifth. To our frustration this, in turn, attracted police attention, and the street was more rigorously patrolled. With that surveillance, our only retaliation was to keep moving as slowly as possible up Bellefield and hope that a janitor emerged exactly as one of our cars was arriving near his spot. Once the janitor was in his car, the police considered it legal to double-park and wait for him to pull out. This was certainly no precise science; many drivers circled numerous blocks several times before identifying an open space. Hopefully the search ended in time for the driver to meet his first class. To make certain that it did, many arrived at 7:30 for a class that met at 9:30. In addition to meeting a class schedule, parkers had to contend with the elevator scramble once they had arrived at the Cathedral.

Parking was merely a prelude to the indoor jockeying that took place in the Cathedral's Ground Floor elevator lobby. Students, faculty, and staff approached the building from all four sides; even those who entered on the first floor routinely walked down a flight of steps to begin their elevator quest because experience had proved that, in the mornings, Up-cars were generally filled to capacity before they left the lower level.

For decades Pittsburghers' most popular meeting place was said to be under Kaufmann's clock at the corner of Fifth and Smithfield. But the hundreds who gathered every weekday morning on the Ground Floor of the Cathedral might contest that distinction. That lobby was a rapidly changing sea of humanity where those seeking express elevators swayed to one side and those needing local cars pushed toward the other. To an outsider the scene suggested chaos with a slight hint of order.

Individuals in no particular hurry contributed to a clogging of the system by stopping in the lobby to greet each other, to arrange transportation home, to plan lunch, to exchange notes, or to check on a meeting time. The faculty was as guilty as anyone else in creating the bottleneck; they adopted the lobby as a fitting gallery to chat about world affairs, politics, a university program, or a forthcoming conference. But, despite all of these imperfections, the system worked; the vertical campus survived, functioned, and progressed through the '40s and '50s until a horizontal campus developed, its size threatening Oakland and its prominence capturing the attention of the world.

AN ADDENDUM OF CATHEDRAL FACTS

A. When the University moved to its Oakland location in 1908, the architectural design for the new campus was first patterned after the Athenian Acropolis. This Greek model was intended to take form on the hilltop above Soldiers and Sailors Memorial Hall. Ten years into the building program, development was stalled by a lack of funds. Shortly thereafter the architectural style was changed. A new chancellor, John G. Bowman, directed construction away from the Acropolis and toward a Gothic model that gained approval. The result was the Cathedral of Learning, and with that decision the die was cast: The original design was shelved, and the University was anchored in Oakland forever. Although the exorbitant cost of city property hindered expansion and although rapid improvements in transportation made flight to the suburbs inviting, such a possibility for the University was only a brief flirtation in the minds of a few; it never progressed beyond the dinner table; whatever glimmer existed died with the appointment of Edward H. Litchfield as chancellor.

B. One of the University's best hidden secrets was the telephone switchboard. Designed to be that way, it was located in a windowless room on the third floor in a passageway running on the Forbes-Fifth axis.

In those pre-electronic days of the '40s and '50s, all phone calls were routed through a single switchboard with live operators who were seldom seen or known to others in the University. All incoming callers provided the operators with the name or extension desired, and all outgoing callers had to supply the operator with the number to be called. The process was cumbersome by today's standards, but the operators were unbelievably efficient and helpful.

I had never thought about switchboards or attempted to match faces to operators. That changed one morning when I was conversing with a student in the Ground Floor lobby. As he departed to catch an elevator, a woman approached me and exclaimed: "Mr. Kehl, I'm pleased to meet you and see what you look like." I had no idea of her identity or why she spoke to me in that manner until she introduced herself as Ann, the switchboard operator. She explained that she had heard me speak to the student and recognized my voice. She had heard it many times on the phone, as was true with most of the faculty whom she knew only by their voices. Now we both had faces to go with our voices.

Ann was one of Pitt's most popular employees, both inside and outside the University. She was recognized on the phone lines throughout Pittsburgh and Pennsylvania primarily by the way she answered incoming calls—proclaiming simply in a clear and cheerful tone: "University" with the crescendo on the final syllable.

C. The Cathedral was on fire at least once. I have a good reason for knowing; it happened in my office during my deanship. No flames shot from windows, and no mass evacuation occurred, but it showed enough potential for a catastrophe to bring the Pittsburgh Fire Department to the ninth floor.

One of the women in the office had decided to enjoy a little tea with her lunch and proceeded to heat a cup of water on the marble windowsill of the conference room by using an immersion heater plugged into an electrical outlet. When the water was hot, she pulled the warmer out, placed it on the windowsill, and neglected both to unplug it and to discern that it was touching the fiberglass draperies, which in a short time were ablaze.

When the fire was detected, someone, probably the same someone who made the cup of hot water, called the Fire Department which responded immediately, driving a fire truck up the sidewalk to the Fifth Avenue entrance and cracking more than a half dozen flagstones in the process. The firemen proceeded to ignore their cardinal rule for civilians regarding fires and elevators—never take the one to escape the other. In full regalia they alighted on the ninth floor. In this instance I was pleased that they had overlooked the rule, because they were able to extinguish the blaze with a minimum of damage. The furniture and carpeting were untouched, but the draperies had to be replaced and the walls repainted.

For the first time I realized how much oxygen a fiberglass fire draws from the atmosphere. Since it was payday and one of the girls was perturbed lest her purse and paycheck be lost, I volunteered to enter the general office, not the conference room where our junior inferno was raging, to retrieve the purse. That was near enough to place a strain on my lungs; my breath was sucked out of me for a minute, but the firemen were eminently successful because of their gas masks.

I had two regrets as a result of the fire. Every time I walked out the Fifth Avenue entrance and observed the broken flagstones, I felt guilty— partially responsible because my office caused the cracked stones. I couldn't wait until the University replaced them and took away my guilt by association. Also I was disappointed that the forgetful woman who caused the incident never confessed.

Only one of two individuals could have ignited the fire; to remove all onus from the other, in my opinion, she should have acknowledged her mistake. Assuming that sooner or later she would step forward, I never attempted to place the blame.

D. Sad to report, there was at least one suicide from the Cathedral, from its 13th floor, but no significance should be attributed to the number. I didn't witness it but came within a minute of doing so.

That section of the floor was composed of a large general room surrounded by individual offices shared by the Geography and Philosophy departments. On this particular Friday afternoon, I was working with Hib Kline, the Geography chairman, on the details of his budget. The discussion lasted longer than anticipated. I emerged in a hurry, anxious to beat the rush hour traffic on my way home.

In that large outer room, I encountered John, a philosophy professor, accompanied by his wife and daughter. John had been on medical leave so I went over, shook his hand, and expressed my pleasure in seeing him back. Knowing that he was an avid tennis player, I asked: "How soon will we see you on the court again?" He smiled and muttered: "Not soon." I continued on my way without inviting further discussion since they too seemed anxious to leave.

John mentioned to his wife that he had forgotten a certain book in his office and returned to retrieve it. When he didn't emerge as quickly as she thought he should, she turned and headed for his office. She screamed, and Hib Kline ran to the scene, finding John teetering on the window ledge. He lunged at John in an attempt to pull him back and succeeded in grabbing only his ankle. He held on for just a minute before his strength gave out, and he had to release his grip. I have often wondered: What if I had taken more time to converse with John and his family? Could this tragedy have been averted?

E.   At various times all of us have jested (or meant it) that we were subjected to a deadly dull professor. I don't think that I fit that professorial category and offer this disclaimer, because a woman did die in my classroom. [With or without my denial, critics are likely to be coy and say: "I thought as much; now we have the evidence."]

During one term I taught an early evening class of 55 students, many of whom were nurses. They were present in numbers because an American history course was a requirement for those who proposed to practice in Pennsylvania's public schools. A woman sitting in the middle of the classroom suffered a seizure that caught me completely off guard. She was a nurse herself, and fortunately those sitting on each side of her were also nurses; this offered a better scenario for an immediate response team than fiction writers could have assembled. The nurses understood the symptoms at once; men scattered the chairs, and they eased her onto the floor.

I ran to the Information Room to summon the University doctor, H. Clifford Carlson, a former basketball coach of renown with whom I had good rapport. Because this was past normal working hours, Doc was not in his office but at home a few blocks away. I informed him that a student, a middle-aged woman, had suffered a seizure in class and that I needed his immediate assistance. His reaction dumbfounded me: "Kehl, I haven't had my dessert yet." I kept explaining how serious the situation was; he kept insisting that he was not going to come.

During that conversation a student came down from the classroom to report that the woman had died. With that information in hand, I asked Doc to come and pronounce her dead. His reply was: "Kehl, your diagnosis is good enough for me. If you say she's dead, I believe you. Now call the police and have her taken to Presbyterian Emergency where an intern will confirm your diagnosis. Let me get back to my dessert." He never came, and I never fully forgave him. The ruddy-faced, bald-headed doctor realized that the incident lingered in my mind. Every time thereafter that he greeted me in the elevator, he would say something light and humorous; when appropriate to the slightest degree, I would reply: "At least I don't have to comb my hair with a washcloth."

F. In no respect is the University of today and that of six decades ago more divergent than in the realm of security. The present security force numbers 74 uniformed officers who are housed in a new Forbes Avenue building of their own, bear weapons, and provide the campus with 24/7 protection. To assist in their assignment and move quickly about campus, a dozen motorized vehicles are at their command. This is in complete contrast to the University's need and concept of security in the 1940s and '50s. Then a part-time marshal, almost as lonely as the Maytag repairman, donned a blue smock with a plain gold-plated button on his lapel, and patrolled the first floor of the Cathedral, primarily to enforce the few rules governing the Commons Room: no smoking, no food, and no feet on the furniture. No other law officer existed.

In those early years enforcement of conduct on the streets, even those that ran through the campus, rested with the Police Department of the city. Today the University police and the Pittsburgh police share responsibility for keeping streets, students, residents, and private property in Oakland out of harm's way. This cooperation has been a happy and rewarding response to the need.

G. The Book Center with its distinguished marquee location on Fifth Avenue serves as a University showcase. Not always a part of the campus "high rent district," it had been known as the Bookstore during its earlier years in the Cathedral. The name change accompanied the change of address.

Originally assigned space on the first floor of the Cathedral, along the corridor running from the Forbes Avenue side to the Fifth Avenue entrance, the Bookstore outgrew those parameters by the end of World War II; since then the area has been refurbished and converted to the Croghan-Schenley conference room.

The Bookstore's second location in the Cathedral was on the Ground Floor, occupying all the space from the Tuck Shop, along the Fifth Avenue side of the building, to the Bigelow corner.

CHAPTER 3

Ellsworth Center

With the vertical campus reaching untenable limits by the end of World War II, long-range relief was still years away. The ever-increasing number of high school graduates seeking a college education and the rapid influx of veterans exposed the severity of the classroom need.

The veterans, in particular, approached the challenge of college with mixed emotions: an eagerness to succeed and a fear of failure. The latter result would mean time lost from their lives in addition to the years spent in the service, but perceiving the GI Bill of Rights as a bonus earned on the battlefield and redeemable only in the classroom, many were determined not to let this educational opportunity slip away; it was a dream waiting to be realized.

In 1946 Pitt, forced to resort to a series of band-aids, rented space in Soldiers and Sailors Memorial Hall, Carnegie Lecture Hall, the Young Men's Hebrew Association (YMHA), the Historical Society building, and nearby churches. Despite all such efforts these supplements were not equal to the demand.

The next year the University took a bold stride forward and created a temporary campus called Ellsworth Center in the original Shadyside Academy building. Pitt had purchased the structure during the war and first used it to train military personnel in the Army Specialized Training Program (ASTP). Although most ASTP trainees were housed and instructed in the Cathedral of Learning, those being prepared as occupation engineers, for duty both during and after the war, were accommodated at Ellsworth.

While attempting to alleviate the classroom crisis with the establishment of Ellsworth, Pitt inadvertently created a potentially hostile minority environment. Initially criticism came from some of the 700 men who were the first students at the Center. They emphasized what they had to forego by not being on the Main Campus, but gradually they recognized that the experience constituted one of the most constructive aspects of their academic careers, particularly for the veterans.

Pitt's situation was not unique. After World War II institutions of higher learning across the nation were faced with an overflow of students compared with the classrooms available. Response to the space problem called for heroic methods, and Pitt answered with the creation of Ellsworth Center, an off-campus campus at the corner of Ellsworth and Morewood avenues (facing on the latter), about a mile from the Main Campus, a site on which Winchester-Thurston later built its private school complex.

Pitt's offshoot campus performed briefly (1947-1951) on the academic stage before the term "Ellsworth Center" was erased so completely from the University lexicon that today, more than 60 years later, almost no one can recall its existence. During that four-year active period, however, Ellsworth was a vital cog in the education of 2500 men in the College of Arts and Sciences.

The late 19th Century architecture exposed the age of the 3-story brick building. Its oiled wooden floors and box-like windows further revealed its longevity, but it did possess the basic essentials to conduct classes. Because it had been a preparatory school for boys, the University was able to effect the necessary remodeling in a short time in order to handle the September 1947 enrollees, but no magician could disguise the fact that this was not the towering Gothic Cathedral of Learning where most of the Arts and Sciences classes were conducted. The small, highly skilled administrative staff consisted of Viers W. Adams as director, Fred Lange as assistant director, Dorothy English as librarian, and several secretaries, all of whom exceeded normal expectations in carrying out their duties. Although more accessible to students than their counterparts on the Main Campus, these administrators couldn't convey to the incoming freshmen and sophomores that they were in a comparable setting to those studying at the Cathedral.

Instruction was delegated to three types of faculty: part-time members whose total responsibility was at Ellsworth; regular faculty from the Main Campus who were designated to teach one or two sections of their departments' basic courses; and faculty whose full-time responsibility was at Ellsworth. Only three departments (English, Math, and History) assigned full-time faculty to the Center. I was the historian chosen for the one slot, and in reflection the appointment was a controlling factor in my career. I had only a master's degree and one year of teaching experience (divided between Pitt and Carnegie Institute of Technology).

Although unaware at the time, I possessed a worthy substitute for both a doctorate and classroom experience. Like two-thirds of my students, I was a veteran of WW II. Because I had been a Navy officer with combat experience and because all my veteran students had been enlisted men in various branches of the service, they had confidence in and respect for my opinions. They often placed different "spins" on war issues than I did; that enlivened informal exchanges that they initiated before class, after class, and during my office hours.

I was 25 years of age when I arrived at Ellsworth in 1947, and a third of the students—all veterans—were older. The younger two-thirds were rather evenly divided between veterans and young men fresh from their June high school graduations. These 18-year olds had presumably retained their disciplined study habits, techniques that many veterans had to recapture after a hiatus of two to six years. In truth, most had never considered college until the GI Bill provided an impetus; to that group, learning the study fundamentals was often a new challenge, more frightening than the substance of their courses.

There was much humor and good-natured kidding as I informally exchanged thoughts with students, but one incident genuinely embarrassed me when I mistook a veteran for an 18-year old. When I implied that he could not appreciate what some veterans had experienced, he felt slighted that I had not considered him to be one of them. He promptly raised his shirt to expose much of his chest and exclaimed: "See that scar? That's where the Japs got me." Whirling around with his shirt still held high, revealing a scar on his back, he added: "That's where it came out." Three years after I left Ellsworth, I was married. When that same veteran became aware of the fact, he and his wife drove 70 miles round-trip to deliver a wedding gift.

My failure to identify this student as a veteran in our first encounter can be attributed to the fact that he did not appear like most veterans who were distinguishable by their dress. Some wore Army jackets with civilian shirts and slacks; others mixed military trousers and civilian shirts or vice-versa. The uniform parts were a badge of honor to some, but to others their uniforms were their best clothing.

Frankly I joined this "cross-dressing" brigade, partly because I am thrifty and partly because my uniform was in excellent condition. Also, the navy blue, tailor-made, J. B. Simpson uniform, with the brass buttons replaced by plastic and the gold braid snipped off, gave the appearance of a distinguished double-breasted suit. Despite this outward impression, I knew that it was basically a uniform.

Perhaps the altered uniform still reminded the students of my Navy days; at any rate my sometimes blunt, provocative comments caused many students, particularly veterans, to view me as their ombudsman. This assumption was crystallized by an incident in which I acted like a Navy officer, not a teacher, when an indignant student interrupted my lunch to explain that the cafeteria personnel had charged him ten cents for a cup of hot water.

Originally he had purchased a cup of tea for ten cents; when he returned to ask for a second cup of hot water only, planning to use the same tea bag, he was charged another dime. Common sense suggested that something was awry, so I accompanied the offended tea drinker to the cafeteria manager who told me in no uncertain terms that a second payment was necessary and that this was none of my business.

Only 18 months out of the Navy, I wasn't accustomed to being told off. I struck back, demanded that the hot water be free and that in the future all others should receive the same courtesy. The manager advised me that I would be reported to the director, the dean, and the chancellor. I added, "Don't forget God!" but my common-sense decision stood without any administrative flak.

Because a significant number of students witnessed the incident, it quickly circulated through the campus grapevine. Despite the trivial nature of the tea affair, I was an overnight hero for championing their cause. Thereafter I seemed to be their choice to discuss issues with the administration. Although the director was always accessible and cooperative with students, they preferred to have me represent them. When they held social functions or recognition programs, they invariably invited me to emcee their events. When they established their own fraternity, the University required that they have a sponsor. I accepted.

In these early years, I was more concerned with my classroom techniques than with the price of tea in the cafeteria or with keeping a fraternity group in check. Specifically I wondered if I objectively presented ideas on which I held a definite bias. I was particularly concerned about the upcoming election of 1948, which had been discussed numerous times in my classroom in the weeks before the November balloting. Pollsters, editorialists, political scientists—all predicted that Thomas E. Dewey would defeat Harry Truman's bid for reelection.

By the morning after the election, everyone knew that a major political upset had occurred. As I walked down the corridor that Wednesday trying to collect a few thoughts about Truman's victory to share with the class, a student walked out to greet me. He blurted out: "We did it! Truman defeated those sanctimonious Republicans. I helped; I'm the first member of my family to vote Democratic since the Civil War."

Assuming that I might pick up at least one version of Truman's triumph, I asked why he, with his family background, had voted to keep Truman in office. His answer shed no light on my immediate concern but was reassuring because it vindicated my possible bias toward one party or the other. "Because of what you said in class the other day" was his reply. I didn't believe that my words had prompted his vote, and I certainly didn't tell him that I had voted for Dewey, but thereafter I never worried much about my objectivity.

Designed only for freshmen and sophomores, Ellsworth Center did a remarkable job of presenting a broad range of courses. Although it offered no courses in Classics (Greek and Latin), Fine Arts, and Geology, the students otherwise made their selections from the same menu of courses available on the Main Campus. That first year I taught four sections of the survey of American History and two sections of the standard Western Civilization course. That translated into 267 students each term or approximately 40 percent of the student body.

Despite the University's most resourceful efforts, it could not prevent the Ellsworth students from claiming that they were being treated as second-class citizens, an underprivileged minority that had to fight for its rights. They accepted their lot, waged an honorable fight, and in the process developed an esprit de corps that carried not only into their years on the Main Campus but also into later life.

Their complaints about being segregated from the center of student activities took numerous forms: (a) They didn't have as many time slots at which they could schedule a particular course; (b) They complained because they couldn't take Latin or Greek but were unable to identify one student who actually felt deprived; (c) Because of their isolation, they were excluded from social activities such as writing for the *Pitt News* and being rushed by fraternities; (d) Science students who had to go to the Main Campus for their laboratory sections complained because of their split schedules; and (e) The litany about having no women in their classes was heard everywhere.

Trying humor as a means of mollifying their discontent over their female-free society, I pointed out that, if young ladies had been present, I would not have supplied the classes with Truman's off-color description of the vice presidency. Likewise I explained that I would have bypassed the reasons for William Randolph Hearst's expulsion from Harvard during his freshman year, but neither seemed to compensate.

Because I had a high percentage of the student body in my classes and was accessible eight to five, Monday through Friday, I heard a repetition of these frustrations, some of which were unsolvable. But, I did help with their fraternity when they decided to create their own. Knowing that Phi Beta Kappa was the most prestigious honorary organization and certain that they did not aspire to that lofty status, the Ellsworth students concluded that they would reverse the letters and be known as Kappa Beta Phi.

Not recognized by the Inter-Fraternity Council, they nevertheless won recognition as an official University organization. Like other fraternities, they held regular weekly meetings, known as Beer Mondays, at a grille on Forbes Avenue, just off Craig Street. As their sponsor, I tried to attend most weekly meetings, put down a buck for a pitcher of beer, and departed as soon as possible.

In those years, the University sponsored spring festivals on the lawn of the Cathedral of Learning. All campus organizations were invited to sign up for a booth or tent. The Kappa Beta Phi men viewed this spring event as an opportunity for this frustrated minority to assert itself campus-wide and arranged to have a tent that featured Princess Lackanooky and her court. (*Nooky* was a slang word used by soldiers and sailors in the Pacific Theater during WW II to denote sex. Like *snafu*, but unlike *fubar*, nooky survived into the postwar world.)

One of the Ellsworth students, a.k.a. the Princess, dressed only in a grass skirt with a pink lei around "her" neck and a fat cigar in her mouth, stood barefoot outside the Kappa Beta Phi tent. When crowds gathered, the Princess performed a hula dance accompanied by a little South Seas music.

As anticipated, the dean of women walked through the various displays to see that decorum was being preserved. Present at her arrival and prepared with my most dignified manner, I introduced her to Princess Lackanooky, who bowed as graciously as she could with a cigar in her face and then added a little hula twist. The dean smiled and asked to be escorted into the Princess's tent where she thought something more risqué might be concealed. As we had scripted it, I was to stammer and then suggest that such a visit would be a waste of the dean's valuable time.

She took the bait and became insistent. Exhibiting reluctance, I led her inside where she observed three nattily attired young men seated at a table and eager to dispense literature on the American Red Cross, the American Heart Association, and the University health and insurance programs. They stood to acknowledge a surprised dean who could only compliment their civic-minded volunteerism. Spoofing the dean, as well as all students who entered the Princess's tent expecting a more provocative display, was the highlight of Kappa Beta Phi's venture.

All of my experiences as an Ellsworth faculty member engendered similarly pleasant memories. Even a sustained absence developed a humorous twist. When a senior professor became ill and no one was available to teach his advanced course in American Political Parties for a month, I volunteered, partly because of my subconscious feeling of remoteness at the Center and partly because of my conscious desire to have the chairman and all the senior professors recognize that I felt qualified and prepared to teach an advanced course.

I was probably given the assignment because I had made myself available, not because I was fully qualified. Acceptance required that I give up one of my survey sections to a substitute instructor for the four weeks because its time-slot conflicted with that of the advanced course. During that month students who were enrolled in the course that I had "abandoned" saw me around Ellsworth teaching my other courses and repeatedly asked when I would be returning.

On the Monday morning when I settled back into my normal schedule, the "abandoned" students applauded, and one came forward to present me with a gift to celebrate my return. I opened a box containing a necktie that this accomplished artist had painted. The tie depicted a nude on a blue and gold background; the class roared. I thanked him but observed that I couldn't wear it around the University unless hidden under a turtleneck sweater. Trying to show my appreciation and deal with reality at the same time, I asked him to take it back and at least provide her with a bathing suit. He obliged and the following week returned it wearing a bikini. I wore it the next day and then retired it to the box where it remains today.

Numerous similarly humorous incidents occurred in the informal atmosphere of Ellsworth. One happened when I discovered that two students had cheated on an examination. Seated next to each other while writing an essay on the Whig Party, they both spelled the party "w-i-g." Their novel explanation was that they had studied together. Seeing the humor in that, I was relating it to a colleague in the corridor when a know-it-all secretary butted into the conversation. Listening for a moment, she blurted out: "Any idiot knows that it is spelled 'w-i-g-g.'" I assured her that she was absolutely correct, and she strolled off almost as self-satisfied with her comment as I was with my retort.

Only when students left Ellsworth's smaller, less formal classes to complete their education on the Main Campus did they start to realize what a forceful impact that experience had had on their minds. Student friendships established at Ellsworth were stronger bonds than any new ones made later; likewise their ties to faculty were more intimate than those developed thereafter.

As time passed, I became increasingly aware of these emerging attitudes. That point was driven home some years after Ellsworth closed its doors; a young man moved into the seat next to mine on the trolley, called me by name, and stated that he was from Ellsworth. At that time I prided myself on knowing the names of former students but had to apologize because I did not remember his. He interrupted me: "I was never in your class, but we were at Ellsworth together." Like others, his tie to the Center was obviously a connection that he cherished and wished to preserve.

I was often the beneficiary of such favorable student reflections on Ellsworth. One became a businessman who took pride in inviting and introducing me as a speaker before his branch of the Chamber of Commerce. Another asked me to be the best man in his wedding in the nation's capital, and I accepted. Later he presented me with an oil painting, his own creation, which hung on our dining room wall for years. He has died, and I am in the process of shipping the painting to his widow, because he created only a few works in oils and the family wishes to preserve this one.

After I completed my teaching at Ellsworth, I took a leave to pursue a doctorate at the University of Pennsylvania. At that point, an Ellsworth "grad" invited me to visit at his family home in nearby Norristown. There I discovered that his family owned or leased a small airplane, and he gave me an aerial view of Philadelphia and later sought my opinion on his forthcoming marriage.

Still years later, another Ellsworth student, separated from his family and almost financially destitute, fell ill and called for my help. He had been admitted to a Veterans Hospital in Central Pennsylvania, where he was thoroughly unhappy. He prevailed on me to have him transferred to the VA facility in Aspinwall. Not familiar with VA procedures, I was nevertheless able to make the contacts necessary to effect the transfer. Once he was relocated, I invited him to spend several Thanksgivings with our family; a fellow Ellsworth veteran extended similar Christmas invitations, but regrettably the poverty stricken colleague died while at Aspinwall.

But one of the most improbable renewals occurred when, after 30 odd years with no contact, an Ellsworth student called with a question. He was moved to pick up a phone because his wife, apparently stymied while working a crossword puzzle, couldn't fathom the clue: a 19th Century American politician. Because the word contained two *Ns*, plus at least one *O*, one *C*, one *I*, and one *L*, she and her husband at first concluded that the answer was *Lincoln*, except that the proper word contained an additional letter.

The former student gave me a big buildup, saying that he told his wife that, if anyone in Pittsburgh could come up with the answer, I could. We chatted for several hours, but I failed to live up to his hype. With the challenge running through my mind, I deciphered the answer the next day and called him with the name of Roscoe CONKLING. Seven or eight years later, I received a call from his wife informing me that Stan had died; she asked if I would speak at his memorial.

Unwittingly by such incidents, I have been involved in the lives of these students only because I was identified with Ellsworth. After their two basic years of instruction, these students looked back with pleasure on their Center experiences. Time had taken them out of Ellsworth, but no amount of time could take Ellsworth out of them.

For all who passed through, Ellsworth had been more than their introduction to higher education. The University had attempted in 1947 to duplicate the academic programs of the Main Campus and succeeded spectacularly. Because of relatively small classes and a closeness of students with each other and with the faculty, these students, particularly the veterans, developed a bond that they needed and appreciated. Thus a University invention that sprang from necessity created for many a significant and enduring sidebar to the learning process.

CHAPTER 4

At the Edge of the Surreal

In the late 1940s American college and university classrooms were inundated with students. The burgeoning population and the enticements of the GI Bill of Rights created a greater demand for qualified instructors than the teaching profession could satisfy. Of necessity faculty members were often engaged without a complete check on their qualifications. Even when such reviews were conducted, evidence demonstrated that the applicants were the best available. The following local account portrays one of many desperate needs to meet the overwhelming staffing crisis.

A FOREIGNER TANTALIZES THE CAMPUS

After World War II when Americans began traveling abroad in larger numbers, Europeans were concluding that many of us were sanctimonious chauvinists. In 1958 that stereotype was validated when captured between the pages of *The Ugly American;* but a decade before that book's publication, Pittsburghers were already being treated to a counter-attack by Reggie Shortstraw, whose antics were sowing the seeds for a sequel, the ugly immigrant.

An Englishman by profession, Reggie joined the history staff at the University of Pittsburgh as an instructor in 1948 through the most improbable of circumstances. Despite his charm and wit, his lack of experience, training, and aptitude, coupled with his unwillingness to change, condemned poor Reggie as a misfit by all standards of the teaching profession, here and abroad, almost before he had a chance to utter his first "bloody bloke."

When Reggie first arrived in America, he carried a bag of confused beliefs including skepticism about the American national resolve. That attitude precluded an easy transition; in fact, his acceptance of reality lagged so badly that he still hadn't come to terms with the American Revolution.

Amazed that in less than two centuries America had achieved unchallenged stability and phenomenal growth, Reggie stood nonplussed but found consolation in believing that our nation "lacked sophistication." His sentiments could have been mollified if only he had stopped at Independence Hall to spit on the bell before completing his journey to Pittsburgh. With such a side trip, he may have not only gained a measure of closure with the past but also modified the negative image of his about-to-be-adopted homeland. Because no such expectoration occurred, an unabridged Shortstraw reported for duty.

Reggie suspected that our democracy was superficial and our quest for money insatiable. Taking delight in pontificating about those assumptions, he, for some naïve reason, concluded that freedom in America signified that everyone was free to act almost according to his own whims, a misconception, but one of the few aspects of American society that he heartily endorsed.

This misreading of reality caused Reggie to exhibit a perverse pleasure in analyzing one situation after another. In addition, his ignoring of custom and defying of order were first interpreted as "cute" and helped him win superficial acceptance because his outbursts were almost always humorous—and after all, he was a foreigner. In time, however, the comedy vanished, and his antics bewildered and bedeviled many who had to contend with them on a daily basis.

The accolades in behalf of diversity, opportunity, and accomplishment in American life that he expressed were often facades for his oblique criticisms. Perhaps justified in pointing out that our nation had not maximized its advantages and that England had done more with less, he simultaneously applauded and questioned American conduct in world affairs. Knowing that he was on our turf, his observations at times were thinly veiled in order to hide his disdain. On one issue, however, he was forthright, encouraged by a few sympathetic colleagues who thought that having criticisms fall from the lips of an outsider gave the comments greater credence. Good-naturedly but firmly, he rejected the growing role of women in society. Long before there was a National Organization for Women's movement in the United States, Reggie was actively trashing its concepts.

He identified an alarming trend: Women were gaining control of the nation. As he interpreted developments, America had assisted England in winning two world wars, but was losing its masculinity because of the fallout from the women's suffrage amendment that had been a part of the American Constitution since 1920. He further warned of the ominous consequences lurking in a statistic that portrayed the hands of widows manipulating the purse strings of major corporations. Likewise he found no solace in the fact that women had doffed their kitchen aprons and were showing little temerity in being pictured in beer and cigarette commercials. But even more disturbing to him was the spectacle of a female depicted as the Statue of Liberty. In addition, he often blundered into snide remarks about sending women to college and escaped being branded a male chauvinist only because he preceded that application of the term. Thus no one can deny that, in his view of the world, the gender issue stood unresolved.

Reggie vacillated on acceptance of American consumer culture. Outwardly he complained that, despite our social reforms, we remained too competitive and individualistic, but he secretly hoped that there was enough "rags to riches" potential remaining in our economy to permit him to make the transition. Reggie had arrived in America low on funds, a condition from which he never recovered, and his financial status was not based as much on a substandard salary as on an inability to manage. As a result he frequently experimented with ways to enhance his income.

In a sense Reggie visited his anxiety about money on the next generation of Shortstraws when he decided that the names of all three of his children should reflect his pecuniary obsession. With the help of names drawn from monetary denominations in three national coinage systems, his children were christened Mark, Penny, and Franc.

Mark, the first-born, was burdened with the task of attracting funds to the family coffers; to achieve this goal, he was assigned two middle names. Thus his birth certificate carried the extended moniker of Mark Williams Deadlock Shortstraw. The "Williams" honored Professor John Williams, the department chairman, who, Reggie hoped, would be charitable in remembering him with salary increases and promotions. The "Deadlock" was to attract his estranged Uncle Roger Deadlock, whose affection Reggie wished to recapture so that his name might be restored to the old gent's will. Unfortunately, neither ploy yielded the dividends anticipated.

The monetary purpose behind the other names was less ambitious. Recognizing that his copper-haired little girl needed a financial boost, Penny was assigned McNickel as a middle name. Franc, on the other hand, was considered a name sufficiently stable financially to stand alone.

Two incidents of financial need, one involving checks and the other cigarettes, vividly conveyed to me Reggie's continuous struggle to remain socially afloat. Having never opened a checking account before his arrival, he attempted to impose his own vacuous theory on the banking system. He thought that banks should be more understanding of individuals who experienced too much month at the end of their money. Expecting banks to indulge his insufficient funds for two or three weeks, he couldn't understand why his repeated overdrafts gave bankers financial apoplexy.

One day as I walked into the office, Reggie was on the phone with the bank manager who reported that his account was once more overdrawn; his only response was, "Ah! Not again!" As a teenager I had been lectured by my parents to the effect that writing a bad check was stealing and would not be tolerated by them or society. Apparently I hadn't forgotten that bit of instruction and stood aghast at Reggie's nonchalance. To him it was the same as being five minutes late for class—it always happened.

Never embarrassed, he always seemed jovial about his plight. In an expansive moment he shared his discovery about cigarettes that greatly simplified his expenses. He noted that smokers impatiently lit up while waiting for an elevator, only to take a few puffs before the elevator arrived; the cigarette had to be extinguished and deposited in a receptacle: thus his deduction that the largest butts were in elevator lobbies. When Reggie lacked the cost of a pack, he made the rounds of the elevator lobbies on various floors of the Cathedral of Learning to procure his cigarette supply for a few days. This was the first of numerous clues that, to Reggie, economics trumped hygiene.

In his mind his salary was never enough; he was certain that he needed an invention such as an electric mousetrap or an intriguing idea that Americans reputedly employed to hasten their ascent up the economic ladder. With no scientific or mechanical skills, he recognized that his financial outlook could be brightened only by creating a novel concept, but on the false assumption that Americans were gullible for any innovation, he completely botched his first get-rich scheme.

At that time television had not yet made a major impact on the local market, and radio was adapting to the newest leisure fad in popular culture—listening to phonograph records. The radio industry was attempting to capitalize on this trend in music by featuring programs on the *music for reading* theme. Shortstraw considered this counterproductive for a nation with a craze for record collecting, because nearly every household possessed a phonograph and every young person spent part of his allowance/salary each week on the purchase of at least one record featuring a favorite orchestra or vocalist.

Individual collections were growing rapidly, styled to personal tastes. Reggie concluded that the radio emphasis should be on reading, not music. Thus he proposed a program consisting of *reading for music* whereby members of the radio audience would play their own records at home while he, with his melodious English-accented voice, would read the classics over the airwaves.

Rather than quash this cockamamie idea, his thoughtless friends encouraged him to pursue it by recommending that he take the next step and personally seek out a sponsor. Armed with this bad advice, Reggie for some undefined reason decided to overlook such local prime candidates as US Steel, ALCOA, PPG, and Gulf Oil and gave a local furrier, Max Azen, the first opportunity to profit from underwriting his reading/music scheme.

With the thought of easy money on the horizon, Reggie was bold beyond normal understanding. He scheduled an appointment with the furrier's CEO to present this new music concept. On the day after his absurd meeting, I inquired about his reception. "I didn't even get in to see Max," a dejected Reggie responded, but this failure didn't end his quest; instead, it launched him on an endless and futile search for a short-cut to affluence, his personal attempt to validate the Horatio Alger folklore.

The root of Reggie's bizarre presence in Pittsburgh can be traced to his World War II duty as a young Royal Navy officer in the European Theater of Operations. During a joint

US-British operation, Reggie met Carroll Amundson, a lieutenant commander in the US Navy who in peacetime was a Pitt professor of English history. On several occasions the two chatted over a few brews, and from their conversations two bits of crucial information became lodged in Amundson's mind: In the prewar years Reggie had been a law student who had emerged from the program without a degree, and he aspired to relocate to America after the war.

When peace came, Amundson returned home to resume his teaching career. Like every other professor at the time, he was overwhelmed with students. Not only the normal flow of high school graduates to college but also a mass influx of veterans stormed the classrooms, enticed into the halls of academe by the GI Bill of Rights. More alcoholic than workaholic, Amundson was not thrilled by the task before him, especially when a high percentage of the GIs wanted as much education as the government would provide gratis and opted for professional, as well as baccalaureate, degrees.

One of the most popular graduate pursuits was the study of law; that placed added pressure on Amundson because a common assumption maintained that his course in the History of English Constitutional Law not only afforded a valuable background, but also served as an eye-catcher for law school admission committees. The result was particularly disturbing to Amundson because this was his least favorite course to teach even though students were clamoring to take it.

When he tried to curtail enrollment by requiring a survey course in the history of England as a prerequisite, his plan boomeranged. Because he also taught the survey course, they signed up for it in order to qualify for the constitutional history. To his consternation that magnified his student burden all the more.

In desperation Amundson sought a quick fix and thought he had found his answer when he spied Reggie Shortstraw's name on a list circulated by the English Speaking Union as one who now formally declared his intention to migrate to the US. Adding this to his recall of Reggie's law school background, the professor mumbled a joyous "Eureka!" Certain that his teaching dilemma was resolved, he hurried, not to be confused with walking, to his department chairman's office with the suggestion that Shortstraw be invited to come to the campus as an instructor in English history. His proposal consisted of two parts: The constitutional course would be Reggie's primary responsibility, and he could advance himself by assuming a student role and working toward a doctorate.

Providing exaggerated statements about Reggie's capabilities based on his brief wartime contacts, Amundson convinced the chairman, and then the dean, to offer him a position. The proposal intrigued the dean because, with no foreign scholars on the history staff, this would give the department an international dimension of sorts.

Shortstraw accepted the terms and thereby consummated an unhealthy alliance that should never have occurred: "One cannot but wonder at such a grotesque a blunder." Before he presented any written record of his law student days in England and before he demonstrated an ability to perform successfully in the Pitt graduate program, his law experience was declared the equivalent of a master of arts degree. Thus having received a degree and faculty status by merely proposing to come to the US, he must have thought "only in America," and the words "land of opportunity" must have immediately taken on an exaggerated meaning. Basking in this prestige that was heaped on him, he immediately began signing his name: "Reginald Shortstraw, MA," an etiquette no-no in American parlance. From that beginning Reggie was special, but soon thereafter the University's unmet expectations, indulgences, and extensions became the primary ingredients of his career both as teacher and student.

At the outset Reggie shared an office with Bob Duncan and me; we three constituted the lowest ranking members of the department faculty. Our new colleague was a conversational delight, a keen observer who asked good questions about the city and campus and in the process offered frequent insights to life and customs in England. Likable, urbane, and soft-spoken, he also assumed that no one in America worked hard, and he was anxious to fit in. Our first serious discussions revealed that he was married to a Dutch girl, Wilda by name, whom he had met in the service and who also planned to join him within several months. We also learned that he was a social democrat enamored with the ideas of the Labour Party leader, Clement Attlee, who served as prime minister between Winston Churchill's two terms.

When Reggie swung into action, we discovered other attributes; he was hopelessly disorganized and suffered from a terminal case of forgetfulness. Chronically late for class, student appointments, and faculty meetings, he also made a habit of losing everything in his possession from office keys to lecture notes, from student papers to his car and from roll books to a day in his life. Of course, he always found the car, frequently with the help of others, but when he would emerge from his office in the Cathedral of Learning, even with key in hand, it was no clue to where the car was parked; he often didn't know in which direction on the street to start looking.

One time he insisted on driving me home, a real imposition for him since he lived within a mile of the campus and I was ten miles out. After declining his invitation several times during our conversation that afternoon, I finally consented to his generous offer. Happily chatting, we descended from our office on the 29th floor of the Cathedral; but as we stepped from the elevator (which he insisted on calling a *lift*), a quizzical look covered his face, and he blurted out: "I'm sorry; I didn't drive today." On another day when a second such invitation was proffered and accepted, we searched for 45 minutes in three directions from the Cathedral before locating the car. That brought to an abrupt end my belief in the concept of free transportation.

The word other than elevator that he refused to say was suspenders. He always wore *braces*, frayed gray ones that age had robbed of their elasticity and thus had little resilience. When he sat at his desk, the braces that held the trousers properly while he was standing pulled tightly against his shoulders, so he flipped them off to the sides. At times he forgot that they were still dangling when he got up and ventured into the hall. One day the department chairman saw him in this state of limited undress and believing that his trousers were about to drop to his knees, gave him a fatherly: "Get 'em up, boy; get 'em up."

Reggie returned to the office with the thought that the chairman's comment was a violation of his democratic right to wear suspenders at half-mast if he so desired. On several other occasions he forgot that they were hanging down when he slipped on his suit coat and went to class. This produced the uncommon sight of loops protruding below each side of his jacket; a few students smiled, but Reggie thought: "What the hell."

Detection was not disturbing to Reggie, who took a perverse delight in snubbing tradition, sometimes irreverently. By some quirk known only to Reggie, he occasionally purchased fresh eggs from one of his students. Once in November, at least he thought it was November, he inadvertently placed a dozen of them in the back of a desk drawer and didn't discover them until March. Coming to the only logical conclusion that these eggs were unsafe for human consumption, he pondered the question: What constructive purpose might they serve? He concluded that he would use them for target practice by throwing them out a 29th floor Cathedral window with the Heinz Chapel door, 250 feet across the lawn, as the intended bull's eye.

Not thinking that he was serious, I made the observation that an egg could not possibly be thrown that far. He accepted the statement as a challenge, picked up the dozen of rotten eggs, went to the side of the Cathedral facing the chapel, threw open the window, and began firing one by one. No egg reached halfway to the stated objective. He came back to the office and said: "OK, Jim, you win," but the idea of tossing objects out the window was not abandoned.

Several months later the department secretary appeared at our office door bearing gifts: a pair of blue woolen gloves rolled into a ball. She was cleaning out her lost-and-found drawer from the winter's accumulation, and because no one had claimed the gloves, she thought that Reggie, who was always in need of everything, could use them the next winter.

He accepted them with thanks, but a few minutes after she disappeared, he turned to me and said:

> These gloves will come in handy in the fall, but by that time I will have no idea where they are. Thus there's no point in keeping them now. I think I'll throw them out onto Forbes Avenue. [Our window faced Forbes.] Some little kid will see them land and think that God dropped them from the sky.

Again I made the mistake of offering an observation. By pointing out that no one could possibly throw a pair of gloves 200 feet out to the street, Reggie once again challenged my statement. I explained that both the distance and the downdraft around the building precluded such a feat. He jumped up immediately, opened the window as wide as possible, flipped a desk chair out of his path to the window, went out the door into the hallway with gloves in hand, ran full speed across the office toward the opening, and gave a mighty heave. The gloves may have gone 50 feet out before they were caught in the downdraft and sucked back toward the Cathedral. They landed about 25 feet from the base of the building, near an elderly groundskeeper resting on a bench. He looked up in wonderment, and the cigarette he was smoking fell from his lips.

Bob Duncan arrived at the office later that morning as the sun was shining brightly through the window that Reggie had closed after the glove episode. The sun revealed how disgustingly dirty the window was. In jest Bob commented: "Reggie, you've done it again; you were supposed to be here yesterday afternoon to let the window washer in. Now we won't have our window cleaned for another four months unless we do it ourselves."

Of course, Reggie didn't realize that the window washer had his own key, and he was so forgetful that he couldn't recall whether or not he had agreed as recently as the previous day to be there. To add to the spoof, I suggested that we not delay and undertake the cleaning chore. As a consequence we drew straws to determine which one of the three did the washing while the other two hung him out our 29th floor window. We used pencils as straws and had the drawing rigged so that Reggie would draw the shortest one. Bob and I thought that our colleague understood that we were pulling his English leg, but when he looked at his short straw, he rolled up his right sleeve, selected a cloth from a desk drawer, went to the men's room to soak it thoroughly, and returned. Not to have a limey call our bluff, we held him out the window, each of us holding firmly around a leg. Today I still get a chill down my spine as I recall our prank.

The inevitable happened. Later in the day after we had "cleaned" our window, the rain came. Actually the rain helped because the one-cloth treatment had succeeded only in smearing the dirt on the glass into a new pattern. During the shower I had to leave, but my car was parked about a half mile away, near Phipps Conservatory, and I had neither an umbrella nor a raincoat. Good-natured Reggie never hesitated and proposed that I take his raincoat that was in the office because he had neglected to take it home two or three rains earlier.

I suggested that that would be inconsiderate, because he would probably need the coat when he had to leave. He countered that argument with two observations; he didn't plan to leave until the rain ended, and he wasn't as particular as American men about keeping a crease in his trousers (perma-press hadn't yet hit the market); he seemed proud to say that a little water wouldn't disturb him. After a modest prodding, I took the raincoat and told him: "Reggie, I owe you one." When I returned it the next day, I asked: "Do you have any idea what's in the pocket of your coat?" Assuming that he had no clue, I was not prepared for his accurate response: "A dried salami. You can't tell where you might be when you get hungry. Did you eat any of it? I also keep one in the glove compartment of the jeep, and another in my desk drawer." That was his concept of being prepared.

No one could challenge Reggie's penchant for the unex-pected. At times he looked neat, presentable, and as normal as anyone, but only moments were needed to alter that image. He had arrived in Pittsburgh with only one suit, which he called "the king's suit" because, when Brits were discharged from the service, they were each given a suit of clothes, not a bonus or mustering out pay that was allotted US servicemen. This was the suit provided by the government, thus dubbed "the king's suit," which remained his sole dress garment far too long.

Several times when the History Department was between secretaries, his wife Wilda substituted. One morning she had come to the office but neglected to put on the five-inch wide, flaming red belt with a large red buckle that complemented her dress. Since Reggie was still at home, she phoned with the request that he bring the belt to the office. She sternly admonished him not to forget as he did with most details. To be absolutely certain that he remembered this time, he imme-diately buckled it around his own trim waist.

Wilda was a tall, willowy, dishwater blonde, and Reggie, equally slender, found no discomfort in wearing the belt. As was his custom, he arrived at 10:45 for a 10:40 class, totally blotted the belt from his mind, and never thought of delivering it to Wilda before heading late to class. Some twenty minutes into his lecture, he noticed several girls looking at his midsection and nudging each other. At first he thought he had neglected to zip his trousers again, but upon surveying the situation, he noted that, with his jacket unbuttoned, the big red buckle was visible to all. Somewhat relieved to know that his zipper was in place, he considered removing the belt, but decided against that and stared down the girls as they snickered. After all, if he had taken it off, he might have left it on the lectern at the end of the period.

No classroom situation seemed to embarrass him. He was so parsimonious that he refused to buy Kleenex and used institutional toilet tissue from the men's room as a substitute when he had a cold. He admitted that the occasional display captured student attention almost as completely as his description of King Henry VIII's marriage problems or his denunciation of American democracy. The latter topic seemed appropriate even in an English history course because, as he had gleaned from the pages of *Time*, the mayor of a small Midwestern town had ordered a local panhandler placed in a public shower for his annual scrub-down. Reggie insisted that such an order ignored the vagrant's individual rights (that harken back to English common law) to remain as dirty as he wanted to be and that students needed to be awakened to the perils of their crumbling democracy.

Reggie's most unusual manner of dress that upset his wife was wearing his shirt tucked into his undershorts. This meant that at times the band of his shorts was exposed above the top of his trousers. Such exposures were so commonplace that every Monday one of his classes conducted an informal lottery on the color of Reggie's shorts that would start off the week.

One year at the highlight of the department's social season, this appearance particularly vexed Wilda. The occasion was a retirement dinner for the chairman, and Reggie appeared with shorts exposed. One of the staff members who was independently wealthy invited all faculty members to a dinner at his suburban home, and the guest list included the Shortstraws.

While we were standing on the terrace chatting in small groups, Wilda first spied Reggie's display of underwear. She came over to our group and began softly to berate him for his appearance. As she spoke, she began pulling his shirt out from his shorts and stuffing it back between the shorts and trousers. Almost oblivious to what was happening, Reggie continued talking, simply raising his arms, glass in one hand and cigarette in the other, as she manipulated his attire. He was so relaxed on such occasions that it was disquieting.

STUDENTS' DAYTIME NIGHTMARE

Pedagogically Reggie Shortstraw was a Neanderthal who found a place to happen, but part of the responsibility must be shouldered by the University that employed him. Having never thought about teaching until Professor Amundson beckoned him to America, he had no understanding of the American education system and was thrust into the classroom with no preliminary except for having a textbook shoved in his hand and a "you-can-do-it" pat on the back. To make failure irreversible, he scoffed at any on-the-job training except for a few self-contrived, half-baked ideas of his own. The results ranged from unbelievable to horrendous.

As Reggie and I walked across campus one afternoon, we passed several of my students, whom I greeted by name. Impressed, he asked, "How do you do that? I not only don't know my students' names; I'm not even sure that I've seen them before when they speak to me."

I outlined my formula for him: On the first day of the term, I allow students to sit wherever they want, but insist that they must sit there regularly thereafter. I make a seating chart of that pattern, arrive at each class session before the students, match names and faces of as many as possible as they file into their seats, and when a student comments in class, I call him/her by name. By the time I hand back the first examination papers, about a third of the way through the course, and make eye contact with each one, I will know 50-70 students in the class, even if the total is a hundred or more.

Although this sounded like a lot of extra work to Reggie, he vowed that he would try the plan. Later when I asked about his progress, he reported only failure. Several times he forgot the chart, before ultimately losing it. As well as those two tribulations, he had difficulty with student cooperation. Once he was about to call a student by the name on the chart only to realize that the name was that of a man, but the waving hand was obviously attached to a curvaceous blonde. On another occasion he called the name of a woman who was expected to be in the front row, but she answered from the back of the room. He gave up in frustration.

Early in his career Reggie concluded that American education was too structured. He couldn't understand why final grades had to be reported by a specific date, or why an instructor had to supply the registrar with the names of students who were not officially registered for courses they were attending, or why instructors were expected to schedule specific office hours, or why textbooks for the next term had to be selected by a specific date. He decided to exhibit contempt for such administrative details by ignoring, as long as possible, the many requests for information that came to his desk. When he left campus for a summer vacation at Cape Cod without turning in the final grades for any of his courses, Reggie so frustrated an acting chairman that the chairman alerted the Massachusetts State Police to track him down. Reggie explained that he thought that it would be relaxing to evaluate his final exam papers with the Atlantic Ocean lapping at his toes.

One day incurable Reggie discovered a form (12 weeks overdue) requesting the names of students not officially enrolled for his course. Gleefully he concluded: "If I turn this in now, it'll only confuse that poor registrar. He won't know if I'm late for this term or early for the next one." And without further deliberation he threw the requested form into the wastebasket. Under similar circumstances in another term, he decided to reverse his strategy and submit the form. Although out of date to the extent that it was meaningless, he commented: "The registrar needs to be confused further; perhaps then he'll stop harassing me."

For most of Reggie's years on the staff, in order for a student to register for a particular course, he had to pick up a coded card from the department to indicate that he was properly admitted. The number of cards cut for a survey course was dictated by room capacity, but Reggie sneaked around to heist 15-20 cards for each of his classes and discarded them to keep his enrollment low. Often unnecessarily disrupting student programs, this practice also shifted the instruction burden to others while Reggie reveled in the knowledge that he had 15-20 fewer students in each section than planned for by the department.

Reggie's action was due both to his laziness in reading student papers and to his dislike for preparing exams. He didn't have a clue concerning the construction of a test capable of measuring student learning. He was adamant that he did not want to schedule essay exams because they required too much time to evaluate. By elimination he arrived at true/false questions, but they always turned into disaster. When he discussed the "correct" answers in class, students were able to demonstrate that three-fourths of his questions were so ambiguous that they could be interpreted as either true or false. Thus with three-fourths of all answers correct, everyone in the class was assured at least a C grade on the tests.

Instead of admitting the difficulty inherent in that type of examination, he decided to perfect it with a little Shortstraw creativity. Thereafter all his true/false statements were direct quotations from the textbook, except that in some he would add the word NOT or remove it from others. Thus if an exam question were the exact duplicate of the text, it was true; if NOT were added or deleted, it was false. Any time students questioned the answer, he simply referred them to the specific page in the text from which the statement was copied—not a recommended examination procedure.

This inept testing contributed to the exposure of another of his unconventional techniques and came to light one evening when I returned to the office we shared. I encountered two students rifling through Reggie's desk—drawers open and papers strewn on the floor. Surprised by the intruders trying to steal a copy of a forthcoming exam, I excitedly asked for an explanation. One began with an obvious lie that they were waiting for Mr. Shortstraw who, I knew, had gone home much earlier.

Because I was not a University policeman, I decided to settle for their names. When I asked the one nearer me to identify himself, he replied simply "Joe." Not accustomed to cute answers nor gifted with a long fuse, I was immediately furious and stepped toe-to-toe with him and demanded: "Joe what?" He quickly responded: "Joe Mikailandrosolonovich." Certain that no one could concoct that name on the spur of the moment, I knew that he had spoken correctly, so I told him that he was dismissed. Angry enough to square off with him because I felt that my office, as well as Reggie's, had been violated, I was relieved that he belatedly volunteered his name, because I later learned that he was a football star who could have clobbered me senseless if the incident had become physical.

I proceeded to ask the other student for his name, but instead of answering, he bolted past me as he yelled to his accomplice: "Let's get the hell outa here." With that they were off down the stairs. Still confident because I had one name, I immediately called Shortstraw at home to report what had happened and to have him verify that Mikailandrosolonovich was indeed enrolled in one of his classes. My adrenalin was still pumping overtime, but Reggie was calm and thought the situation called for a little levity. "I don't have any 'viches' in my classes" was his reply. In my excited state I didn't understand what he meant; exasperated that he had to explain, he responded: "I have no student whose name ends in *vich*." Although he was generally wrong on such details, he was correct on this one.

Not happy that I had been outsmarted by a clever student, I nevertheless felt obligated to report the details to the dean, because the students obviously had a key. In an effort to identify the culprits, I asked Reggie if his records indicated that a mediocre-to-poor student had performed above expectations. I suspected that earlier tests may have been pilfered. Luck was with us; he identified a student who scored 98 per cent on one of his true/false crazies taken from the textbook, but I wasn't prepared for Reggie's explanation: "Yeah, I was suspicious of that guy. I took that test myself and only made 94." That must be a first—an instructor who could only score 94 per cent on his own test.

I asked Reggie if he could think of a pretext by which the individual with the 98 score might be summoned to our office. I wanted to walk in while he was there and determine if he were the one who passed himself off as Mikailandrosolonovich who, by the way, was a real person, a football waterboy, who was not near our office on the night in question. Apparently when I demanded "Joe what?" he was the first Joe who flashed across the intruder's mind, and he spit it out—all of it.

Reggie volunteered that the 98 per center still owed him his class notes. In disbelief I asked: "His class what?" "Sure," responded my office mate, "I ask students to turn in their semester notes at the end of the term, and he didn't submit his." I advised Reggie that his procedure was "juvenile—even high school mentality," but he assured me that the situation was not as bad as it seemed because he didn't grade the class notes as I had assumed. In reality the practice had a far more disconcerting purpose as he explained:

> You know that I often lose my lecture notes and need to build some protection against that. Also a few conscientious girls in every class will type their notes, especially if they think the notes will be inspected. I give everyone else's notes back almost at once, but I tell the girls with excellent sets that I would like to retain theirs as models to show students during the next term. Actually I can use their notes to lecture from, and even have a spare in the event I lose a set. I've already lost some of mine from this term.

That is among the saddest, most amateurish approaches to effective teaching that I have ever heard, but that's what makes him Reggie.

In a more humorous and less manipulative vein, Reggie in all sincerity attempted to prepare me for impending disaster; in his view I was about to be fired, and he wanted me to be forewarned. When I asked him what he knew that I didn't, he explained that, since the department's enrollment had dipped steadily for two years, the loss equaled the approximate number of students assigned to an instructor. Because Bob Duncan had previously taken a position elsewhere, Reggie and I remained the two lowest ranking members of the staff, and he reasoned that one of us was "ripe" for a pink slip.

He knew that I should expect the worst because he had taken out an insurance policy to protect his job. By that he meant that he had borrowed a thousand dollars from the department chairman to rehabilitate his garage apartment. As he observed: "The chairman's no fool. He won't fire me when I owe him a thousand bucks, so I'm warning you." Of course, my position was never in danger. Although Reggie's solicitude should be commended, it was not rooted in reality.

At times his perception of scholarly matters dipped equally low. On a Friday morning just before a summer term was to begin, Reggie asked if I could allot an afternoon to him. I hesitated and wanted to know if he had a specific one in mind: "Yeah, this afternoon. I need to know American history."

He explained that, months before, he had coaxed the department chairman into assigning him to teach a course in Anglo-American Relations so that he might earn a little extra money, but as with everything else, he forgot to prepare. Now he admitted: "The problem is that I don't know anything about American history and want you to teach me this afternoon." I advised him that for us to chat for three or four hours about the subject would not serve his purpose. I did think, however, that his assumption of what could be done was bred of a European ignorance. Since the history of that continent is much longer than ours is, he assumed that ours could be condensed to a few hours.

In attempting to analyze his plight, I inquired about the structure of the course: Was the focus to be diplomatic? Or was it to be a social-cultural study? When he replied that the theme was his to choose, I suggested several volumes that could introduce him to both possibilities. Claiming that time did not permit the luxury of reading, he argued more strenuously for a quickie synopsis from me. Still inexperienced myself, I refused to consent to what I considered a futile session and recommended that he advise the department to cancel the course, because he was not adequately prepared. He dismissed that proposal because it would curtail his income. He would rather make a fool of himself before a class than forego the money.

Knowing that I was not about to change my mind, in all seriousness he wanted to know: "Tell me this, was Washington president before Lincoln or was it the other way around?" My response was one that he probably didn't understand: "That's what makes a single afternoon session useless." The discussion ended with: "Well then, this will have to be a cooperative course. I'll teach them English history, and the students can teach me American history."

The course was held, and I was sorry that I could not attend as an auditor, not to learn but to laugh, and to add to my storehouse of examples of what not to do in the classroom.

OFF-CAMPUS LIFE

During his Pittsburgh years Shortstraw lived in four locations, including the one with a path down the hall, where he had subsisted in the months before Wilda arrived.

One wintry day while returning from lunch, Reggie asked if I would like to see "his quarters." I accepted the invitation; we turned a corner or two, and quickly I was ushered up to this third-floor tenement located between Fifth and Forbes avenues just east of Dithridge in the campus, or Oakland, district. Mercifully it was soon to be razed, and no one who ever saw it doubted that the change was in the name of progress.

Stark in appearance, the room grabbed my attention immediately and after sixty years still hasn't let go. Spacious, relatively bare, and so cold that I could see my breath, it was austere by any definition—containing only a paint-splattered poster bed, a small table with chair, a scarred veneer chest of drawers, and two faded rag rugs that covered less than a third of the unpainted pine flooring. It was the most inhospitable, almost forbidding room I have ever seen.

I feel that this is an accurate description although I was far from an experienced evaluator. I had never before seen a one-room flat; in fact, I had never been in an apartment of any size or quality. By chance my family members, as well as my high school and college friends, had all lived in houses. Thus I always had a kind of romantic image of life in an apartment, but this visit rendered me speechless.

As my eyes surveyed the barren walls, Reggie, seeming to accept the situation as normal, sprightly asked if I would like something to drink. Seeing no food, no refrigerator, and no possible storage area, I hesitated to answer. After a pause my host followed up with "beer or Coke?" Because he seemed insistent, I opted for the latter whereupon Reggie threw open his one window (making a cold room actually frigid), peered down the outside wall, and tugged on one of several cords attached to the window handle. At the end of each three-footer dangled a container; one sported a six-pack of Coke bottles that he was in the process of drawing up. I went over and looked down at his open-air refrigerator but could not decipher what was at the ends of the other two cords. As I drank the Coke, my mind wandered from the lack of amenities in the room to the chilling cold and to the challenge of trying to study there.

That night I described Reggie's pad to my mother, who at once insisted that he be invited to dinner. He accepted and came a few days later. During the conversation that evening, he explained that he was about to move to better surroundings because Wilda was coming.

That led to the revelation that they possessed zero goods with which to set up housekeeping. In deciding to take the first step to remedy that, my mother promptly went through the house collecting sheets, blankets, and pillows, along with a full set of cheap silverware, a few dishes, pots and pans, and a living room chair. Because Reggie was not yet able to invest in a car, I had to drive him back to Oakland that night. Like gypsies the two of us loaded this loot into the family car and transported it to his room for storage until Wilda's arrival. Reggie was overwhelmed with gratitude, and although he forgot most things, for several years he regularly inquired about my parents, to whom he referred as my "mama and papa" with the accent on the second syllable of both.

The Shortstraws lived only briefly in their first apartment before moving to the Clyde Street brownstone. The change of address was accomplished almost without incident and was cost-free thanks to helpful friends; the only casualty was the couple's secondhand washing machine. Painfully aware of the difficulty experienced in lifting and twisting it up the stairs to that third-floor apartment when they had moved in, Reggie devised a plan to simplify its removal. Rather than lug it back down the two flights, he proposed to lift it onto the window-sill and lower it by rope down the side of the building. This was a comedy about to happen, and it proceeded to write itself into history. No sooner had Reggie and his helpers swung the weighty appliance free of the window ledge than the rope snapped, sending it on a free fall to the pavement below. Parts littered the sidewalk, with a few stray pieces lodging in the shrubbery—most of which a sad Reggie reclaimed.

This minor debacle put the Shortstraws in the market for a replacement, and coincidentally Sears was having a sale on a coin-operated model with a five-dollar discount to anyone with a trade-in. Reggie immediately recognized an advantage in the coin-operated feature; neighbors could be invited to come to the Shortstraw basement, use their washer by inserting quarters, and thereby let it pay for itself. Acting on this theory, he nevertheless expected to find it difficult to qualify for the five-dollar discount, because his pile of twisted metal, supplemented by a bucket of bolts, bore little resemblance to any washing machine and possessed the same probability of being reassembled as did Humpty Dumpty after his celebrated fall. When he casually mentioned to the salesperson that he had a trade-in at home, he was automatically given the five-dollar reduction, sight unseen. An astonished Reggie couldn't comprehend that this was a part of the promotion; to him failure to inspect the merchandise to be reclaimed had cost the store a five spot.

Pleased with his purchase, Reggie explained the deal to me and warned that, if this was typical of American business practice, the nation was far down the road toward bankruptcy, and he wanted me to note that I heard it first from him. I stored that bit of worthless information in my mental wastebasket, along with his earlier proclamation that American businessmen were inattentive to public demand because there was no bar where one could order a glass of warm beer, a missed opportunity by Reggie standards.

The Shortstraws were exceedingly pleased with their new brownstone. To celebrate their good fortune, they invited

friends to a housewarming on a hot, humid Saturday afternoon in September. This first-floor apartment was the result of
subdividing a two-level dwelling. The Shortstraws had three
rooms and a bath—two average-sized rooms, one behind the
other, followed by a bath and small kitchen side by side. The
front room was obviously the living room, and the second one
doubled as a dining/bedroom.

The Shortstraws could have entertained a dozen guests
comfortably if most had been willing to stand throughout
their visit. Invitations for the fateful Saturday were extended
by word of mouth with no check on the exuberance that
overcame Reggie and Wilda. They invited approximately
a hundred people, all of whom came, some with friends.
Within minutes of the first arrivals, space was at a premium;
with limited success the front porch and small yard accommodated the overflow; the large front window was kept open
so that those on the inside and on the outside could feel a
sense of attending the same party. Mingling temporarily
became a lost art.

Most of the guests were in their twenties and found satisfaction in the camaraderie; from our standpoint the party was
a success; the only older guests that I recall were Professor and
Mrs. Guy Chapman. He was a distinguished visitor from the
University of Leeds, who for the year had exchanged lecterns
with Carroll Amundson; Mrs. Chapman was a noted novel-
ist who wrote under the pen name of Storm Jamison and was
teaching for the year in the University's English Department.
All of us budding historians stood in awe of her publication
record, because the only thing that any of us had published
was our vitas.

Reggie prepared mysterious drinks in advance. Several times he attempted to describe the contents of each for his guests; that only added to the confusion. Some couldn't hear, and others didn't understand, but that was only secondary to the frivolity. In one group of empty quart milk bottles, he had poured an elixir of fruit juice and something designated vaguely as spirits. Known as Isaly's Special, which he pronounced as Is-ALL-ees and the locals knew it as ICE-lees.

In less distinctively marked milk jugs, he provided a concoction defined for the occasion as Reick's Special, which he pronounced to rhyme with pike, whereas everyone else knew that it rhymed with pick. To add to the joviality of the afternoon, all drinks were requested according to Reggie's pronunciation.

Those on the porch or in the yard were at the mercy of the window tenders who had to relay requests for drinks to those inside. Delays, mix-ups, and actual loss of contact were normal. In time heat took its toll on everyone; the most anyone could hope for was something cold; then the ice supply was exhausted, and finally even warm drinks ran out. That was the unspoken signal that the party was over, but it had been a boisterous affair while in progress.

Before the end a coffee table incident in the living room left a young lady in tears. She was standing next to the table filled with trays of olives, potato chips, and pretzels when she accidentally kicked one of its legs; at least that's the way it appeared to her and those nearby.

The table had been a gift from someone's attic, and the Shortstraws had been forewarned that one leg was totally detached and required two screws to be rendered safe. The day before the open house, Reggie assured Wilda that he would make the necessary repairs at once. She placed the trays on the table in good faith that her husband had followed through with his commitment—always a false assumption until checked.

As he crawled around the floor to reclaim the olives that had rolled in all directions, Reggie assured the young woman that this was no tragedy. He admitted that he had knocked the leg out of place at least a half dozen times. As fast as Reggie placed the munchies back on the trays, Wilda dispatched them to the kitchen. He thought that they were still edible and should have been served to the guests, declaring that, if no one else would eat them, he would.

Later that month a group of us planned a Sunday outing to Cooper's Rock overlooking the Cheat River near Morgantown. The Shortstraws were invited, but Reggie held up acceptance until the departure time was verified. He insisted on nothing earlier than noon—when Sunday School at the Church of the Ascension ended. He had arranged for his wife to teach Sunday School there because it was the only church in town, according to his survey, that paid its teachers, and he didn't want her to miss work. In fact, he managed to keep her employed seven days a week; Monday-Friday she taught at the Ascension Academy and rounded out her week by serving as the History Department's secretary on Saturday mornings.

We accepted Reggie's conditions, and it was agreed that he and Wilda, along with another couple, would ride with me. On my way to pick up the others, I had to pass the Clyde Street apartment and considered it the better part of discretion to stop and make certain that Reggie was up and functioning because Wilda was off at church.

Not only was he up, he was up painting the ceiling. Startled by the spectacle, I stood dumbfounded. Alert to the crispness in my voice when I asked: "Do you know that you are supposed to be ready to leave in fifteen minutes?" he decided to go formal:

> James, I was just lying there in bed, looking up at the dirty ceiling with its blotches of brown and streaks of gray. Then I remembered a can of paint in the basement and a ladder leaning against the wall. I decided that this morning was the time to bring paint and ceiling together, but I haven't progressed as expected because of unforeseen difficulties.

During this recitation Reggie stood barefoot on the second rung of the ladder; in fact, his only clothing was a pair of rust-colored corduroy trousers. Gesturing with a partially emptied bottle of warm beer in his left hand, he kept the other free for painting. He explained that, after ladder and paint were in place, he couldn't find a paintbrush. The closest unreasonable facsimile that he was able to turn up was a wallpaper paste brush, but that was too wide to fit into the paint bucket. Undaunted by such detail, he had poured the paint into Wilda's large skillet.

After surveying this incongruous portrait of "artist-at-work," I was too overwhelmed to comment on the painting extravaganza and in departing reminded him that I was about to pick up the others and expected him to be ready in fifteen minutes. I returned on schedule; Wilda had arrived from church; and surprisingly the Shortstraws were waiting on the porch. I have no idea what was said about the project or the skillet or how Reggie made the transition from painter so rapidly, but I did notice that he pulled on a long-sleeved shirt to cover his paint-dribbled arms.

The subject of painting never came up again for months—until the Shortstraws decided to have a family and needed more space. Always on the alert for good deals, Reggie learned that a garage apartment behind one of the Forbes Avenue mansions in Squirrel Hill was available rent-free for a year to anyone who put up a thousand dollars to make the necessary alterations. That's when he borrowed the money from the department chairman and suggested that I might be fired.

In addition to the money, the new tenant was expected to paint the total interior, and Reggie asked if I could sacrifice a Saturday or two to his painting project. I agreed, but decided to pull his English leg in the process. I asked if he had already selected the paint. He took the bait, answered in the negative, and immediately wanted to know if I had a source through which he might buy it wholesale.

With tongue in cheek, I advised him that I would do better than that. Since his apartment was newly remodeled, he should be a little bold and modern in his choice of colors. At the same time I explained to him that a keen competition existed among paint manufacturers and that Sherwin-Williams had won the race in the laboratories and was about to revolutionize interior design. It was on the verge of bringing to the market a new plaid paint destined to be a wave of the future. Of course, I informed him, this was going to be expensive because of the refining expense. He interrupted my presentation at that point to insist that he couldn't possibly afford it.

But, I stressed, there was a flip side that provided for a free paint deal. The major competitor to Sherwin-Williams for this breakthrough came from Pittsburgh Paint & Glass (the name had not yet been reduced to PPG), a loser by a narrow margin, but it had nonetheless developed a polka-dot paint that the company was trying to rush to the market. A friend in the paint industry had told me that Pittsburgh Paint was quietly giving three gallons of free polka-dot paint to select individuals who could pick it up at their downtown store. The one stipulation was that the individual allow the company photographers to come into his home to photograph the rooms decorated with the polka-dot design. Thus the photos could demonstrate that their paint had already achieved public acceptance and had, in fact, won the race with Sherwin-Williams.

When Reggie wanted to know if he qualified as a select individual, I assured him that all that was necessary was to walk into the store and ask for "the dotted paint." That bit of information made his day. He was in the mood to throw kudos indiscriminately and praised Americans as an astonishing breed with these advances in paint.

Elated with this tip, he asked for the address of the store where the free paint could be picked up. He ruined my fun when he asked me to accompany him to the store; I was forced to burst his bubble and admit that I had painted a grand farce, but I assured him that I would come with my own paintbrushes to apply whatever he acquired by whatever means.

A satisfying camaraderie prevailed throughout the subsequent painting sessions that, in turn, provided the Shortstraws with a bright, cozy apartment, their home for the remainder of their years in Pittsburgh.

A Tale of Two Cars

While at the University, Reggie owned two cars, each the source of at least one bizarre story. Before acquiring either, his principal auto transportation was provided by an English friend, known to me only as Hughes, who possessed a strange model of his own. Hughes claimed that he had liberated it after the war from Marshal Hermann Goering of the Third Reich. I can't vouch for the car's pedigree, but outwardly it was formidable in appearance: tank-like with bulletproof glass all around, including the interior panel between the front and back seats. As a two-time passenger, I was impressed by its luxuriously detailed upholstery, elaborate intercom system, and intricately designed instrument panel.

No such display of opulence intrigued Reggie; he was thoroughly content with two used vehicles, the best he could almost afford. The first was a jeep acquired from Harold Wiand, an instructor at Slippery Rock State Teachers College. Reggie and Harold had met in an English history seminar and struck up a friendship that led to the latter selling the car-less Reggie the jeep that had been housed at Harold's summer home near Emlenton, 75 miles north of Pittsburgh.

Reggie and Wilda were invited to spend the Labor Day weekend at the Wiands' residence with the thought of driving the jeep home after the visit. The plan contained an uncorrectable flaw; neither Shortstraw held a driver's license. Wilda's lack was deliberate; her husband did not approve of a woman's right to drive. Reggie himself was armed with a learner's permit, and with his proclivity of dalliance, he had postponed taking the driver's test until the day before the scheduled departure for their Labor Day holiday. He was certain that he would pass for two ironclad reasons: He had held a license in England, and Americans were lax enough to allow vast numbers of women to drive; if the test was simple enough for them, in his mind, success was assured.

Unaware of this certainty, the Pennsylvania State Police examiner flunked poor Reggie. Not particularly daunted by this result, except for the knowledge that some women had passed on the first attempt, he proposed to drive the car home without the presence of a licensed driver, but Harold convinced him that this was not only foolhardy but also against the law.

Reggie pondered alternatives and concluded that I was the answer to his dilemma. Thus he called me that fateful Sunday afternoon. He began the conversation by being solicitous about my holiday. I immediately suspected that a proposition was forthcoming. When I told him that by design I was doing nothing, he suggested that I needed a little spark in my life and proposed that I come to Emlenton that evening by bus. After pouring out his sad tale of buying the jeep and flunking the driver's test, he said that Harold would be pleased to have me as a guest and that we could ride back in his jeep the next day.

With no desire to go, I responded negatively to his comments. Then he turned on the charm and explained how simple it would be, because he had checked the schedule and found that a bus left Pittsburgh late that afternoon at 5:00 PM and arrived in Butler at 5:55; then there would be a delay until 8:00 PM, when a bus on another line left for Emlenton, arriving at 8:45 PM. When he promised "on scout's honor" not to screw up, he said that he and Harold would meet the bus. These details, although markedly simple, represented far more planning than Reggie had ever put into anything. I was astonished and realized how much this meant to him. Because I wasn't sacrificing anything specific, I agreed to come to the rescue although I wasn't fully aware of what that meant.

With a minimum of toiletries and clothes stuffed into a brief case, I was downtown in time to depart on the five o'clock for Butler, but on arrival at that destination, I encountered my first problem. Reggie had read to me from the weekday schedule; there was no bus service to Emlenton on Sundays; there was no return bus to Pittsburgh; there was no phone in the Wiand summer residence. Not panicky, I decided to walk to the edge of town, about a mile along Route 38 that led to Emlenton, put my faith in my trusty thumb, and was eminently successful.

I was in Emlenton by 7:10, a quiet spot on the Allegheny River, with more than an hour and a half to wait for Reggie to ride into town. With no public building open on a holiday weekend, I decided to keep improvising, while also becoming a little angry at Reggie. I elected to pursue my own techniques to reach my destination rather than endure a lengthy wait standing on a street corner. If successful, that would prove how resourceful I was and how unthinking Reggie was, but the thought of that embarrassing him was wishful thinking.

I simply stopped people I encountered on the street and asked if they knew Harold Wiand. After unsuccessful queries, I ran into two elderly ladies who held the answer to my puzzle. They reported that he lived about three miles out of town and that I had to re-cross the Allegheny, retrace my route up the long hill, and continue straight at the top rather than turn left heading toward Butler and Pittsburgh.

With no desire to climb that hill on foot, I again resorted to hitchhiking. Almost like magic, a local in a pick-up truck stopped; on the way uphill I explained my plight, and the driver was able to supply the essentials but did not convey the idea that Harold didn't live *on* the highway. He knew only the entrance to Wiands' lane, and his route took us past it. He dropped me at what he termed the entrance although at first glance it appeared that he was simply inviting me out of his truck along the highway. No mailbox, no name printed on a board, no indicator of any kind except two parallel vehicle tracks that came out to the edge of the pavement gave this spot any distinctive marking; even the area between the tracks was grassed over with weeds 10-12 inches high. My benefactor did not say, and probably did not know, that the lane was almost a mile long.

I thanked him for his assistance and began to trudge up the lane. After the first 50 yards the foliage from the trees came together forming a canopy overhead and almost instantly blocked out all light from a setting sun. To this point I was quite pleased with my ability to improvise and meet the travel adversity that Reggie had thrust upon me; but as darkness closed in and I was alone in an unfamiliar forest with only two wheel-tracks as a guide, I became less certain of the wisdom of bowing to Reggie's entreaty.

While I could still follow the map provided by the tracks in the semi-darkness, I reached a point where a fork in the road presented my first dilemma. Deciding which branch to follow in order to reach my desired goal became all-important. After a minute or two of reconnoitering, I concluded that the set of tracks to the right was more heavily traveled and must lead to the cabin. I headed in that direction with an added spring in my step in wishful anticipation of finding some sign of recent human habitation. I wanted to conclude my trek before nightfall had totally eclipsed my literal *road* map. My thoughts also wondered; could the truck driver have mistaken Harold's lane for a path leading to an old lumbering operation?

Facing the alternative of proceeding or sitting in the woods for the night, I elected the former course. The judgment finally paid dividends. Dimly I perceived the proverbial light at the end of my tunnel of foliage. I could see the partial outline of a house from an outdoor candle that was burning to ward off insects. Soon the sound of laughing voices made me aware that I was in contact with civilization again. As I walked, I vaguely saw a woman whom I could not recognize.

For a moment I thought I could have traveled down the wrong lane, but shortly I recognized Harold's bald pate reflected in the candlelight. Probably a minute passed before any of the revelers noticed me approaching. As Reggie looked up, his face registered total disbelief before he blurted out: "We aren't scheduled to leave to pick you up for another half hour. I've been looking at my watch regularly." He looked again, and after a pause asked: "Where did I screw up?"

Over a beer I explained the no-bus problem and the applied ingenuity in reaching the cottage. Harold assured me that I was most welcome and that under the circumstances he was grateful that I had consented to come. When he pointed out that he had space for me to sleep, Reggie objected and said that he, Wilda, and I would be leaving in a few minutes. For the moment I thought that he wanted to drive back to

Pittsburgh at 9:30 that night, but he had nothing as sane as that in mind. He explained: "We're going to rough it like those hearty American pioneers we read about. We're going camping."

I couldn't believe that the idiot had struck again. Harold tried to dissuade him, but Reggie changed the rules that all of us had accepted. Even Wilda was completely uninformed. He wanted me to understand that I would be well provided for: I could sleep either on his army cot or in his sleeping bag. He and Wilda had each brought bag and cot. The revelation came in reply to my argument that in the dark we might pitch our so-called camp in the midst of poison ivy.

I found it uncomfortable to press further my preference to stay in the house to which I had been invited under such bizarre circumstances. Since Reggie was determined that we could not remain in these serene surroundings, Harold convinced him that we should leave the jeep, walk to a location on his property, and return in the morning for breakfast and for the use of toilet facilities before heading home. Reggie accepted the first part of that compromise although all others assumed that he had bought the package. Without knowing better, we were off.

About a half mile into the wilderness, guided by a flashlight that was about to lose its charge, our dauntless leader identified what he divined as the ideal camping spot. The area was a small open clearing half surrounded by a dense stand of trees. This afforded us an opportunity to enjoy sleeping under "the great canopy of the stars." (He liked that phrase.) I opted for the army cot, took off my sneakers and converted them into a pillow partly to keep them free of crawling critters, and stretched out. At the same time I tried to blot my two companions and the whole weird situation from my mind.

As I reflected, I realized that during my entire Navy career, even in war zones, I always slept on a mattress. How, in less than ten hours since Reggie called me at home, had I permitted myself to be trapped into "roughing it?" As I pondered where I had gone wrong, I drifted off to sleep with only the distant sound of the waters of the Allegheny lapping against the rocks as they rolled on their way to Pittsburgh. I was sorry that I was not going with them, but not as sorry as Reggie was going to make me.

During a fretful sleep I didn't realize that day had dawned until I felt something nudge my shoulder. As I rolled over, Reggie gleefully exclaimed, "breakfast in bed," and thrust a paper cup filled with canned orange juice into my hand.

On our trek to the campsite, I had helped carry the gear, with no idea what was in the large gunnysacks aside from the sleeping bags and army cots; but as I looked around, I saw Reggie tending to a small kerosene stove, frying me an egg. That was both the minimum and maximum capacity of his cooking apparatus.

I was surprised by the presence of the stove, a few utensils, rations of food, and the inevitable bottles of warm beer. Aware that the Shortstraws had come to Emlenton by bus, I queried Wilda: "You must have looked like a couple of gypsies leaving home. Were you allowed on the bus with such large bundles?" Wilda spoke up: "That's nothing. He has made me hitchhike with this much equipment." I thought that I wasn't seeing or hearing what was before me, but my only consolation came from the fact that the charade would be over in a few hours when we were back in Pittsburgh.

Reggie was as happy as a male dog with a five-gallon bladder that had just discovered a row of new telegraph poles; he flitted about his kerosene campfire, invigorated by the brisk morning air, while planning our day's itinerary in his mind. Wilda was almost as nonplussed as I was, but she had no excuse; she had lived and traveled with this madcapper for a few years. As she had done the night before, she submitted docilely to his proposals for scenic exploration.

Once breakfast was "served" and devoured, all three headed back to the Wiands' cottage to reclaim the jeep. At this point Reggie set forth the first phase of his plan for spending Labor Day. He suggested that we visit Cook Forest State Park before heading home. Because it was early in the morning and we could take that route home, I agreed. The trees of Cook Forest failed to impress Reggie with their towering splendor; the river, the nature paths, and the overall beauty also left him cold. Insisting that the description of the forest that had been painted was far more impressive than the forest itself, he suggested after an hour that we move on for Brookville "to see a real country town."

That likewise proved to be a disappointment for Reggie. I took heart in his reaction and interpreted it as a signal for an early departure for home. Without further ado I headed down Route 28. When Reggie realized where I was going, he dropped another bomb: "We can't go home without spending another night in the woods." At first I protested mildly by saying that I was expected home before nightfall. To Reggie, being 24 hours late was the same as being on time, so he dismissed my plea that we head south for Pittsburgh.

My second approach was to point out that rain was a distinct possibility, and with no curtains for the jeep, we had absolutely no protection from the elements. Reggie rebutted by saying that we could sleep in a farmer's barn. Since I had heard horror stories about vagrants, drifters, and drunks seeking shelter in farmers' facilities, I advised him that no farmer would consent to having strangers take up residence in his barn. When Reggie questioned me about the reasoning behind a farmer's reluctance to be hospitable, I pointed out that too often these intruders had lit a match, torching the barn and destroying the animals inside.

Not convinced of the accuracy of my statement, Reggie noted that sleeping in a barn was only a backup measure in the event of rain. He was intent on communing with nature one more night, but I continued to harp on the threatening skies. If rain came, I had no desire to spend the whole night in a jeep with the nature-crazed Shortstraws.

Reggie insisted that it would not rain, but I told him that, if I had to sit all night cramped in a wet jeep, "I will curse you on the hour every hour." Still intent on roughing it, Reggie asked if I would stay provided a farmer agreed that we could sleep in his barn if a shower developed. On the assumption that no farmer would welcome us, I relented. I thought that Reggie would be willing to set the compass for Pittsburgh after he struck out a few times.

Unfortunately we came across a clump of trees a short distance off the highway that I had to admit was as good as any spot if we needed to pitch camp. I still had hope of escaping another lost night, because we had to locate a barn nearby to serve as our safety valve. One came into view about a mile down Route 28. Reggie suggested that I was the logical person to request permission to enter the barn if the rain interrupted our sleep because, as he said, "People think I'm odd because of my British accent." I thought he was damned odd, and his accent had nothing to do with it. I flatly refused because I considered it an inane and inappropriate request.

When I remained adamant, Reggie understood that the task of gaining the farmer's permission rested with him. To his advantage only the farmer's ten-year-old daughter was at home, and he proceeded, I am sure, to confound her. He explained that we really did not want to sleep in the family's barn, but rain might make it a necessity. The young girl pointed out that only her parents could sanction that request, and they would not be home for several hours. Knowing that I was ready to head home if he "struck out," he rephrased his proposal to the bewildered girl: "We won't sleep in the barn unless it rains. In that event I'll come to your window and whisper: 'It's the campers,' and you'll know that we are going in the barn." Without giving the girl a chance for a rebuttal, he thanked her for her courtesy and left.

Because the girl gave no answer, I could not interpret his account as an affirmative response, but Reggie declared that it was all arranged. I was nevertheless certain that I could not turn to that barn at night no matter what the weather conditions, but during Reggie's negotiations the sky cleared and my rain argument evaporated. Thus I reluctantly surrendered to Reggie's whim; we headed back to Brookville, not for dinner, but to purchase a few rations that we could take back to the clump of trees that Reggie had designated as our campsite. There he proceeded to cook them on his portable mini-stove. Except for a can of baked beans, I cannot remember what delicacies our erstwhile leader had purchased. After being heated, the can was passed around the three of us with a common spoon, not unlike a group of Depression hobos around a fire. As the so-called guest, I was permitted to sample the beans first. Despite this honor the whole incident so overwhelmed me that I was already hoping for an early dawn.

Once we had partaken of his culinary achievement, we played word games until nightfall. I again selected an army cot and was happy to rest after a day of mental torture. By 10:30 PM traffic at our campsite became congested. Apparently this was the favorite spot where all the young couples of the area came for romance after an outdoor movie or other social event; on second thought that may have been the main event. Several times the headlights of approaching cars shone brightly in my face and woke me from a half-sleep. With no desire to disturb my rest, the drivers of every car without hesitation turned quickly and departed as though our jeep was a symbol of the law in those rural parts; perhaps the local police operated one, but for whatever reason the parkers never stayed around after glimpsing the jeep surrounded by three bodies spread out on two cots and a sleeping bag. They may have concluded that the three of us were the victims of a mass murder.

After all had quieted down and eight or ten cars had come and departed in haste, the final one appeared but did not beat an instant retreat. From my cot I could see the driver get out, and immediately I thought that we were in big trouble—trespassing violations, robbery victims, or something more sinister. The driver, however, totally ignored us, went to one side of our stand of trees, methodically removed a few pieces of brush that covered a roadway (reminiscent of Harold's lane) that led over a small crest, returned to his car, and drove about a quarter mile along the edge of the trees.

Reggie came stealthily over to my cot and whispered: "Did you see that?" When I nodded my head, he suggested that we follow on foot down the path that I had vaguely noticed in the daylight before we had settled down to a strange summer night's nap. Confused as to why he was anxious to make contact with these strangers, I waited for him to elucidate: "Do you think they might have a still down there, and do you think they would be willing to share?" I assured him that these were not the hills of Kentucky, that liquor was not their motivation, and that he should settle back into his sleeping bag.

Aware that that car was down there, I could not sleep until it returned after an hour and continued down the highway. All was peaceful until morning, when Reggie again served me breakfast in bed. Before he could leave the area, his curiosity forced him to go down the path that the car had taken the night before. His hope was that the occupants had left a little alcohol behind.

He went, surveyed the situation, found no still, only a used condom, and remarked: "Must have been Susie Sex." With that remarkable deduction we at last headed home with Reggie driving the first leg of the trip. He did well except for the first car that came toward us. As the car approached at a safe distance, Reggie announced: "That idiot is on the wrong side," until I shocked him into reality with a few cryptic words to the effect that we were in the US, not England. With that, he moved into the right lane.

I was driving when we reached their brownstone on Clyde Street. Before the jeep came to a complete stop, Reggie bounded out one side and Wilda the other; they hit the pavement running, with the basement door as their destination.

Apparently they had been thinking the same thoughts, and one was determined to outmaneuver the other.

For a moment I thought that I had contracted the worst case of BO known to mankind based on the speed with which they abandoned me. I'll admit that these two days had left me dirty, unshaven, and urgently in need of a shower. When they returned within a few minutes to explain their conduct, I realized that my unkempt condition was not their concern. They had moved into the brownstone only a short time before this sojourn to Emlenton, Cook Forest, Brookville, and points north. Having literally grounded their old washing machine in the move from their previous apartment, they had installed the new coin-operated model in their basement. Enterprisingly they had placed leaflets in all their neighbors' mailboxes inviting them to enter via the outside basement door to use the washing machine in their absence.

The race to the basement was to collect the booty in quarters that they hoped had accumulated from the neighbors' use. Wilda explained that, if she got there first, the money could be used to pay off the washing machine purchased on credit, but if Reggie won the race, it would undoubtedly be converted to beer money. With that explanation I left the jeep parked in front of their apartment, headed home via public transportation, and my relationship with Reggie was strained, not ruptured, thereafter.

Determined that my acquaintance with his second car would not be so intimate, I nevertheless experienced an indirect encounter. This acquisition was a Dodge business coupe acquired through the generosity of Dr. Leland Baldwin, a senior history professor. Equipped with a large shelf rather than the rear seat characteristic of most sedans, it created a seating disability for anyone intending to transport more than three people on a front seat.

The professor had purchased the Dodge new shortly after World War II and operated it for six or seven years before deciding to replace it because of age. He had spent two of those years on leave with the coupe up on blocks; as a result the mileage was much lower than normal for a car of that vintage.

Baldwin was aware that Reggie's Jeep had coughed its last, and, after having the Dodge checked by a mechanic and pronounced to be in good health, he offered it to Reggie for a mere $100, provided that he take a solemn pledge: "Never mention the Dodge in my presence no matter what good or bad fortune it brings you." Reggie knew a good deal when he heard one and without reservation took the oath.

This cost, plus other indebtedness, placed a strain on the Shortstraw budget. Resourceful Reggie devised a plan whereby the coupe could work to pay for itself; he secured a daylight moonlighting venture that was simplified by a car. Declaring himself a physical education specialist, he was engaged by the recently inaugurated Ascension Academy, the forerunner of St. Edmonds, to teach phys. ed. to boys in the first four grades. In cramped temporary urban quarters, the new school possessed limited athletic facilities, but that proved no impediment to Reggie, who was nimble of mind, as well as of foot.

With Schenley Park and its famous Oval less than two miles away, the new instructor decided to exercise his charges there in a series of soccer scrimmages. When Reggie described this second job to me, I asked how he transported the boys to and from the field.

Shortstraw: In my car.

Kehl: How many boys do you instruct at one time?

Shortstraw: 10 or 12

Kehl: How many trips do you make? You must spend at least an hour hauling each class to and from the field.

Shortstraw: It's done in one trip.

Kehl: That's impossible. How do you handle it? Do you have most of them run behind the car?

Shortstraw: No, everyone rides. It's not impossible if you have a little ingenuity.

Reggie went on to explain that he divided the boys in his charge into two teams. Because the end of each scrimmage always produced a winner and a loser, the result determined the transportation. "Those on the winning side ride back to school in the car with me, and the losers are sentenced to the dungeon." Of the winners, three or four sat on the front seat, on each other's laps, while the others crawled onto the shelf or stood bent over in the limited space behind the front seat. The losers accepted their fate willingly, climbed into the trunk, and as Reggie slammed the lid, they were banished from sight for the ride home. And I might add, they retained their exile for the return trip to Schenley Park on the next soccer outing.

I stood in shocked disbelief as Reggie recounted his busing technique. I asked if he realized that a defect in the exhaust system could cause a tragedy. The least that could occur would be a lot of sick kids, and a major carbon monoxide leak could have been fatal. Reggie shrugged off my admonition and declared me an alarmist. He also defended his action by concluding that the boys "loved it," as though their approval would lessen the dangers of his potential gas chamber.

He further defended his practice, noting that the boys were so enamored of the dungeon concept that they were happy losers at soccer, because he suspected that some were pleased to "throw the game" just to serve their sentence. With the trunk and seat kids yelling at each other as they traveled to and fro, the rides generated more enthusiasm than the games.

I am certain that neither academy authorities nor the students' parents had any knowledge of Reggie's improvised system. He gave new and secret meaning to the concept of being bused to class. Since the school served some of Pittsburgh's more prominent families, the administrators would have been embarrassed and the parents outraged if they had been aware of the potential horrors lurking in Reggie's car caravan. Reggie would have expressed a totally different view: It all turned out well, so what's the big deal?

Those boys, now pushing the sixty age bracket, might recall these trips in the portable dungeon fondly, because they were introduced to soccer long before it became popular; they were, in turn, able to teach their sons and daughters the finer points of the sport with more aplomb than their contemporaries, thanks to Reggie and a secure exhaust system.

SHORTSTRAW'S LAST HURRAH

After more than eleven years Shortstraw completed his doctorate in 1959, a task requiring most part-time students approximately five years. During his extended travail he gave no evidence of becoming a research scholar and, to prove the point, wrote a pedestrian dissertation that met the minimum standard for a degree.

After belatedly admitting to itself that Reggie possessed no potential to serve on a major university staff, the History Department continued his appointment on a year-to-year basis. The purpose was to encourage his departure by having him complete the doctorate, thus making him more competitive for a less challenging position elsewhere. Acceptance of the dissertation was the final preparatory step. The department elected not to renew his appointment again. Everyone even vaguely conversant with the situation, except Reggie and a small coterie within the department, expected the ax to fall when it did. His advocates expected inertia to be renewable into infinity.

But even Reggie had to be fantasizing his role when he pictured himself as a permanent member of the staff. Distraught, he whined to the press that he had been "fired without explanation" and that graduate students were destined to suffer. Of course, the next time he influenced a graduate's program was going to be the first. The newspapers responded with modest recognition, primarily their way of saying that all was not serene in the halls of academe.

I felt sorry for Reggie personally, but professionally I knew that his conduct had sealed the department's choice. For years I had lobbied for his termination, because his scholarly profile was inconsistent with everything the department maintained that it wanted to promote. Furthermore, he was denying space to someone who could fulfill the departmental standards.

Following several dead-end appointments after he left Pitt in a snit, Shortstraw responded to a publicized vacancy at Currville State College, where the generic term for faculty, students, and administrators was Currverts. The college, in turn, wrote to me for a professional assessment. I was perplexed by the request, because a friend, Art Johnson, was a member of the Currville history faculty, and he surely knew that in good conscience I could not write anything favorable. My first reaction was that Art did not want to make a negative decision because he knew Reggie from earlier days. What I didn't realize was that he was on sabbatical that term and was playing no role in the appointment process. I pondered this strange request, but proceeded to draft a thoroughly truthful response.

In a letter dated December 15, 1965, I explained that Reggie was "urbane, witty, and likeable," a man whose eccentricities in the classroom made him more "a campus character than a faculty leader." I literally stated that this one had to be seen to be appreciated. My purpose was either to quash his candidacy without further expenditure of Currville time and money or to force the college into a personal interview if my word wasn't sufficient.

In due course I learned that the department preferred both—to conduct an interview and then blunder. Reggie was hired despite my letter. When I asked Art how that had come about, with my statement on file, he gave me a candid reply: "They threw your letter in the wastebasket and requested another from someone who was not nearly so honest."

During his leave Art had remained at home and was aware that the Currverts had invited Shortstraw for an interview. Because Reggie and Art had shared an office at Pitt years before, the latter courteously invited his old office mate to dinner the evening before his department visit. Reggie accepted.

Over the years my friend had recounted snippets of Reggie-isms for his wife's amusement, but his excerpts concentrated on his ex-office mate's penchant for the humorous and unorthodox. She also had been given enough evidence to conclude that Reggie was no purveyor of fashion, but her knowledge fell short of understanding the full range of his repertoire. She quickly realized that, in Reggie's scheme of life, her preparation of a roast beef dinner complemented by red potatoes and mixed vegetables was a futility of effort, one that her guest affirmed with his first words of greeting.

Amid typical Reggie fanfare, he arrived proclaiming that he had "brought dinner." In free translation that meant that, while en route down the highway, the car in front of his struck a low-flying pheasant. Reggie leaped from his vehicle, dodged on-coming traffic, and retrieved the dead bird, which he now proposed to convert to pheasant potpie. The Johnsons were suddenly transformed from gracious hosts to confused guests in their own home, with chef Reggie about to do the unthinkable.

Despite objections from his hosts, Reggie insisted that this was his treat. Repeated protestations and explanations that a dinner was already prepared in anticipation of his arrival did not dissuade him. For some strange reason he saw this as a once-in-a-lifetime opportunity—pheasant delicacy in their own home at no cost; what more could a couple ask?

Injecting his opposition as forcefully as possible, Art was unable to disrupt the flow of Reggie's spirited determination. In a weak moment, he took the first and fatal step toward fulfilling Reggie's madcap plan—thinking that it might awaken him to the fact that it was totally unfeasible. Art provided a bucket of boiling water that the self-styled culinary genius carried to a vacant lot across the street where he proceeded to dunk the bird and pluck its feathers in preparation for road-kill potpie.

Art accompanied him—keeping up his patter of protest as Reggie de-feathered the fowl with an air of great anticipation. The agitated host argued that the bird probably suffered shattered bones and that there was a danger of eating the splinters, but the new chef conducted his own autopsy, debunked that theory, and gave the bird his own "Good Housekeeping Seal of Approval." With that declaration they walked back to the Johnson homestead for the next phase of impromptu meal preparation.

The bird was dressed, boiled whole, then de-boned and poured into a large casserole dish for baking. Our chef extraordinaire spied the mixed vegetables that Mrs. Johnson intended to serve and added them to the pheasant meat, with no regard for the fact that they had been cooked and would now be overcooked. He also asked for flour to make a crust to cover the mixture. Once provided, he appropriated a little extra to bake a few biscuits that actually turned into rocks before their eyes. What's a pheasant delight without a hard biscuit to pour it over?

After almost three hours of this erratic behavior, Reggie announced: "Dinner is served." Described as "inedible, detestable, indigestible, and heated garbage," chef Reggie's highly touted *piece de résistance* proved to be the worst meal Art and his wife ever ate—and in their own home—with a delicious roast beef on the back burner to become tomorrow's leftovers, all as a reminder that Reggie had passed their way.

For me the finale to this weird Shortstraw tale came five years later—unexpectedly like everything else about Reggie; that was the secret of his superficial charm. Visiting on the Currville campus, I was introduced to President Bumpchin, who had ascended the administrative ladder via such acclaimed academic posts as assistant dean of men and director of admissions, without any direct contact with the classroom or departmental faculty meetings. As an immodest Currvert, he let me know immediately that he administered a highly professional institution.

Upon hearing that I was from the University of Pittsburgh, he smiled and said: "We had one of the boys from your elite, urban school down here and had to fire him." (I guess he put me in my place before I had a chance to say a word.) Knowing nothing about Reggie's tenure at soon-to-be Currville U, I was not going to be surprised by any litany, so I inquired about what had gone wrong. The president was pleased that I asked that question, because he was about to answer it anyway.

It seems that Reggie went to class one day only to find another instructor in the room. Believing that he had entered before the professor from the previous hour had gathered his papers to leave, Reggie proceeded to pass out exam booklets to a surprised class. When the instructor asked Reggie what he thought he was doing, he replied: "I'm going to give my class an examination as soon as you get yourself out of here."

To Reggie's amazement his colleague refused to leave— declaring that this was his course, and he was about to teach it. Obviously someone had screwed up, and without knowing any of the details, my money would have been on Shortstraw. The two checked their watches and neither one was out of sync; they also looked at the number on the door, and both agreed that they were in the proper room; they even identified the building as the proper one without finding a solution to the problem. Before the impasse was resolved, pleasantries escalated to unpleasantries.

To the extent that students were aware of the discussion unfolding before them, they were amused. Charged words between the two instructors prompted a call to campus security. The crisis ended with Reggie being escorted off. As the president said: "He was drunk as a skunk." Somehow poor Reggie had lost Tuesday that week. It was 3:00 PM and the room was 125, but the day was now Wednesday.

The president loved his rendition but couldn't appreciate the egg that covered his face. I said little, but when I returned home, I sent him a copy of my letter that identified Reggie as a campus character, and that portrayed his "boys" as too dense to understand the words or to recognize an academic farce when one had appeared before them for an interview.

In this one instance, at least, the president was definitely off base in belittling supposed big university arrogance. Perhaps he was equally wrong in assessing Reggie's state of sobriety. Reggie had repeatedly demonstrated that he was fully capable of such an oversight as losing a day even when completely sober.

Almost everyone who has ever enrolled in a college program has encountered at least one instructor suspected of having a loose flywheel. No one did more to foster this loose flywheel concept than Reggie Shortstraw. As an instructor his gears didn't always mesh.

Unfortunately, early in his career his potential was thwarted by frivolous schemes, improper shortcuts, and a lack of commitment: all foibles that he never developed a will to overcome. That failure condemned him as the zaniest, wackiest, and at times the most outrageous colleague I experienced in more than forty years. Thus before the "ugly American" was defined in print, Reggie was hard at work demonstrating that the concept knows no national boundaries. He was entertaining but exasperating, proof that the American abroad had at least one worthy competitor.

PART TWO

THE ADMINISTRATION PHASE

(1955-1969)

An auto mechanic sets the timing so that an engine will run smoothly. Likewise, the comedian times the punch line of a joke to achieve the maximum response. Both mechanic and comedian agree that timing is "everything." The same analogy can be applied to academic administration, because the timing of an appointment can strongly influence the long-term success or failure of an appointee.

For Edward Litchfield, who accepted the chancellorship in 1955, the timing was superb. There had been no permanent chancellor in more than a year, and the previous chancellor was inclined to accept the status quo whenever possible. The faculty meanwhile yearned for leadership and direction.

Because of Dr. Litchfield's innovative ideas, this was an opportunity befitting his talents. His programs to expand the physical campus, to raise the level of student admissions, to develop a more diverse student body, to initiate a program of Mellon professorships and fellowships, to introduce a trimester calendar, and to propose challenging developments in other areas of the University were all met with faculty enthusiasm.

When Wesley Posvar assumed the chancellorship in 1967, his arrival was eagerly awaited by students and faculty. The timing was different, however. The new chancellor had hardly felt comfortable behind his desk when he was placed on the defensive; he was forced to confront societal problems that engulfed not only the University but also the community and all America.

Student uprisings, centered at other institutions across the nation, spilled their acrimony onto the Pitt campus. After the assassination of Dr. Martin Luther King in 1968, African-Americans also intensified their drive for equal rights. At the same time, with less physical pressure, the women's movement entered a new phase in its search for equality: equal pay for equal work. The chancellor could defer none of the three and had limited opportunity to insert his personal program for University advancement.

By the time Posvar had brokered campus solutions and restored a modicum of calm, the time for innovative proposals was slipping away. He became more and more absorbed in personal proposals and withdrew from University-wide goals. Gradually the faculty sensed that it was headed in a different direction than where the chancellor wanted to lead, but an extended period passed before either felt compelled to confront the emerging crisis.

My own brief career in university administration overlapped the terms of Litchfield and of the two interim chancellors before Posvar took office. Although the terms of both Dr. Stanton Crawford and Dr. David Kurtzman were short, the impact of both produced wide respect among the faculty. The former appointed me as dean of the College of Arts and Sciences, but his untimely death brought Dr. Kurtzman to office, who agreed to serve until a permanent successor, Dr. Posvar, was appointed.

Edward H. Litchfield, Chancellor 1956-1965

Photo courtesy of Archives Service Center, University of Pittsburgh

CHAPTER 5

The Undiscovered Chancellor

The vertical university came to an abrupt end with the appointment of Edward H. Litchfield as chancellor in 1955. Not only did the University assume an expanded physical presence, but it also cast a much broader net in search of quality students and faculty. New programs and new professional schools gave added dimensions to the campus.

Litchfield was a creative, competitive, self-motivated individual who exhibited little self-doubt. His accomplishments are worthy of a biography, but this vignette is not an attempt to provide one. I enjoyed a unique relationship with the chancellor that might assist any would-be writer in analyzing and documenting his career. Never an insider to the Litchfield decisions, I merely witnessed his achievements from an uncommon perspective.

Early in 1958 I was summoned to the chancellor's office without a clue concerning the purpose. I knew that I wasn't about to be fired because I was too low on the academic totem pole to be dismissed by the "big boss." Protocol suggests that an underling could have performed that task with no difficulty.

At that point I met Chancellor Litchfield for the first time. Ticking off a few details that he had learned about my conduct at the University, he asked if I would consider serving as his assistant. He was quick to add that this was not the typical flunky job where I carried the briefcase, opened the door, wrote the thank you notes, and escorted prominent women to special events.

His proposal outlined a plan by which I would spend a year in learning how the University functioned. Although he never expressed the purpose behind this experience, he suggested that I work in four different offices (three months in each) in the process and that I was to have access to every document and every decision pertaining to that office while I was assigned there. Failure for anyone to comply with those rules was to be reported to him immediately. With the proviso that I could continue to teach one history course in order not to become detached from the teaching profession, I accepted.

Immediately I volunteered to work for one period in the financial area, because my knowledge about such matters was sub-par. The chancellor agreed and added that, when I moved into that field, he would like to know why his [the University's] monthly telephone bill was so high. For the most part I discovered numerous ramifications of the problem, not solutions. One minor aspect that I did detect involved a woman who phoned her husband in Germany and her boyfriend in Bermuda at least three times a week on the assumption that this was a fringe benefit. That fringe was easily eliminated.

The chancellor and I also discussed the other three assignments that I would undertake. In so doing, he pointed to a stack of documents on his desk pertaining to power struggles within the physical education areas of the University. All were unsolicited papers and letters sent to him, mostly from outside the University, praising or condemning the professional standards of members of the Pitt staff and advising him to act on these alleged and conflicting statements. He wanted me to untangle the mess and tell him what to believe. That investigation was an eye-opening venture that included interviews with everyone from Captain Tom Hamilton, the Director of Athletics, to the men and women who conducted the required phys. ed. courses for freshmen.

The third part of the study took me to the office of the Dean of the Faculty, who had been instructed to analyze the undergraduate college curriculum and suggest possible improvements. A comparison with other programs, known nationally for their success, was expected to provide the guidelines for improving our programs.

Selected duty for the final three-month period pertained to a subject close to the chancellor's heart: the introduction of the Trimester System. With this proposal the University was attempting to revive and energize a plan that had been employed with limited success at various times in the American past. It projected an academic year of three (Fall, Winter, Spring) terms, each equal in credits to the existing semester.

When I accepted the appointment in the chancellor's office, the decision to adopt this new calendar had already been reached; and in the 1958-1959 year, final adjustments were implemented for full operation the following year. The chancellor was particularly desirous for this conversion to occur with as little disruption as possible, because he knew that the academic world was observing, and he was anxious for Pitt to make a positive impression. Seeing this as a wave of the future, I wanted to be a part of it.

Ultimately the Trimester made a major impact on the calendars both at Pitt and throughout America's academic world. The most thoroughly accepted aspect of the Pitt pattern maintained that the Fall Term would end in December, not be continued into the month of January as had been true in the past. Also in many institutions the end of the following term, à la Pitt, was moved to sometime between late April and mid-May rather than extending graduations to sometime between late May and mid-June.

Both at Pitt and elsewhere, the substance of the Trimester was not enthusiastically embraced by either students or faculty. The latter failed to develop courses for the Spring Trimester that were appealing enough to attract sufficient numbers of students to make it financially feasible. On the other hand, there is no evidence that any program was going to keep the bulk of students in class for eleven-plus months per year. The students welcomed a Winter Term that ended in April because it provided a longer summer in which they could be gainfully employed to meet the ever-increasing tuition rates. Furthermore, the Russians had successfully launched Sputnik in October 1957, and that brought an abrupt change in federal assistance to education that was predicated on a two-term year. That combination blunted the progress of the Trimester.

The chancellor accepted this disappointing outcome, quietly blaming inadequate preparation. One day he remarked to me personally that "we must be more thorough in the next phase," but the meaning of that remark never came to fruition. He considered the Trimester as part of a larger adjustment, a calendar revision that would encompass the primary and secondary school years as well.

In the late 1950s Edward Litchfield viewed television as primarily an instructional medium limited only by the inventive minds of the nation's leaders. This version completely overlooked the commercial appetites of an entrepreneurial society. The power of business/advertising, not education, proved to be the dominant forces in the television age.

That development relegated Litchfield's idea to an unreality that could never emerge even in a formative stage. His scheme was based on the assumption that, because of television, children would be better prepared for formal education than in the past.

Toward that end his plan called for all students to enter First Grade at the age of five. Thus the first six grades could be completed at age 11. The next three grades (7-9) could be telescoped into two years and concluded by age 13. With the high school years (10-12) following, a student would graduate from high school at age 16. If the Trimester plan were fully operational, as he then expected, a student would have his college diploma when he was 19.

On the other hand, the student who did not elect a college program would have completed an apprenticeship in a skills program at approximately the same time. By age 21 all would be firmly placed in a job or have at least two years toward a degree in a professional field. The purpose of this accelerated calendar was to capitalize on the individual's most productive years in a way that would benefit both student and society.

The program never emerged, because the chancellor and the trustees parted ways before any progress could be made public.

Calendar revision was not the chancellor's only visionary idea to fall short of maturity. He believed that the industrial, commercial, educational, military, and hospital organizations adhered to the same generalized administrative processes. Thus he undertook the ambitious, exploratory task of discovering a new discipline—administrative science—that served all. Aware that political science, sociology, and psychology, for example, had been gradually defined as distinct disciplines for viewing and understanding the social processes, he hoped to add administrative science to that list.

Convinced that such a body of knowledge existed that delineated this separate role, he sought to link the various parts together. With this in mind, he organized a seminar, which he would lead and for which he would select all of the students. With Dr. James Thompson as his seminar assistant, Litchfield deliberately identified his students from among leaders in widely divergent fields: a hospital administrator, a public school superintendent, a bank vice president, a corporate official, a lawyer, and several others including me. The group was to meet every Tuesday at 4:00 PM for one term in the chancellor's office.

I fought hard diplomatically to be excused from the assignment. Having completed a PhD a few years before, I did not look forward to reading assignments, paper presentations, and weekly discussions. The chancellor was adamant; he declared that I could give up everything that I was doing that term as long as I was in his office every Tuesday at 4:00. I complied.

Reflectively I must confess that the experience improved my teaching. The seminar presented a new tool with which to examine party politics, particularly in regard to decision-making. I came to realize that oftentimes the level at which an organizational decision is reached may be more significant than the decision itself. When adjustments are necessary, and frequently they are, they can be undertaken with greater deftness and less disruption if the original level of action was the appropriate one.

Of course, the seminar reaffirmed much that was already known; administration is a montage of information gathered from numerous disciplines such as economics, sociology, philosophy, accounting, finance, and business principles. Some combinations performed better in some organizations than in others, but we never discovered that one body of information fits all.

This limited success, I'm sure, disappointed the chancellor. He at least hoped to identify one or more of us who would commit to the pursuit of administrative science as a separate discipline, but no one could see that as a career objective.

From the seminar experience I did discern that the chancellor, like most successful administrators, was more interested in the bottom line than in details. When he assigned a task, he wanted to know only that it had been accomplished, not the arm-twisting, exaggeration, or rule-bending that may have played a role in achieving the desired goal.

I had to employ this interpretation of the chancellor's wishes when he gave me an assignment concerning the appointment of a new dean. In the negotiations the University agreed that the appointee would receive a room exclusively for his book collection. The only stipulation was that the room be provided with adequate shelving to accommodate 600 linear feet of books. The simple green, unsightly steel shelf units (4 ft. long by 6 ft. high) with diagonal reinforcing strips across the back (like those many of us have in our garages and basements) were designated as appropriate.

My assignment was to see that the room was properly equipped by a certain Monday. Purchasing was no problem; the shelving was delivered six weeks in advance, and a work order to assemble them was immediately sent to the unionized ground crew that possessed the sole right to perform this task. When no action on the work order was taken within three weeks, I called and also sent a note restating the deadline.

I also enlisted the assistance of a graduate student to be on standby in case of an emergency. When Friday before the scheduled completion date arrived, the work order had still not been fulfilled. I gave the student a key to the room with instructions to erect the shelves over the weekend. That task was carried out, and on Monday I reported to the chancellor that the room was prepared.

That was all that he wanted to hear, and I was glad. Individuals had informed me that the union could have shut down the University for taking away a union job. Personally, I was more angry than perturbed but realized that the incident could have embarrassed the University. I was certain that I had followed legitimate procedures and didn't give a damn about union protocol because adequate opportunity to act had been given. Fortunately the subject of the shelves never resurfaced.

Although the administrative science venture and the proposed revamping of the public school calendar never became noteworthy, they were not alone among the chancellor's concepts that failed to reach fruition. He also promoted a plan to restructure the University's academic programs, which was eventually aborted and never reached the public ear. Under this structure the undergraduate Arts and Sciences program would remain relatively small (approx. 2500) but become truly elite in character. Expansion was to occur in all graduate schools and professional programs. Thereafter Pitt's major strength would reside in those areas, with regional and smaller schools throughout the nation serving as feeder institutions for Pitt's advanced programs.

When I was first asked to be a Litchfield assistant, he had no thought, in my opinion, that I was being groomed for any position at Pitt. Instead, he expected me, along with several others, to become presidents of colleges/universities that would direct students to Pitt's burgeoning programs. Shortly after my appointment, I received invitations, I suspect on Litchfield's suggestion, to interview for presidencies where I knew no one and where no one knew me.

Evidence that such invitations were chancellor-induced became clear at the LaGuardia Airport one night after such an interview. I encountered a Pitt friend who was returning from an interview at the same university. The school's authorities did a skillful job in keeping our paths from crossing during the day's activities. The redesigning of the University structure achieved limited success because of numerous crosscurrents, and this idea of placing Pitt personnel in college presidencies to benefit its graduate programs failed to pay the dividends expected.

The causes were multiple. The National Defense Education Administration (NDEA) came into existence, focusing its funds primarily on specific programs. That trend was buttressed by newly available state and federal government loan programs, which encouraged more students to pursue undergraduate degrees. At the same time Pennsylvania State University was moving forward with its two-year Commonwealth campus program that encompassed the whole state, including Western Pennsylvania.

Pitt responded by adding regional campuses at Greensburg, Titusville, and Bradford to the one at Johnstown, an idea that was not enthusiastically received by Pitt faculty. At one point I suggested to the chancellor that greater faculty support for the regionals could be enlisted if, like me, the faculty had a constructive explanation for the expansion. For the benefit of a few administrators, he stated the purpose in four words: "To stop Eric Walker," the president of Penn State, who was supplying the thrust for the Commonwealth program that potentially threatened a basic source of Pitt students.

The philosophy for this movement had been revealed in generalized terms a few years before. Penn State officials had requested, and were granted, an opportunity to come to Pitt to explain their newly defined mission. At the time Pitt was still a private institution, and Penn State was state-related.

I was among those invited by Dean Stanton Crawford to attend the meeting held in the Cathedral of Learning. The visitors pointed out that, as a state school, they had an obligation to provide communities with the best locally available educational services possible. Their proposal called for the delivery of skill courses, as well as academic ones. This step was the precursor of the Commonwealth System.

It was a little jarring to Pitt people to learn that another university was planning to offer courses in our own backyard.

One speaker emphasized that, if ten or more people requested a course in a given area, Penn State felt an obligation to respond. A little angry at that perceived aggressiveness, I asked what Penn State would do if a group requested a course in safecracking. At first I thought that Dean Crawford might ask me to leave the meeting for being rude to a visitor, but that didn't happen. The comment brought laughter, especially from the Pitt group including the dean.

The speaker did not back down from his stated desire to be of service to a community. He explained that there were constructive reasons for breaking into a safe and added that the University would certainly explore the moral implications before proceeding. Most of us at Pitt exhibited little reaction to the Penn State proposal, but shortly thereafter the Commonwealth System became a reality to fulfill its mission, as well as to offer skill courses as needs were identified.

Although Penn State's Commonwealth Campus System influenced Pitt's resurgence in undergraduate education, the Trimester remained Pitt's most heralded contribution to undergraduate learning. It aroused greater interest nationally than any activity since Jonas Salk had developed his polio vaccine in 1955, but the University enjoyed a brighter spotlight in 1959 when Chairman Nikita Khrushchev of the Soviet Union visited the United States on an eleven-day transcontinental tour.

Pittsburgh was the last stop of Khrushchev's state visit. As Robert C. Alberts noted in his history of the University (p. 272): "No comparable event has ever been held on the Pitt campus." Ours was the only university at which the Soviet leader spoke, and every effort was exerted to capitalize on the publicity. Responsibility for that honor rested solely on the maneuvering of Dr. Litchfield.

One of the chancellor's outside organizations was the Governmental Affairs Institute in Washington of which he was the founder and president. Part of the Institute's duty was to determine itineraries for America's state visitors. In this case it naturally followed that Litchfield would select his own university campus as the only one at which Khrushchev would speak.

Elaborate logistical security and protracted protocol preparations were necessary to stage the stately luncheon planned for the William Pitt Union. Almost 500 guests, including local and state leaders, were invited; also on hand were 325 American and foreign journalists who were served lunch in the University cafeteria where they also watched the proceedings on television. For the benefit of students, 35 television monitors were placed throughout the campus so that they might hear the speeches not only by the Soviet Chairman but also by Governor David Lawrence, Mayor Thomas Gallagher, and Chancellor Litchfield.

Security precautions were more detailed than the city had ever witnessed. During the morning and luncheon hours, no one was permitted to stand before any of the Cathedral's windows on the Bigelow side (facing the William Pitt Union). This was tighter security than that afforded President Kennedy during his fateful Dallas trip four years later.

A special reception for the Khrushchev caravan was staged at the Fifth Avenue entrance to the Union. All of the invited guests received personalized invitations instructing them to enter via the Forbes Avenue entrance. Accompanied by a Secret Service agent looking over my shoulder, I was charged with the task of checking the credentials (personal invitations) of the guests. The procedure ran smoothly, until a man approached whom I recognized immediately from the many photos I had seen over the years; it was none other than Soviet Foreign Minister Andrei Gromyko.

I have no idea how his car became separated from all the others in the entourage that arrived at the Fifth Avenue door. I don't know if his driver failed to follow instructions, or if he deliberately took the wrong turn so that Gromyko might observe what the University was doing on the less celebrated side of the building, or if he was frantically looking for a Men's Room.

I was awe-struck, and the Secret Service agent had disappeared. I did manage to stammer: "Sir, a special welcoming ceremony is planned for you at the other side of the hall. I will have someone escort you there." Agitated, he looked me in the eye and grunted: "Me Gromyko" and charged by me. I heard no more; he undoubtedly found his destination whatever it was. I did observe he was on the dais in time for the luncheon.

The speeches took longer than planned. The real excitement, however, did not come until near the conclusion when Khrushchev decided to ad-lib a few boastful remarks. In the process he conceded that the grain fields that he had toured in the Midwest were superior to those in the Soviet Union's wheat belt, but proclaimed that the Soviets were improving, would catch us, salute us, and pass us. Likewise after viewing the steel mills at the Mesta Machine Company in West Homestead, he found them more productive than those at home, but insisted that the USSR was becoming more efficient, will catch you, salute you, and pass you.

That's not the exact account as reported in Alberts' history of the University (pp. 273-275). He adhered closely to the formal speeches of both Khrushchev and Litchfield, but I was there and can only report what I saw and heard. In this final exchange the chancellor challenged and rebuked the Soviet leader more decisively than he had ever been criticized in a public forum before or later.

To Litchfield, Khrushchev's remarks sounded like a challenge to a competition, and he reminded his guest that the Americans have been well acquainted with the concept of competition for more than a hundred years. He then challenged Khrushchev to a novel competition from which all mankind could benefit. He proposed that the two national giants compete to see which could be the first to eliminate the slums in its cities, which could first find a cure for cancer, and which could lead the way in eradicating heart disease. He could have added, but did not, that the US had already taken the first step with the Salk vaccine.

As these words were being relayed to Khrushchev by the translator, he frantically motioned to have the microphone returned so that he could respond. Litchfield meanwhile calmly announced: "This meeting is hereby adjourned" and turned to open the door behind the podium which was the exit for those on the dais. Khrushchev had no alternative except to follow the chancellor's lead. They walked out together amid the audience's applause.

The session was over, and the Soviet delegation shortly left the city. Comment and reaction continued for weeks, but to me the media failed to exploit the chancellor's remarks and give him the accolades he deserved.

On most of these matters, I was on the fringe of the strategy, but being a political historian I always tried to discern what connection, if any, specific events and individuals had to the political scene. As a result of this kind of thinking, I concluded that Litchfield and the business leaders of Pittsburgh were part of a legitimate game called "president-making." There is no reason why the Mellons, Falks, Scaifes, Hillmans, and even Litchfield should not be part of this practice. For more than a hundred years, this game has been played in various cities, and Pittsburgh had a right to play.

According to the theory, city and state leaders frequently identify a young, aggressive, appealing politician whom they groom and support financially for high office. The ultimate success for this protégé is the White House, but most often such players must settle for something less—a governorship, a place in the US House of Representatives, a seat in the US Senate, a cabinet post, or nothing at all. Although he was not a politician, Litchfield possessed the attributes of a young (41 years of age when he came to Pitt), successful leader. A good debater with a charming manner, he looked and dressed like a man of stature because he had already demonstrated his ability to deal with businessmen, governors, and other influential leaders.

The principal factor that caused me to link Litchfield and the trustees with president-making was the unnatural series of offices that Litchfield held concurrently with the chancellorship. He was not only chairman of the board at Smith-Corona-Marchant, but also an executive with AVCO Manufacturing Company and Studebaker-Packard Corporation, as well as a director of *Fortune* magazine.

The faculty and some trustees questioned the heavy administrative burden that this combination of duties placed on one set of shoulders. They wondered if the chancellor was on a frantic search for power and/or money at the expense of the University. Leading the institution to the excellence he had proclaimed seemed to be a mammoth undertaking in its own right. To my political eye these positions outside the University were designed primarily to achieve national exposure for political purposes. I have no idea whether these assignments were with or without the blessings of the Mellons and fellow leaders. My hunch is that the trustees at least helped to make them possible.

When Bob Alberts was writing his history, he and I discussed this theory several times. I asked if he found any evidence in the documents that either the city's leaders or Litchfield himself hinted that they were a part of this president-making practice. On page 250 of his work, Bob alludes generally to this idea, but falls short of a definitive statement.

The question became moot when the trustees forced Litchfield's resignation. Either they no longer agreed with the chancellor's management of the University or became disenchanted in their perception of his political potential. But, excitement was always there; it was impossible to predict the chancellor's next headline.

CHAPTER 6

A Logical Progression

My first academic administration venture crept into my career almost unnoticed. If I had realized that it would be central to my life for the next 14 years (1955-1969), more forethought would have been given. Unplanned as it was, administration proved challenging and always exciting. Because I continued to teach part-time, it was always viewed as an extension of the classroom.

In 1954 my friend and mentor, Russell Ferguson, was named chairman of the History Department, but only several months passed before he was diagnosed with lung cancer in an advanced stage. Weakened by the cancer treatments, he needed help in handling departmental details and asked me to serve as his assistant. I accepted, but sadly by the end of summer in 1955, Professor Ferguson had succumbed to the disease.

For the next five years, the department operated without a permanent chairman. During the first three of those years, I administered the department with the title of executive officer. In the third year (1958), I was invited to serve as assistant to Chancellor Litchfield as described in the previous chapter. That appointment was for one year, but I remained on the chancellor's payroll for a second year, during which the University underwent a major organizational change particularly crucial to the arts and sciences.

Before this reorganization the dean of the College had been the pivotal figure—with supervision of both the faculty and the undergraduate program. The revision separated the arts and sciences departments into three divisions: Humanities, Social Sciences, and Natural Sciences, each with its own dean. These deans assumed responsibility for the relevant faculty and for their own graduate programs.

This structure fitted into Chancellor Litchfield's strategy to expand graduate study greatly in the future (see previous chapter) while holding undergraduate enrollment to a slight increase. In this arrangement a dean of the College remained, but that role was diminished, because he now had only an undergraduate program to manage. He was responsible for students but had to rely on the divisional deans to provide the instructional faculty. (As we said in jest, he was a dean without faculties.) This placed undergraduate education at a disadvantage, because the divisional deans were primarily interested in developing a faculty that strengthened their graduate programs with only a secondary regard for faculty appointments with an undergraduate emphasis.

Almost as soon as the new organization was agreed upon, Professor Max Lauffer of the Physics Department was named dean of the Natural Sciences, but no deans were immediately identified for the other two divisions. Their graduate programs nevertheless had to continue, because students admitted under the old system, as well as those admitted currently, required record keeping and administration. I was chosen to oversee these programs for both divisions (Humanities and Social Sciences), whereas the Vice Chancellor for the Academic Disciplines took direct charge of supervising the faculties.

In 1960 John P. Gillin, an anthropologist from the University of North Carolina, was appointed dean of the Social Sciences. Part of his acceptance package required that I be assigned as his assistant dean to continue to administer the division's graduate programs while he managed faculty affairs. I was happy to accept the assignment, but apparently I carried a jinx, because after a year, Dean Gillin became a victim of lung cancer. He survived the surgery but never regained his full strength. Resigning the deanship, he remained at Pitt as a professor of Anthropology.

During Dean Gillin's illness and convalescence, I was the representative for the Division of the Social Sciences. Ultimately a new dean, Richard Park, a professor of Political Science from the University of Michigan, was appointed as Gillin's replacement. I served as his associate dean, but he too became ill, and I was again the division spokesman.

In 1965 Dr. Park returned to the University of Michigan; at the same time, I was named dean of the undergraduate college by Stanton Crawford, who had become chancellor when Litchfield resigned. The college had been without a permanent dean for more than a year; that created a favorable climate for change and for the introduction of new procedures.

During my four years in the deanship, a change of historic note occurred. At a Commons Room ceremony in the Cathedral of Learning on August 23, 1966, Governor William W. Scranton affixed his signature to a measure passed by the Pennsylvania Legislature whereby the University of Pittsburgh was officially transformed from a private institution to a state-related one. The most notable aspect of this change took place in the School of the Liberal Arts (the new name assigned by the reorganization to the undergraduate college, but while I was dean, it was changed to the College of Arts and Sciences, and still later to the School of Arts and Sciences; throughout the remainder of this volume, it will be referred to as the College).

Accompanying the legislative enactment came a marked reduction in tuition, which, in turn, produced an immediate enrollment increase, both in freshman applications and in requests for transfer from private and state-owned colleges. As one transfer student said to me: "Now, for practically the same tuition, I can earn a Pitt degree."

Even the wife of one state senator found the opportunity so tempting that she transferred from a home economics program elsewhere to the College. After the first glow wore off, neither the senator nor his wife was content with the amount of transfer credit that she had been awarded. In a cryptic note the senator requested an opportunity to review every course for which his wife had not been given full credit. He added that he wanted to deal directly with me, not with the staff member charged with that responsibility. I promptly agreed to such a discussion, which did not proceed as he had planned.

Central to the issue was the fact that his wife had received no credit for a course in which she had attained an A grade. He knew that that was an error despite the title of the course: Use of Cooking Utensils. This problem came to the forefront after the substance of other courses had been discussed and determined. Even those had caused the senator to become a little testy, and I too was annoyed at having to repeat the position of the College on certain types of courses.

The senator seemed to have no appreciation for the philosophy behind liberal education and was unwilling to learn. When he rebuffed my arguments for the umteenth time, I replied: "Look, we do not give credit for pots and pans in the College; the quality of your wife's performance in the course is a non sequitur. It's like breathing; it's good but doesn't carry College credit." That ended the discussion and may have brought the senator to a slightly higher understanding of the meaning of the liberal arts.

One of the first additions that I brought to the College in 1965 was the creation of the Executive Council, composed of two representatives from each of the three divisions. Together that council and the College staff achieved several enduring changes: (a) designation of the Self-Designed major, (b) addition of plus/minus and pass/fail grades to the student record system, (c) establishment of the Academic Integrity Guidelines, and (d) establishment of the predecessor to the Career Guidance Center, which originally was known as the Post-Baccalaureate Educational Services Office (PESO).

In its first years PESO served only College students. Its creation was my attempt to provide a service to College students generally that was similar to the committee that aided only students applying to medical schools. Why shouldn't all potential graduate school applicants receive the same support in their efforts to find suitable programs, especially if such assistance would enable them to compete for scholarships and fellowships?

I also appointed a faculty committee on Admissions that did not survive my tenure. I was interested both in faculty input and in having a particular faculty member as chairman. He was a volatile professor of English who by some means, certainly with no assist from the University administration, procured an appointment to write a Sunday column for one of the Pittsburgh dailies. Often his weekly dissertations waxed elegantly critical of Pitt officials.

When I informed my associate and assistant deans that I planned to invite this professor to chair a committee, they were certain that I was placing the College in jeopardy. I explained that I would prefer to have him on the inside shooting out rather than on the outside shooting at us.

My ploy succeeded. The professor accepted the appointment and, as expected, performed diligently in the assignment—never offering in public a negative word about the College. He was transformed into a happy camper, because we had recognized him as a talented individual. Unfortunately for him, his past rants against the University were undertaken with only partial information. Those outbursts had kept Pitt officials off-balance, because they didn't know what to expect next. The College was not subjected to such conduct, because we had taken him into our trust.

Throughout my years in administration, my office was always intent upon carrying its share of any joint project. As a result I had good rapport with other offices, including those of both chancellors Crawford and Kurtzman. For various reasons (see next chapter), the same cooperation did not develop under Chancellor Posvar. Undergraduate education did not appear to gain Povar's attention, and the administrators who stood between me and him chose, despite my urgings, to overlook College needs.

Early in my deanship, I also succeeded in activating the College Alumni Council, which held regular meetings that I attended. My task was to keep its officers abreast of College developments, explain controversial issues to them, and field their reactions. They appreciated the involvement, and at the end of my four years, presented me with a Distinguished Alumnus Award at a banquet at which US Senator Hugh Scott was the featured speaker.

SECRETARIAL SALUTE

One of the major reasons my office, both in the Social Sciences and in the College, functioned so smoothly and efficiently can be attributed to the succession of quality secretaries that I was able to recruit. They were all gracious, courteous, and helpful to students, faculty, and administrators alike. I often volunteered their services to other offices, because I respected their abilities and wanted to compliment them by giving them opportunities to help others.

Often secretaries were new or new to a particular procedure, and I would advise them that they could call our office for assistance. Many were grateful, but one created a humorous moment when she thought she had a problem and called. She reported that the word *pursue* was missing from her dictionary and asked if my secretary shared that problem. In reply my secretary said that her dictionary was not deficient in this manner, because the word is not spelled *p-e-r-s-u-e*.

From my contacts in many University offices, I realized that Pitt was blessed with many high quality women serving as secretaries, office managers, and administrative assistants.

Sometimes I also became acquainted with them in the class-room. Because I generally taught a course at night, these women would take advantage of the University's generous tuition break to earn an undergraduate or graduate degree. They invariably proved to be superior students.

Although my evaluation may be slightly biased, I feel that my five secretaries were always among the elite. Each was the backbone of the office during my tenure. They were all quick learners who derived pleasure from representing the University well. Varying in age from 21 to 66 when they first came through my office door, they made my life a joy.

Alice, a pleasant 30-something former school teacher, represented my first official encounter with a secretary. She was inherited from two former chairmen when I took over as the executive in the History Department. As an undergraduate while studying in the School of Education to become a teacher of secretarial/business subjects, Alice had served as a half-time secretary in the department; the budget in the austere 1930s could provide no more.

Exceeding the expectations of the senior staff, Alice created a serious loss when she earned her degree and departed for a teaching assignment in rural Pennsylvania. While away from Pittsburgh, her family suffered a major tragedy that stirred the empathy of the History Department. As a patient, her father was beaten to death by a local hospital employee. The trial, court appearances, delays, and newspaper publicity were calamitous to the family. This caused Alice to resign her teaching position to be at home with her aged mother.

History's secretarial slot meanwhile was upgraded to full-time and without hesitation the department, with the same chairman, invited her to return. Faculty members understood

Alice's grief and welcomed her reliable presence back, and she appreciated the opportunity to work among sympathetic faculty. I learned this part of Alice's background from senior colleagues. In less than a decade, the chairman resigned. His replacement was a faculty member whom she also respected and admired. Both chairmen were 25-35 years older than Alice; she was comfortable with them as father figures; but within months of taking office, the second chairman died of cancer. This was the vacancy that I filled, and Alice had the misfortune of being eight years my senior. At first she was outwardly apprehensive about her ability to work with a younger man and also about my ability to provide the same competent leadership she had come to respect.

For three years Alice and I survived happily together. She worried about everyone's problems. Because Pitt was a private university at the time, near the end of every fiscal year, budget cuts, particularly in office supplies, were standard, sometimes real and sometimes only an alarm. Alice feared that faculty members would ask her for supplies that she could not provide. I repeatedly assured her that such shortages, even if real, did not reflect adversely on her managing skills.

With an expanding department and young instructors feeding the mimeograph machine as though it were on an alcoholic binge, she feared that the supply of ink would be exhausted before the new budget kicked in. She lamented not only to me but also to her regular lunch companions, who included secretaries from the offices of the dean and chancellor. She didn't complain about the cuts, only about her ability to manage. They told her, as I did, not to worry, but she kept reinventing the argument about the dwindling supplies on her shelves.

One day these friends decided to poke fun at her fears. From their various offices they collected a ream of paper, a box of paper clips, a pair of scissors, a stapler, and a bottle of the precious mimeograph ink. The items were all boxed as one parcel, labeled "Care Package," and delivered to Alice's desk personally by a chancellor's assistant. She understood that they were encouraging her to relax and go with the flow.

A professional worrier, Alice fretted that I worked too hard; I stayed after five o'clock to catch up on paperwork. Because neither of my predecessors followed that routine, my conduct was disconcerting and unnatural.

From me she had learned that my wife worked outside the home and followed a weekly menu so religiously that tuna casserole dinners were as predictable as Tuesday evenings. Alice knew that this was my least favorite dish. As a result, late one Tuesday afternoon, Alice said good night, walked out, and locked the door; within minutes I heard her key in the door, and with a twinkle in her eye she said: "Don't work too late; remember this is tuna casserole night."

When I was about to leave the History Department to become assistant dean in the Social Sciences, I informed Alice of my decision. She advised me in all sincerity that I was making a major mistake. From her vantage point she concluded that I was one of the most popular instructors in the College and believed that I should capitalize on that. She summarized not only what students said about me when they came to her office but also what she considered a more concrete reason for her advice.

In those days students registered for courses by obtaining official class cards from the department in which they intended to take each course on their schedules. Alice was in charge of the History class cards but could not authorize more students per section than there were seats in the classroom. Once a room was filled, students could only enroll in that section if someone surrendered a card via a schedule change.

Alice kept a waiting list of students desiring a particular course. Because of that role she informed me of something that I was hearing for the first time. Students offered her five dollars to put their names at the head of the list for my courses, and one offered ten dollars if she would assure him a card. She was so honest that she was flustered by the prospect of someone attempting to corrupt her in that way. I made light of the situation when she explained it to me and told her that students probably didn't want me personally; they only wanted a class that came at the popular hour at which my course was being taught.

Although Alice's tenure in the department office preceded mine, I was totally pleased with her professionalism. Her four successors in my secretarial history, however, were all my own choices. Two of the four were recruited from the chancellor's office, a feat that to my knowledge has never been duplicated.

June was the first of those two; she actually recruited me before I recruited her. One day she phoned my office, introduced herself as a not-too-distant neighbor of mine, and stated that she worked for the chancellor. She explained that she saw my name in the University directory and recognized that we both lived in the Whitehall area. In need of transportation, she asked if there were a possibility that she could travel to and from the University with me if she walked to an intersection that I passed each day.

June and I became fellow travelers. We discussed the details of her assignment in the chancellor's office, her career goals, the education of her kids, and her theories of education. During these conversations I expressed my thoughts on these subjects, as well as on a few others. In the process I learned that she was not particularly happy with her role as the one in charge of the chancellor's mail. She logged in every piece, routed some to the chancellor, diverted others to certain administrators, some to be answered directly and others to be drafted for the chancellor's signature. It was a repetition that became boring.

At the same time, as assistant dean in the Social Sciences, I was looking for a new secretary for a new dean who was coming from outside the University. I preferred an experienced secretary from within and considered June a worthy candidate. I explored the situation with her, and she literally jumped at the prospect. The immediate challenge then was to determine how to broach the subject to the chancellor. At that point Dr. Litchfield was unaware that June and I knew each other, and I didn't think that this was the propitious moment to apprise him of the fact. Knowing that the chancellor always preferred the direct approach, I simply asked with a smile if he would object to my attempting to lure one of his office staff away. Never desiring to hinder anyone's progress, he said: "If you can convince her to join you, be my guest." Thus June came to the Social Sciences.

My arrangement with her was that, if she and the new dean were not a compatible team, she would remain as my secretary, and the search for a dean's secretary would be activated. She worked with me for months; the new dean ultimately arrived, and they formed a highly workable team.

Thus I was again in the hunt for a secretary, and the personnel gods smiled broadly on me. A friend in the Human

Resources Office called to report that a 21-year-old girl on her first job interview was in his office eagerly seeking employment. My reply: "Send her down," and he did. While she made her way from near the top of the Cathedral of Learning to the tenth floor, the friend called and said: "I'm impressed, and I think that you will be too. By the way, ask her where she got those big blue eyes; they're the biggest I've ever seen." To this day I remember the phrase "big blue eyes," but I forgot to ask.

She arrived a little nervous but not flustered like most on a first interview. She had completed three years at Allegheny College but came to Pittsburgh to be close to her fiancé, who had already graduated from the same school and was attending Pitt's School of Law. Sue had taken a speed-writing course in preparation for a secretarial post and felt comfortable with the problems of an academic office. I quizzed her about leaving college with only a year to complete a degree, but obviously she had considered all angles. She was determined to work for me or for someone else; she was in Pittsburgh to stay.

Sue's qualifications were perfect for my needs. She worked for me for the three years that Doug was in law school. During that period they married; my wife and I attended their wedding in northeastern Ohio. I have remained in contact, Christmas-letter style at least, over the last 40 years. In the course of Sue's tenure, I became the dean of the College of Arts and Sciences, and Sue moved there with me. She was super-efficient in all her work; reports, bulletin information, correspondence, and surveys from the department chairpersons were always on time. I never asked how; I was simply satisfied. Years later a chairman revealed Sue's technique; anytime a department seemed to be lagging on a request, Sue would say: "The dean is going to be disappointed," and she achieved her goal.

While I was still in the Social Sciences office, a need arose for an assistant to evaluate the academic credentials of students applying for graduate study. The task required an individual who could interpret transcripts from many different undergraduate institutions. The assignment also called for a person who could collect all documents, including GRE scores, required for admission and compute the applicant's grades in terms of our admission procedures. This position called for abilities that were not common among university personnel, but fortunately I identified a fully qualified woman already on the payroll; in fact, she had been there several years before I was born. She had worked in this particular field for the dean of Graduate Study, but reorganization divided this responsibility among various offices including the Social Sciences. Thus that dean had no need for her special talent but she remained on his staff without any challenging assignment.

In years Juliette was the most experienced person in the University. She came to Pitt directly from high school and was now 66 years of age. Her salary was well in excess of that budgeted for the Social Sciences slot although certainly not exorbitant. I went to the budget director who was as savvy as anyone and explained that Juliette's talents were being wasted in her present position. If he added $3,000 to my budget, I could have a task expertly carried out, and the University could save the remainder of Juliette's salary. The director bought my argument; Juliettte was anxious to be productive, but she was hesitant about working for anyone as young as I still was. We nevertheless became fast friends, and she remained in the office until her retirement—actually longer than I was there because of my transfer to the deanship.

Juliette was a very proper lady whose dedication could never have been questioned. No one except me, who was responsible for it, ever heard a word that could possibly be considered offensive drop from her lips. At times the office became a little hectic. When several people wanted my attention at the same time, I was known to remark: "And they want ice water in hell, too."

Juliette was familiar with my comment. One day she appeared in front of my desk with a question, but I didn't acknowledge her immediately. I had just completed a phone conversation and wanted to jot down my notes from the call before I left the subject. Apparently I took too long in writing; Juliette, a little disgusted and tired of waiting, turned to walk out and said in a soft voice: "I know." Still writing, I looked up and asked: "You know what?" "They want ice water in hell" was her response as she continued to her desk. I roared in laughter, and she gave me a little smile.

One evening several years later when Juliette invited me and my wife to dinner with her and her blind sister, I was telling the sister about making Juliette so angry that she swore in my office. Juliette insisted that the incident occurred only in my mind, but I joked with her about it several times.

When Sue's husband graduated with his law degree, the couple took off to fulfill his ROTC commitment. Of course, I was aware of this inevitability and was prepared with a secretarial replacement for Sue. From June and other secretaries in the chancellor's office, I learned that Grace was another who would consider a change. At the time she worked three days a week transcribing dictabelts and wanted to increase her hours because her second daughter was entering college. In fact, that daughter and Chancellor Mark Nordenberg were later in German class together. Furthermore she wanted a job that offered a greater challenge and more varied duties.

Grace and I knew each other slightly, because we often walked together to a University parking lot (now the site of Crawford Hall) in the late afternoons. She was enthusiastic about my proposal to come to the College, but now I had to attempt the same tactic on Chancellor David Kurtzman that I had successfully employed on Dr. Litchfield. He gave me permission to talk to Grace but, in so doing, suggested that my chances of receiving an affirmative response were slight. Like the situation with June, he didn't know that the two of us had worked out our deal and needed only his blessing.

Aside from Juliette, Grace was the oldest of my secretaries but not as old as many assumed. This false assumption was prompted by her prematurely gray hair. She was probably 50, but in mind and movement she was a young professional woman. For at least a month in advance, knowing that she would be coming to the dean's office, she read all the literature that she could find to familiarize herself with the office. Aided by a few transition sessions with Sue, she felt prepared to step in.

When Grace and I talked about her new duties, I informed her that I had a policy of always attempting to see department chairpersons at their earliest convenience. It was my experience that, when one of them called, the issue was probably pressing and needed a quick resolution. I wanted the meeting to take place at his/her preferred time if my calendar could possibly be so arranged. With this in mind, Grace decided to memorize the names of all chairpersons so that, if one called, she was prepared to be as cooperative at possible.

During her second day in the office, she identified what she construed as a need for this chairperson information. She received a call from an individual who she thought was Professor Alan Pfeffer, chairman of the Germanic Languages Department. The caller remained haughty and demanding, even after she explained that an appointment could be arranged within ten minutes; it would take him that long to reach the office.

Grace immediately alerted me that he was coming, but after the ten minutes elapsed, she came to the door again to apologize, saying that it wasn't Professor Pfeffer in the outer office, but Assistant Professor Pepper, whom I did not know but was about to regret coming to know. She was unnecessarily embarrassed by the name confusion and apologized immediately to Pepper, who was in no mood to forgive anyone anything.

Pepper came to complain. Outraged that I had filled his class with incompetent and rude students, he exploded almost before he sat down. Although I explained that I played no role in assigning students to any specific course or section, that didn't stop his rant. He was on a roll and had to let it all hang out. He was upset about having students in a general education course that could be elected by very diverse groups within Arts and Sciences, as well as by students from outside the College.

This incident took place three weeks into the term, and 29 of the 55 students originally registered for his course had already transferred to other courses or simply dropped out. He found the remaining 26 unable to perform at the level he demanded; as evidence he gave a quiz and only two passed and then only with Ds. Expecting me to attend his class and "read the riot act" to the students because they were disrespectful to him, he claimed that they talked when he talked; they talked to each other in class; they read the *Pitt News* during his lectures; some sprawled over two or three chairs; others chewed gum "and burst the bubbles in my face. It wasn't very sanitary." Not seeing this as a glaring indictment of himself, he was too obtuse to recognize that he had painted a disquieting picture of his classroom.

Pepper had been hired at the eleventh hour when a member of the staff became ill. He was obviously unprepared for any position in academe; he didn't realize that students, in part, were dramatizing how disgusted they were with his conduct. Although Grace was temporarily embarrassed by her inadvertent mistake and although giving him an appointment on the spur of the moment massaged his self-importance, I told her that knowing Pepper's temperament provided an advantage, because it alerted us to his problem. Thereafter when I was in a teasing mood and Grace would come to the door to announce a visitor, I would ask if she was sure that it wasn't Pepper.

When I had originally discussed the position with her, I did not consult either the associate or the assistant dean, largely because our discussions could have no official status until cleared by the chancellor. At lunch a week or so after Grace began working, they both advised me that I had taken a false step, because they believed that a gray-haired woman could not function harmoniously with the younger women in the office. A month later they both changed their opinions and admitted that Grace was the best thing that could have happened to the office. Of course, I agreed.

Grace remained in the dean's office for a month after I resigned. She left the University without another paycheck on the horizon, but one readily appeared. My wife and I remained friends with Grace and her husband for the last 30 years of her life—visiting in each other's homes and going to plays together; we have continued to maintain contact with her husband and other family members after her death.

I would be remiss if I permitted any reader to leave this chapter without realizing two salient facts: The talents of all five secretaries were exemplary, and I was fortunate for the opportunity to work with them. Although I don't think that I will ever forget either, both of these points were reaffirmed for me only months before I retired from teaching in the History Department. At that time the department was suffering through a secretarial crisis that it didn't deserve and that I witnessed from the sideline.

A faculty member had received a research grant permitting him to hire a half-time secretary. The chairman meanwhile thought that the department workload was such that an additional half-time secretary would ease the burden. Thus to satisfy both requirements, the department requested a full-time secretary from the Office of Human Resources.

In due course a candidate, obviously chosen from the bottom of the application file folder, arrived and was put to work with the usual 60-day probation period. When I first saw a new face in the main office, I stopped, introduced myself, and welcomed Whinetta to the department. On successive days I greeted her when I passed through the office and always received the same blank stare, silently asking: "Who the hell is he?" I didn't take offense, because I noticed that she gave the same look to her typewriter every morning when she uncovered it.

With the end of the probation period came the moment of truth. Human Resources requested a written appraisal of Whinetta's progress. Both the research professor and the office supervisor were reluctant to admit that she was a colossal failure. Thus they labeled her progress as "fair" and "average" in order to permit her to continue in that slot. The two failed to recognize that often there is truth in the adage: No good deed goes unpunished. Whinetta decided to provide them with a reminder so dramatic that they will never forget its potential wisdom.

Rankled that her performance was rated as only fair, Whinetta became a greater liability as time passed. Apparently assuming that everyone in the department was against her, her learning curve remained flat. First, her typewriter let her down; it proved it could spell no better than she could. She quarreled with other secretaries, botched assignments, and was reprimanded by her supervisor. Both unwilling and incapable of accepting guidance, she decided to seek gratification in another direction.

Writing to the Equal Employment Opportunity Commission (EEOC), she was informed that, unless she had been fired, it had no basis to intervene. By being "a good guy" and not dismissing her, the department became the ultimate bad guy because, through its generous evaluation of her record, it had taken away her leverage with EEOC. Running out of options, Whinetta thought that she was still holding one ace. In a 318-word letter to the chancellor, she poured out her misfortunes at the hands of the History staff.

Containing 35 writing errors, Whinetta's masterpiece of self-incrimination proved that she was an equal mis-user of all aspects of the English language, twice misspelling the chancellor's name (thus high marks for consistency). In one of the best examples of how to make a negative impression that I have ever seen, her letter adroitly illustrated her lack of knowledge; spellings, capitalizations, punctuation, grammar, and the use of numbers were all accorded widespread misuse. In addition, without realizing it, she threatened the chancellor; after informing him that she had consulted EEOC, she slipped in the remark: "I hope you can help to somehow resolve this problem before it gets any worse, or I have to do it legally."

Via a note from the chancellor, the department first heard the shocking news that Whinetta had launched her offensive. For his part the chancellor alerted the legal eagles. This was overkill akin to swatting a fly with a sledgehammer. There was no indication that the employee had been mistreated; nothing of gender, race, or physical/mental abuse was evident; the incident simply reeked of abject incompetence. Once the chancellor had read Whinetta's ode to incompetence, he should have acknowledged her letter with a one-liner: "Your diatribe is self-evident; you're fired." The fact that some such response was not taken demonstrates how seriously the University perceived even the wildest of charges.

The only person with whom I ever spoke concerning this issue was the supervisor. Thoroughly distressed, she believed that she had precipitated it. She felt that she had let the department down, because she knew that it prided itself on presenting a united, dignified front to the University at large on all issues. Internal problems were to remain within the department, but this one made a resounding thud on the chancellor's desk. Frustrated and dwelling on her perceived failure, she was indeed troubled when she mentioned it to me.

Trying to assure her that hers was simply a noble gesture to train an unteachable employee, I decided to cheer her by writing a cynical and humorous letter on the subject, addressed to the chancellor but with the only copy given to her. After explaining the basic facts of the incident, my letter read as follows:

> Whinetta should have been shown the door before the end of the probation period, but the professor and supervisor chose to discriminate—to extend the normal learning period—to provide constructive criticism beyond the expected time limit—to be compassionate—to be charitable by calling her performance "fair" when it was not. I must confess that I would have adopted the same course of action, but for that conduct these two became victims. But they were wrong and must be punished. As I survey the options, you have two:
>
> (a) You may continue this ridiculous charade and sentence them both to a public flogging with a wet noodle. May I suggest that this punishment be delivered at midfield between halves of the next Homecoming football game with you personally applying the lashes.
>
> (b) On the other hand, you could award Whinetta a Chancellor's Medal at the next Honors Convocation for her thoroughness in documenting her incompetence and for providing you with an opportunity to demonstrate to the Pittsburgh community that, being born in the shadow of the Chicago stockyards, you know real bull when you see it.
>
> I'm confident that this information will assist you in reaching the proper decision on punishments. I'm also sure that

you are aware that this is a rare but not unique phenomenon; every so often someone insists on jumping (in this case squeezing) into the electric chair and personally pulling the switch. Even though we applaud this do-it-yourself, take-charge attitude, we expect the self-server to receive the shocking experience of her life.

All this advice comes to you absolutely free, but no honorarium would be considered too large. As the evidence clearly reveals, I am a specialist in absurd solutions to absurd situations. It's always a privilege to serve.

Yours in Collegiality,
James A. Kehl
Professor of History

The supervisor smiled politely at my attempt at humor, but I don't think that I relieved much of her anxiety. As it should, the incident passed almost unnoticed until now. I have been accused of being an elitist in reacting to other people's abilities. If the details of this incident so define me, I'll wear the badge proudly.

Wesley W. Posvar, Chancellor 1967-1991
Photo courtesy of Archives Service Center, University of Pittsburgh

CHAPTER 7

Fame, Fortune, Failure

ABOUT-FACE

On an ordinary day in 1989, Wesley W. Posvar met with the local media amid confusion concerning the agenda. Because Posvar had already served as chancellor of the University of Pittsburgh for 22 years, the journalists incorrectly assumed that he was about to reveal his retirement plans. The chancellor, on the other hand, expected the session to be devoted to the highlights of his long career. With the reporters more intrigued by a new story than by a rehash of an old one, they pressed for comment about his retirement.

The chancellor was coy, acted surprised that they would introduce the topic, and proclaimed that he had given no thought to stepping down. Thus the remainder of the interview focused on the accomplishments of his stewardship.

The chancellor's first eight years (1967-1975) had been tumultuous not only for the University but also for higher education nationwide and for American society at large.

During that period the drive for gender justice, relief from racial tensions, and recognition of widespread student unrest were all activated, the latter two being potentially militant. The student demonstrations were the most disruptive in the history of American education. Almost from the day he took office, Chancellor Posvar was thrust into the local version of these complex and volatile issues.

All three elements of social unrest, fueled by emotion as well as by fact, burst on the national scene in the 1960s and '70s. All demanded immediate deliberations and responses. Internally the University community was convulsed by the assertiveness of these groups. The chancellor had no time to gain a consensus. Resolving the demands set forth by these aroused forces, all of which had justification for exerting pressure, was a daunting task.

The student outburst, led by faculty and student Vietniks, perceived the Vietnam War to be unjust if not outright immoral; this movement was potentially the most dangerous of the three to life and property. At nearby Kent State University in Ohio, four students were killed; major universities across the nation, including Berkeley, Columbia, Chicago, Wisconsin, and Cornell, experienced extensive property damage, and nationwide 900 students were expelled. Under Chancellor Posvar's leadership, Pitt suffered no loss of life, no expulsions, and minimal destruction of property. Details of the chancellor's actions in confronting these contentious issues are fully reported in Robert C. Alberts, *Pitt: The Story of the University of Pittsburgh*, pp. 382-419.

Frustrated that they could not stop the war, Pitt's Vietniks turned their emphasis to tangentially related topics designed to abolish credit for ROTC courses, cancel ROTC programs on the campus, alter the College grading system, change academic requirements in the College, and investigate faculty research contracts with federal agencies to determine if they were contributing to the war effort.

Overlapping some of these concerns were the more deep-seated and longer festering issues that rankled African-Americans. In the name of preserving democracy, they had been drafted, along with young white men, to wage World War II only to return home to witness the same segregation that existed when they volunteered their lives. A few years later under similar circumstances, Black soldiers came home from Korea to find minimal changes in their segregated status. Two decades after that Black soldiers returned from Vietnam, while many of their brothers were still there continuing the fight, and found similar conditions.

Despite Civil Rights acts of 1957, 1960, 1964, and 1968, buttressed by the Voting Rights Act of 1965, segregation was still prevalent throughout our society. The most galling condition apparent on American campuses, including our own, was that the percentage of African-American students and instructors was far below the Black percentage of the population, a plight also reflected at most workplace levels. At the apex of these statistics was the indication that the African-Americans were bearing an unequal burden on the battlefield in this questionable Vietnam war. To alleviate these conditions, African-Americans, like the Vietniks, relied on lock-ins, sit-ins, teach-ins, demonstrations, and marches that, in turn, kept the University administration off balance.

Less flamboyant, but as determined to succeed as these struggles, was the quest of women for equality in the workplace. After World War II women's access to educational opportunities improved grudgingly; with even greater exertion they were accepted into the job world, but on a much lower pay scale than that accorded to men with equal credentials. At Pitt women organized and set forth their demands for equality in hiring, promotions, tenure, and fellowships. They exposed the fact that the University lagged behind the national collegial average in providing such opportunities to women and persuasively argued their case before the University Senate and the Senate Council, and ultimately by letter before the United States government. The chancellor admitted the institution's shortcomings in this area and moved swiftly to correct them, but his directives were variously interpreted by those entrusted with compliance. Thus this problem, like the others, was not readily solved.

Through the ordeal of these three social movements, Posvar called for tolerance and patience. He himself moved to keep the lines of communication open and appeared to listen sincerely to all arguments. He encouraged the right of groups, even the radicals, to assemble peaceably on campus and steered a personal course that guided the University safely through these troubled waters. The chancellor brokered programs, agreed to procedures, established deadlines, helped staff committees, provided funds, and joined in every endeavor to heal the embattled campus.

Success came at a cost. All factions carried scars from these years of turmoil; even those who achieved the most suffered—perhaps because they hadn't achieved enough. This high intensity period for all three social movements rose and fell during Posvar's first eight years; in fact, the student uprising literally collapsed with the withdrawal of American forces from Southeast Asia in 1973-1974. The racial and gender problems, however, have continued in subdued form into the present; needed refinement and continuous monitoring followed, at times with less dedication than was essential to insure that intended advances be made permanent.

Those first eight years of the Posvar administration stood in sharp contrast to the final sixteen (1975-1991). During the earlier period the chancellor was in the limelight constantly, whether or not he and/or his public relations staff preferred such exposure. In the longer second period, he pursued a low profile—sharing as little governance as possible with the faculty and, at times, with the trustees as well. This transformation in his *modus operandi* became more annoying to faculty as the years passed, because it produced an authoritarian chancellor.

Reasons for the about-face in administrative style are not readily apparent. Posvar may have personally preferred an imperious style from the outset; on the other hand, he may have felt compelled to adopt a centralized policy-making procedure in order to advance basic University objectives that had been temporarily stymied by the social movements. If he had permitted the faculty to share in all University governance, debate would have delayed action. Encouraged by those closest to him to accept an authoritarian role because that, in turn, would enhance their own power, Posvar grew comfortable in utilizing this technique.

What happened after 1975, constructive or disastrous, cannot be attributed to one individual. Posvar's staff, plus his top academic administrators, either favored the high-handed approach or, without consciences of their own, told the chancellor what they thought he wanted to hear. As evidence, releases from the chancellor's office on issues of faculty importance contained more boilerplate than substance. Speeches by these subordinates and their participation in joint administrative-faculty committees conveyed the same attitude. With each year they had to know that the faculty was growing more restless, or they were totally inept at detecting obvious signs, or they believed in their infallibility in suppressing popular opposition.

Weeks after his 1989 conference with the media, the chancellor in all seriousness reaffirmed that he had "absolutely no plans" to retire at any specific age. (*Univ. Times*, 05-11-89) If he did not feel totally secure in his relationships with both the faculty and trustees, he would not have sounded so certain. Meantime, at a University Senate Council meeting in the chancellor's presence, Professor Sarah Thomason, had castigated him for failure to discuss real University issues: "What I hear from the [chancellor] of the University is very little about strictly academic 'things.' I hear about your role in revising the [West Point] military honor code, about new sports facilities... about executive parking lots...." (*Univ. Times*, 04-13-89)

With ample justification Posvar bristled at these remarks. Senate Council meetings were not an appropriate forum in which to discuss teaching and learning as implied by Thomason's comments. Such "esoteric" topics could best be explored within the individual schools. Despite this assessment, failure to identify these sharp words as pent-up frustration shared by her faculty colleagues and to debunk them as an isolated case of carping widely missed the point.

With this explanation and Posvar's no-retirement statement, the anti-Posvar genie escaped from the bottle in February 1990, never to return. The chairpersons of the Faculty of Arts and Sciences (FAS) departments gave the chancellor a unanimous no-confidence vote that was forwarded to the Board of Trustees. In taking this action, one of the group later reflected: "FAS has been very dissatisfied with Posvar for a very long time and nobody listened to us." (*Press*, 06-04-91) Days after the chairpersons' vote, in a letter to the editor, Douglas E. Ashford, the Andrew W. Mellon Professor of Politics, expressed a personal frustration when he denounced the administration's "mindless assumption that a faceless, unresponsive, and often uninformed managerial style is appropriate to a complex university." (*Press*, 02-24-90)

When faculty-administration relationships did not improve over the following months, Professor Donald McBurney, chairman of the Budget Policies Committee of the University Senate, declared: "I've seen grade school parent advising committees that have more influence than the faculty here at Pitt." (*Univ. Times*, 10-29-90) At this point Professor Ashford restated his disappointment in stronger language: "I don't see any point to the kinds of negotiations we have now, where administration people lie about salaries and lie about faculty salary policy." (*Univ. Times*, 10-25-90)

As these incidents were unfolding, the chancellor re-thought his future and announced his retirement effective in the summer of 1991. An unthinking Board of Trustees failed to grasp the gravity of the no-confidence action and subsequent faculty comment. The trustees realized that Posvar's psyche had been stung by this vote and sought to buoy his spirits. Eschewing ANY investigation into the depth and breadth of the feelings behind this faculty vote, they expressed their unanimous confidence in the chancellor and sanctified their opinion by granting him a 29 percent salary increase.

Not content with this arrogance, John Marous, chairman of the Board, referred to Posvar in his May 1, 1991, memo to the University community as one "who has served this University with such high distinction and outstanding leadership since 1967." The combination of this trustee vote and the Marous statement was interpreted as defiance. The trustees either were misled by Posvar or on their own decided that the faculty had no justifiable right to an opinion. This set the stage for more dramatic rounds yet to come.

The Board's responses heightened the tension. The anti-Posvar genie was still on the loose, but unfortunately this was not perceived by some well-intentioned individuals. Naively, dedicated University staff members set in motion elaborate arrangements to celebrate the occasion of the chancellor's retirement. To initiate the festivities, a Farewell Reception was planned for April 17, 1991, with all staff and faculty invited. Individuals were encouraged to attend because "Dr. Posvar's presidency of twenty-four years has made an indelible, powerful imprint on the history and future of Pitt." Jazz artist Nathan Davis even prepared a special salute for the occasion, an original piece of music entitled "Goodbye Dr. P."

This function was so successful that within five days a second farewell gala, set for June, was in the planning stage. The total Pittsburgh community was to be invited to the Commons Room of the Cathedral of Learning "to witness the end of an era," a "cocktail dress" event "in this honorable salute to a man who has positively affected all of our lives and many others."

Before the invitations could be distributed, the well-meaning planners had the event explode in their faces; the anti-Posvar genie went public in May and June, plastering the local and national press with one shocking revelation after another. Amid embarrassment to the planners, Posvar wisely asked that the gala be canceled as he struggled to react to the published accounts that emerged over these months.

As the nightmarish two months began to unfold, even the chancellor's sharpest critics had no inkling that the administration was about to fall like the proverbial house of cards. His opponents had not scored a significant victory; they had leveled serious charges, but produced no smoking gun; their adversary was truly the Teflon chancellor.

Receiving little sustained flak, Posvarites were still exhilarated over his alleged achievements of establishing the University's financial independence while moving the institution from a regional school to one of international renown— a goal achieved by Chancellor Litchfield years before. No one wanted to challenge Posvar's claim; no one seemed to care that undergraduate education had not been shored up or that football scandals continued to capture headlines or that the no-confidence vote had wide-ranging merit. University life experienced few ripples of change until the anti-Posvar genie struck a crippling blow. That came when Bill Moushey, a reporter for the *Post-Gazette*, delved into the chancellor's retirement package. His investigation produced a fall-out extending from Posvar's office into numerous aspects of the administration.

Moushey discovered that, as written, Posvar's golden parachute endowed him with four principal ingredients: a retirement salary, two annuities, a guaranteed mortgage, and an elaborate insurance program. Even the chairman of the University's Board of Trustees, John Marous, was surprised to learn that Posvar was scheduled to receive an annual retirement salary of $201,000 (for officially doing nothing) while his successor would receive only $200,000 a year to administer the University.

The two annuities with TIAA-CREF were more complex. The first vaguely followed the retirement pattern for faculty and staff whereby the annuitant paid $1.00 for every $1.50 contributed by the University, but that ratio was altered for Posvar; for every one of his dollars, Pitt invested $4.00. The second part of the annuity plan, called a "collateral fringe benefit package" in which the University paid the total premium, was even more lucrative to Posvar. The rationale for this supplement varied. Some claimed that the trustees wanted to compensate him for his low salary in previous years. Others pointed out that for the first time Posvar claimed that he had offers from other universities and the federal government, and the trustees were simply demonstrating that they wanted to retain his services. As a result of this total annuity package, Posvar was entitled to a lump sum of $938,000 at retirement, plus a $108,000 annual pension for life, with a generous allowance of $8,850 per month for his wife after his death. (*Press*, 07-26-91 and 09-26-91)

Posvar defended this part of the package by claiming that he "could have made a lot more money elsewhere" if he had worked for a major corporation or another university. To Bill Moushey he declared: "Some people get paid more and have less fun. I'd rather be a university president than the president of a steel company." (*Post-Gazette*, 05-23-91) An accurate translation would be that he wanted to be a university president who was paid like a steel company executive.

Under the Key Employee Mortgage Program (KEMP), originally known as the Faculty Home Purchase Plan although it was never available to faculty, Posvar borrowed $740,000 but never had to pay off the principal, only an annual five percent interest on the total—and that was tax deductible. The University carried insurance on that mortgage and, when he died, a benefit of $740,000 was earmarked for his estate. This was a one-of-a-kind exception to an exclusive mortgage plan for which eight administrators qualified for a less greedy form of KEMP. They were granted mortgages up to 80 percent of the value of their homes on which they paid only the five percent interest. In all, during the life of this noble plan, the participants borrowed $2.8 million to be repaid when they left the University; the life insurance on these mortgages cost the University $70,000-80,000 per year. (*Press*, 06-07-91 and 09-15-01)

The fourth and last part of the package was a $424,000 life insurance policy payable at death with the premiums paid by the University. Only Frank Lucchino, Allegheny County Controller and University trustee at the time, questioned the fairness of the program. "It seems to me," he said, "that if he is going to get it [his salary] from the University, he can pay his own medical and life insurance," especially since the life insurance coverage for faculty at the time was limited to $10,000. (*Pitt News*, 09-26-91)

Revelation of these details spawned a widespread public rebuke and elicited a response from Posvar that didn't assuage anyone. He pointed out that, aside from the lavish package, "I just have a few thousand bucks." That was about the saddest tale I've ever heard. I wanted to cry, but I couldn't find an onion to start the tears flowing. When he played the sympathy card, I broke down and sobbed unabashedly. He revealed that: "If I provide for my children, start making contributions for six [now seven] little grandsons, that of course will reduce our estate." (*P-G*, 05-23-91) That's about as heart-wrenching as it gets. After rereading that sentence, I was almost prepared to endorse the concept of university welfare for all three generations of Posvars.

Before the public could fully assimilate this retirement bonanza, their attention was pulled in numerous directions by tangential disclosures. A potentially costly faux pas occurred when the University lied to the state legislature. The Senate Appropriations Committee pointedly asked the University Director of Commonwealth Relations about Posvar's retirement package; he, in turn, sought the answer directly from the University chancellor. In response Posvar revealed that he would receive some salary below his current level and that he was participating in the TIAA-CREF pension program. Without amplification this implied that he shared in the plan whereby the University contributed $1.50 per every $1.00 by a participant. Nowhere did he even hint at his secret annuity, in which the University picked up the total premium. The Director of Commonwealth Relations reported the details to the legislature exactly as they were revealed to him by Posvar and didn't learn the truth until he read the Pittsburgh newspaper account. (*Press*, 05-26-91)

One plausible explanation for the chancellor's aversion to the truth pertained to campus politics. At the time that the legislature requested the retirement information, the Pitt faculty was about to vote on whether or not it wished to unionize. According to this theory Posvar feared that, if the details of his package were leaked through the legislature and ultimately to the faculty, the vote might be tilted toward unionization and away from the administration's non-union preference. The legislature was not moved by any of Posvar's motivations, only by the fact that he had been less than candid. To demonstrate their displeasure, the legislature temporarily held up the University's state appropriation, but ultimately Posvar apologized to the legislature and the funds flowed again. Unfortunately the University's eye had been blackened by this incident.

With each piece of dirty linen that flapped on the line, the reporters anticipated that Pitt records could be mined for even more delectable tidbits to titillate their readers. The searches were intensified, and one revealed that Wesley Posvar had discovered the most efficient means to balance the family budget: Let the University pay for it. His system went through several stages before being perfected. The first phase was discovered during a campus tour early in his administration; he learned that the pantry at one of the University hospitals stocked staples. One day when the family ran out of ketchup, he sent an employee from the residence to the hospital for a bottle, although a grocery store was half as far away. This surpassed the ultimate in retail advertising: Not "buy one, get one free; no coupon needed;" just get one free.

Shortly he convinced the Trustees to assume the total grocery cost directly, making the ketchup run unnecessary. Thus during his 24 years, more than half a million of Pitt dollars put groceries on his table and provided other supplies for his personal residence. This tab was separate from the cost of official parties and receptions that were covered by another account in his office. Posvar explained how the family grocery system worked: "I would leave a note on the [bulletin] board that we needed... milk, and the chef ordered it along with other items on the board through the University food service," with the University covering the cost, approximately $433 per week. (*P-G*, 05-24-91)

Why would a household that employed a chef require the householder to record the need for milk? Is this called micro-management or an inability to delegate authority? Does this provide a clue concerning University administration in these years?

About the same time an audit by the US Health and Human Services revealed that the University had wrongly claimed $259,089 in overhead expenses on federal research grants in 1990. A high percentage of these funds was charged to Posvar's office and included items so far removed from the research field that they had to be deliberately misplaced. No self-respecting graduate of Accounting 001 could have charged a research budget with alcohol (listed as "special merchandise"), or travel for the chancellor's wife to a foot-ball game in Ireland, or pagers for staffers, or symphony and opera tickets, or Posvar Christmas cards, or engraved station-ery, or chocolates for a sick employee.

Despite the absurdity of all such charges, one deserves special attention: the cost of travel to the Cayman Islands for Mrs. Posvar. Within days after the federal auditors arrived on campus (more than a year after that travel), Posvar reimbursed the University for this item. Another angle on this expense is the fact that the insurance companies in the Caymans paid Mrs. Posvar's travel according to James H. Watters, the University's assistant vice president for finance. In that instance why was there any need to bill the University for the trip in the first place? (*P-G*, 05-10-91, *Press*, 07-30-91, *Univ. Times*, 11-07-91) In his update of June 10, John Marous disingenuously declared that the charges were based on "shifting rules and perhaps some Belt-way demagoguery." He who takes comfort in that explanation believes in the Easter Bunny. That also brings to mind the chancellor's alleged double dipping with Eastern Airlines (discussed later).

Related to this misappropriation of funds that had been brought into the University coffers by faculty research grants was the attempt to direct funds designated for the library to a program (KEMP) to provide luxury for Posvar and his preferred subordinates. This Posvar end run began in 1973 when Trustee William Rea donated a property assessed at $110,000 to Pitt with the stipulation that it be sold and the proceeds applied to the library's book endowment. Pitt retained this Westminster Place home until 1985 when it was sold for $341,356.

At this point Posvar again demonstrated his warped definition of the honor system; the library would have the public honor of expanding its collection to the extent of $110,000, the value at the time acquired, and under this system the excess ($231,356) over the value when acquired would be diverted to help fund his secret $2.8 million Key Employee Mortgage Program that came to the rescue of nearly destitute top University administrators. To the uninformed this maneuver might create the impression that the chancellor was blessed with an ambidextrous talent—left-handed and underhanded.

After weeks of exposure in the press, this issue reached the University lawyers, who sauntered down from their Mt. Olympus and proclaimed what every rational being already knew: Funds directed to the care of impoverished administrators represented money that had been improperly diverted. (*PG*, 06-14-91) Such a ruling was as necessary as calling a symposium of eminent scientists to certify that water is wet. The lawyers' advice was adopted, and the total funds were belatedly assigned to the library book fund.

Simultaneous with the focus on the manipulation of funds in the chancellor's office, two employees of the University food service were also charged with a misuse of funds. One told investigators that he had financed travel for Pitt administrators to various equipment and food shows from food service accounts; by happenstance these shows were held in such dull places as Las Vegas and Chicago. That probe was quashed before it reached the embarrassment stage for those officials.

The other employee was charged with theft by deception and criminal conspiracy, both felonies, for allegedly billing ten personal trips to University food service accounts. Although the district attorney was quick to label the financing of these trips as felonies, he was unable to make the mental leap to similarly improper charges by Posvar: namely, his wife's trips to Ireland and the Caymans. Incidentally, one of Mrs. Posvar's trips, charged to a research grant, was to Dublin to watch a Pitt football game, the same destination to which the employee charged one of his own trips. His was a felony; hers wasn't.

From the lighter side of this financial tangle came accusations about the use of University funds to procure prostitutes for school officials. Posvar described them as "completely unsubstantiated," and Trustee D. Michael Fisher, then a state senator, declared this to be "a matter that's already been handled." Fisher's choice of words was a little unsettling; he didn't say that there was no truth to the rumor, only that it had been resolved. (*Press*, 05-05-91) I am proud to say that, before either Posvar or Fisher spoke out, I came to the chancellor's defense and stated unequivocally that he had no role in the alleged incident. My definitive statement was based on simple logic; Posvar was too busy manipulating the University.

Despite the confusion engendered by the whole sorry mess, Posvar remembered and applied a basic rule for all administrators on the defensive: Protect yourself personally at all costs. In my opinion he retreated to such a last-ditch effort at damage control by authorizing special severance packages for five University officials. They were guaranteed a year's salary if they lost their jobs at the end of his tenure on July 31, 1991.

The most favorable interpretation that can be assigned to this outrage is bad manners. Any administrator should be entitled to enlist subordinates of his/her choosing, but automatic retention or severance pay was an attempt to deny the new chancellor the freedom to control his own administration. I would prefer to conclude that these individuals were chosen for special attention because they knew where the skeletons of the Posvar years were buried. The chancellor gave no reason for singling out these particular five except that they were "certain close individuals."

As these revelations captured headline after headline, the average faculty member read in shocked disbelief. Those who had been involved in University governance shared a less surprised feeling of the unknown but were stunned by many of the emerging details. They derived little satisfaction from the exposures and were embarrassed, as we all were, to see them in print. I was less startled than others, because I had been forewarned. Days before the Posvar appointment was announced in 1967, my own knowledgeable "Deep Throat" had revealed certain of Posvar's personality traits that were hidden from public view, but I was not prepared to accept the bluntness with which they were described in a phone conversation.

THE VITA BEHIND THE VITA

"Hi, Ace! Just called to tell you that you are not going to like your new chancellor—he's definitely not your kind of guy. He's the proud owner of a merit badge in ego-mania, but he's clever enough to disguise it when necessary."

That phone outburst on a Saturday morning in January 1967 succeeded in getting my heart started for the day. Still at the breakfast table, I wasn't yet committed to anything constructive for the weekend, but unknowingly those startling words marked the beginning of a 24-year sentence not only for me but also for the University of Pittsburgh.

The greeting was normal enough. Only my friend Rick regularly called me "Ace" on the phone; it was his trademark for announcing who was calling without using his name. The substance of his remarks, on the other hand, chilled me more than the day's sub-freezing temperature. Every fiber of my being wanted to shout: "It's a lie! It's a lie!" If the caller had been anyone else, I would have considered it a bad joke and hung up.

From my vantage point I had to believe that the next chancellor of the University was going to be an unselfish, dynamic leader. Annoyed by Rick's unnerving declaration, I thought for a moment that he was taking perverse pleasure in supplying me with what in all likelihood was the result of rumor. I shot back: "He [the new chancellor] has to be good; nothing less will do."

After that comment the conversation settled down to a frank exploration of the message. Although Rick was several hundred miles from the campus, his information was more up-to-date than mine, despite the fact that I was the dean of the College of Arts and Sciences. Wesley Posvar had indeed been appointed Pitt's new chancellor.

The previous day I had heard talk that a decision had been reached on the appointment, but made no effort to confirm it. I knew that the Search Committee had exhausted its list of top five candidates without finding a worthy nominee. With that in mind, I didn't think that there could be much validity in Rick's report but was wrong on that score.

From Rick I heard the Posvar name for the first time. His elaboration indicated that my new boss, an officer and professor at the Air Force Military Academy, had graduated first in his class at West Point; partially based on this distinction, he was awarded a Rhodes scholarship to study at Oxford. That military background information stirred a little of the disbelief that I wanted to feel, but Rick's information was nonetheless unnerving because he was always "on the money." I couldn't shake that from my mind.

I was encouraged to think that Rick's evidence might be suspect, because student unrest nationwide, as well as on our campus, had already begun in earnest by 1967, and the establishment, including universities and the military, was a favorite target. I assumed that Pitt trustees and administrators would be inviting student confrontation if a military person were at the helm and that they would not risk that potential. Again my interpretation was wrong on all aspects of the appointment. At the same time, I had faith in the committee's ability to choose wisely. I looked forward to applauding their actions whether or not the chosen candidate presented a military background.

I noted that Posvar reported having served as a co-pilot during the Berlin Airlift, a strategic maneuver carried out between June 1948 and May 1949. Again my friend suggested that someone was a little loose with the truth on that claim. Because the Airlift coincided with the period in which Posvar was studying in England as a Rhodes Scholar, he was available for such duty only during two weeks between terms. (Alberts, p. 347) His only flying experience prior to assuming student status at Oxford had been as a test pilot for fighter aircraft.

Rick observed that many months, not a few days, were required to retrain a fighter pilot to handle a jumbo transport; thus if Posvar ever saw Berlin, it was most likely as a co-pilot's co-pilot, otherwise known as an observer. It would also make eminent sense to speculate that he flew small aircraft while in England in order to log the requisite hours to keep his flying status intact during the period of his study abroad. Today it must be a judgment call, because there is no written record to confirm that he ever flew in the Airlift.

In my opinion, accepting even the most negative interpretation of his involvement in the Airlift did not in my opinion disqualify him for the chancellorship. Believing that none of this information was germane, I shifted the subjects of discussion in subsequent phone calls with Rick to other aspects of Posvar's career.

While Rick and I periodically hassled over these aspects of Posvar's vita, the new chancellor arrived at Pitt amid much fanfare. The press tossed kudos fast and furious in their interviews with the newcomer. Every effort was exerted to make the transition a positive community experience. I personally took new hope in every favorable article. After all, Rick's skepticism was the fruit of a grapevine that unofficially kept tabs on what was happening at the service schools which, with the opening of the Air Force Academy, had been expanded to three in the 1950s. In a sense my friend's portrayal emerged from a rumor mill that thrived, in part, on unverified statements, half-truths, and speculation.

Furthermore, Rick's qualifications had not been tested; he had never served as an administrator, military or academic. He nevertheless stayed with his argument that, as far as the University was concerned, "This guy is bad news, an aggressive little man" who would hot-wire his grandmother's pajamas if necessary to appease his own selfish appetite.

Although a well-reasoned and plausible portrayal, this image of the incoming chancellor lacked the capstone of a systematic, documented analysis. Still retaining my faith in the integrity of the Search Committee to have chosen wisely, I remained optimistic about the University's new leadership.

That optimism suffered a jolt from an unexpected source when I attended a high school reunion. Not expecting the subject of Wesley Posvar to pop up at such a gathering, I was dumbfounded when it did. While greeting a classmate whom I hadn't seen for 20 years, I asked the most commonplace of reunion questions: What has been exciting in your life? Judy replied that she was the proud mother of five and the grandmother of three. With just one ten-year-old son, I didn't have much to compare in the population derby, but Judy promptly turned the conversation to what she had done outside the home.

She was a staff secretary assigned to the team that undertook the exciting and challenging task of creating a new academic institution. The team's assignment was to assemble the faculty, administration, and supporting staff that became the United States Air Force Academy. Her surprise mention of the Academy prompted me to inquire if she had encountered the name of Wesley Posvar. To my amazement and without waiting to discern anything about my sentiments concerning his talents, Judy launched into a vitriolic outburst against the most egotistical s.o.b. she had ever met.

Only a high school graduate, Judy was equipped with fewer skills for evaluating Posvar than my friend Rick. She was also operating in an entirely different environment, but she arrived at the same basic conclusions as Rick—more picturesque and less scholarly, but she had nailed the same individual.

She explained that Posvar had gratuitously offered his services to the team to become the Academy's first academic dean. That overture demonstrated his academic naivete and was unceremoniously rebuffed because he was a 32-year old who could present neither a doctorate nor any administrative credentials. In addition, he had limited teaching experience to offer in support of his request. To appoint such an inexperienced executive officer was unthinkable for an institution that would be immediately thrust into the national limelight.

Rejection of his application was taken as an incentive to recast his quest for a position at the new academy. According to Judy he merely shifted to Plan B and proposed to join the Air Force faculty as the department chairman in the Social Sciences. That too received a cool response from the organizing team, but undaunted he ultimately condescended to accept Plan C, an appointment as a faculty member in

Political Science. In time he was elevated to the department chairmanship, but when the deanship that he had coveted for a decade opened, he was literally advised not to apply.

Reeling from that shock to his psyche and feeling a lack of appreciation for his talents, Posvar decided in haste on a career change. Having already accumulated enough time to qualify for a service pension, he elected to seek validation of his abilities in a nonmilitary sector. Placing his name in the hopper with a national "head hunter," he had the distinct fortune to select the same group that had been enlisted to find a new chancellor for Pitt.

Pitt also acted in haste. For some strange reason the chairman of the University's Board of Trustees, Gwilym Price, who was "about to retire" in a few days, labored under the delusion that it was paramount to name a new chancellor before he left office. Perhaps this was to be his crowning legacy, but prudence dictates that it would be more important to have the new chairman and the new chancellor in sync; after all, they would be planning a future together.

That logic didn't prevail. When Posvar made himself available, Pitt was the first to be informed, and Price acted with undue dispatch. As he gleefully reflected: "I called for an end run" and caught everyone off-guard. With a minimum of warning, the faculty Search Committee was summoned to meet a candidate whose background and identity they didn't know. Within minutes of receiving his vita, they were thrust into a four-hour interview session with Posvar.

With the interview complete at 11:00 PM on a Sunday evening, the Committee reviewed the session among themselves for only 30 minutes, because they were expected to report their acceptance or rejection of the candidate to Price the next morning at 9:30 AM. The response was favorable to Posvar, but in a written statement they grumbled: "We agree with what you have done. But we do not approve of the way you did it. You didn't give us much time to consider such an important matter." (Alberts, p. 348)

Less than 48 hours after the Search Committee first heard the Posvar name, he was appointed chancellor. Neither the candidate nor the institution should have favored a decision in such a brutally demanding time frame; this was not a life-or-death situation for either. On one hand, a madcap candidate believed that he could mentally absorb the essence of the University of Pittsburgh in 48 hours and at the same time snub his Air Force superiors. On the other, University trustees were overly anxious to select Posvar, with whatever baggage accompanied his appointment, before any institution, including their own, could examine his credentials in detail. Time for a more diligent appraisal may have prevented Air Force officers from drinking a toast "To Our Gain and Pitt's Loss" when the appointment was publicly announced.

With no chance to contact sources that might have offered insights into Posvar's career, committee members were severely handicapped. Numerous physical traits and personality quirks eluded them in their brief exposure. Time passed before many understood that, although he had attended West Point where the honor system was in effect, he had evolved a new perception and magnanimously wanted to share the benefits of the code with the University. He slyly implemented procedures whereby the University had the *honor* while he had the *system*.

When conversing, he also had the noticeable habit of swiping his index finger past his nose. Some dismissed this as an unconscious motion, but I concluded that Posvar suffered from "Pinocchio Syndrome," because he strained the truth on occasion. Logic suggests to me that various statements nagged at his conscience and his repeated hand-to-nose motions were used to determine if any growth could be detected. I could be wrong.

The credentials that the Committee were able to analyze were, in part, ten years old, having been developed at the time of Posvar's appointment to the Air Force faculty. They contained the kind of glowing assessments of a new chancellor that I wanted to hear. In addition to his academic attainments, the record revealed that he had been identified in 1959 by the United States Junior Chamber of Commerce as one of the ten young men in America most likely to make a national impact, not the petulant little aggressor that Rick and Judy had portrayed.

When Posvar applied to the Air Force Academy, those who knew him best gushed with words of praise. They filled his dossier with statement after statement demonstrating that he enjoyed "a constant record of outstanding performance." One letter declared that he had "impressed his tutors at Oxford with his intelligence, the breadth of his intellectual interests, and his engaging personality." Another writer expressed equal enthusiasm: "I sincerely believe it would be difficult to overrate Major Posvar's potential as an Air Force officer." Paraphrasing that accolade, another wrote "Posvar is one of the genuine top-drawer intellects in the Air Force," followed by a similar comment that: "Few officers with three times his military service can boast an equal measure of maturity."

Another writer cited his "wealth of leadership ability and the type of pleasing personality which accommodates him to any group with which he has to deal." After he had been at the Academy for a year, his first performance report echoed all of these sentiments: "No other professor on the faculty can match Colonel Posvar for his sound and logical thinking and for his exceptional grasp of the total situation in solving problems."

This presentation of an unblemished record and sterling character was the basis for the Search Committee's whole-hearted endorsement. Undoubtedly this was a young man from whom the Air Force, and later the University, expected a career that sparkled with superior leadership. All of these praiseworthy evaluations were predicated, however, on a continuing career in the military, but Pittsburgh presented a more diverse setting, where certain personality flaws could bubble to the surface more readily. Realization of the Pittsburgh potential set Posvar's career on a different course.

Hindsight suggests that the Committee should have been more demanding. An update of the superlatives set forth when Posvar went to the Academy should have been requested. The absurdity of being given a 15-hour period in which the Committee members knew the Posvar name before being required to report their decision to Chairman Price should never have been agreed upon. More time should have been requested.

The result was embarrassing. As a lone, detached scholar, my friend Rick registered a more accurate judgment of Posvar in his first phone call to me than that reached by the Committee. With his ear to the inter-academy grapevine, Rick possessed the crucial element to arrive at an insightful interpretation of the chancellor's talents. He knew not only that Posvar's egotism could cleverly be concealed but also that there would be unguarded moments. Thus for the brief exposure to trustees and the Committee, Posvar kept this significant personality trait in check.

Public awareness of the true Posvar character remained a secret. Throughout most of his 24 Pitt years, his staff, mostly non-academics, skillfully and deliberately provided the public with only positive accounts of his actions. They succeeded in insulating him from the unpopular and derogatory and in the process molded a true Teflon chancellor. But, as the skeletons in the closet came tumbling out, a reverse scenario began to unfold. Time and an inquisitive press, along with the acid of his deeds, gradually burned through the Teflon coating and exposed incidents that encouraged further research and disclosures.

Not one of the chancellor's subordinates was capable of ever rising to the level of whistleblower, either because of his own little power trip or because of a misguided sense of loyalty to the University. In my own naivete I remained skeptically loyal to the chancellor for more than a year, but a specific incident abruptly changed that.

In 1965, while dean of the College of Arts and Sciences, I had directed the University's first program for disadvantaged high school students, one of the first three in the nation to be so identified and thus eligible for federal funds. With assists from the Admissions and Financial Aid offices, the grants that I had received carried the program through 1967. By then it was more prevalent for urban colleges and universities nationwide to conduct outreach programs for high school students in need of special incentives to pursue a college education.

By definition such programs were expensive, beyond the means of the College's regular budget. In January 1968, I began asking the chancellor's office about the amount of money, if any, that could be expected for renewing the program in September. Although there was now competition among academic institutions for these students, I was adamant that Pitt would not advertise any program to the high schools without knowing that the funds were available to deliver what was promised.

The chancellor's office remained noncommittal to our repeated requests through January, February, and March; the only response was "we're working on it." In April the assassination of Dr. Martin Luther King finally moved the chancellor to action. Rioting rocked the city, and Black groups seized the crisis to make demands on the University. That Posvar understood.

He immediately converted the program for disadvantaged students, Black and white, to a Black only initiative. Blacks demanded to be an integral part of any program planning, so the chancellor and his minions hurriedly sketched out a program in cooperation with Black leaders composed of some students and some Black activists from the community. As the dean of the College, where any such undergraduate program would logically be administered, I was not invited to participate in the formulation of these new courses.

The program that Posvar and his cohorts conceived was communicated to all the undergraduate deans and directors by one of his "Talking Heads," who riled me with the preface to his presentation. Trying to be affable and disguise his doctrinaire message, he said with a smile that he would answer no questions because this is "not something to be discussed and modified, only a dictum to be carried out." These words prompted me to respond in kind, and even today I offer no apology for my comments. Never before had I spoken so harshly against any program. I was angry both because of the disregard for protocol and because of the stupidity of the program concept.

I had no thought of taking the offensive at this meeting, but the nonsense presented and the Talking Head's demeanor brought out my true feelings. Actually, when I spoke out that day, I foolishly believed that I was defending the chancellor from a major embarrassment—suspecting that his minions had unwittingly agreed to an unworkable program. It contained three parts. With all attendees at the meeting silently accepting all that the Talking Head presented, I alone rebutted each of the three parts as he stated them, but I did not succeed in drawing him, even briefly, into a discussion until the third commandment had been set forth. He had his orders to state the ridiculous and leave.

The first dictum mandated that a course in remedial reading, carrying three credits, be established for all Black students who needed it. The College, I am chagrined to report, already offered such a course that carried no credit and was open to all students in need. My reaction: I was not going to administer a common course that awarded three credits to some students and none to others. This was creating, not relieving, discrimination. At that point I didn't think that a sane chancellor would knowingly endorse such a dichotomy, but the Head perceived no conflict and moved to his next item. In the spirit of cooperation, I could have agreed to award three credits to all students who enrolled in a remedial reading course, but I had no thought or power to do so without faculty discussion and approval. I was still operating under the standard belief that faculty exercised control over academic programs.

His second commandment called for a three-credit course in Afro-American History to be added to the College curriculum. Course additions to the curriculum by fiat were serious departures from tradition. I limited my objection to urging caution. I stressed that nothing labeled "history" should be projected without the concurrence of the History Department; professional courtesy demanded no less. Until that was done, I could not consent to the course.

The third commandment provided for a special Black adviser for Black students to be appointed by the Black leadership. I pointed out that I had already appointed an adviser for the following year to assist such students and that he was Black. I asked pointedly why he wasn't satisfactory; he was an experienced adviser and an advanced graduate student who shortly became a professor at a prestigious mid-western university.

The Head was prepared for that question and stated that Black activists did object to him in very specific language: "He's regarded as a white man's nigger, and he'll do what you tell him." I couldn't believe that any rational man who had served in academe could utter such nonsense. I shot back: "You're damned right; any adviser will follow my instructions. It doesn't matter whether he's Black, white, pink, or green; as long as I am the dean, I will be the ultimate arbiter." Otherwise I wouldn't have control over the area of my responsibility.

In all fairness it should be noted that the Talking Head did have a conscience, but at this stage I would have preferred a backbone. Although he had served as a faculty member for more than 25 years and although he reaffirmed his endorsement of the chancellor's program, he resigned from the University only days after delivering the three commandments. Ill health was declared the reason; you be the judge. Was it conscience or health? He's still living 40 years later.

When my comments reached Posvar, he concluded both that I was not a team player and that I was anti-Black. Until this confrontation occurred, I had considered myself a team player, but admittedly the task was challenging. Likewise, I never perceived myself as anti-Black but as pro-education within the guidelines established by the College faculty. Posvar and I never spoke again. He was so furious with me that he advised his administrative group to avoid me because I was a disruptive influence. One and only one in that group exhibited enough character to inform me of his little rebuke. I obviously resigned as dean.

Since "the team" had ignored my input in structuring the program, I felt obliged to place my criticisms on the record. I also believed that I had a responsibility to the integrity of the College program, to the students at large, and to the faculty who had been given no voice in these curriculum decisions. In my opinion, the University inequities toward Black students were real, should have been acknowledged, and followed by a serious effort to redress them within University guidelines.

To many Blacks, their initiatives had been ignited at a high cost: the life of Dr. King. Understandably they did not want his death to have been in vain. Some feared that relying on decisions wholly within the University framework would sap their momentum. That was probably true, but compromise and consensus are always preferable to wild program ventures. Refusing to admit any validity to my objections to the three commandments, the Posvar group developed its Black Program outside the College. To retain control and at the same time keep faith with commitments to Blacks, the administrators' program enjoyed mixed results.

To insure success on the record, they adopted a novel grading system for their program. In the College a 2.0 (C average) was necessary for good academic standing, but their new requirement was 1.5. This was a reasonable change, except for the caveat that all F grades would go unrecorded. That meant that a student with 1 B and 4 Fs was in good standing, but a student, even under the 1.5 scale, with 2 Cs and 3 Ds was subject to dismissal. Both the College and Black students suffered for years until sanity was restored, but undoubtedly the chancellor had identified the crisis accurately. He recognized not only that it required his personal intervention but also that the need was immediate and compelling. By my analysis he placed too much emphasis on an immediate solution and too little on the compelling substance.

This little program tiff with me was a mere bump on Posvar's road to fame, fortune, and failure. Somewhere between the Air Force Academy and the three-martini lunch, changes in personality had occurred. Still arrogant and brusque, he became impatient with detail, unhappy with routine, disillusioned with results, and frustrated by the lack of anticipated adulation; he seemed to focus more and more on himself.

Gradually he showed less genuine interest in University goals. As one of his provosts so aptly phrased it, he viewed the University as "an arena that enabled him to be notable, something of a star—where he could do what he wanted when he wanted. In short, Pitt was Wesley Posvar's giant playpen." (Weingartner, p. 350)

Posvar always possessed a social awkwardness that was not easily overcome. (Weingartner, p. 350) Recognizing this as a distinct handicap for one in his position, he was resolutely determined to remedy it, but in one type of situation he failed because of an appalling lack of finesse. He had learned that a cocktail party provided an effective means of transacting a little informal business, but in the process his technique irritated many guests.

He would attend receptions with an obviously well-prepared agenda and tried intently to identify those with whom he wished to speak. While making small talk with one guest, he would typically not look that person in the eye; instead he would gaze over his/her shoulder in an effort to catch a glimpse of one of those on his list for an exchange of comments. That lack of individual attention was most disconcerting. Certainly not alone in exhibiting this disturbing and impolite wandering-eye habit, he was never able to correct it in the public forum of the chancellorship. This social barrier between him and the University community was partially responsible for his looking elsewhere.

From time to time rumors circulated through the campus that various high-ranking positions in the nation's capital were available to Wesley Posvar, but lunches with military and governmental officials netted no invitations. These leaders may have been willing to discuss vacancies but had no thought of inviting an application. After all, the military contingent included some who had drunk the "Our Gain is Pitt's Loss" toast at the Air Force Academy, as well as others who were apprised of this salute via the academy grapevine.

Frustration on this front converted Posvar into a global junketeer. Traveling with an entourage, at University expense, but with no obvious benefit to his institution, he was only massaging his ego. Expecting to attract the attention of others of prominence, he apparently hoped that they, in turn, would attach significance to his perambulations and possibly recognize his talents. (Weingartner, p. 350)

In addition, an interaction of emotions helped to create a well-disguised schizoid personality. Although reluctant to leave behind the privilege that came with military rank, he loved the prestige that accompanied the chancellorship of a great university. At the same time he coveted the power of corporate America that he identified in his board of trustees. He never conceded the impossibility of capturing and retaining for himself only the qualities he preferred from all three roles; it took time, but frustration ultimately surfaced and tragically disrupted his career.

PIE IN THE SKY

Despite Eddie Fisher's crooning, most Americans give no credence to the theory that there's a gold mine in the sky. Wesley Posvar wasn't so sure, went in search, and happily found at least a reasonable substitute in the form of Eastern Airlines. This venture began innocently enough when he invited former Astronaut Frank Borman, then president of Eastern, to deliver a commencement address. A classmate of Posvar's at West Point, Borman was a good apolitical choice guaranteed not to arouse faculty criticism.

Shortly thereafter Posvar was appointed to a position on Eastern's board of directors. I'm not prepared to call this a quid pro quo, but superficially at least, it possessed the ingredients. When I heard about the Posvar appointment, I cynically remarked to my wife: "Sell your stock in Eastern! With Posvar on the scene, it can only be headed for trouble."

At that time I had no clue that Eastern's financial outlook was already bleak. I simply wanted to vent again my complete lack of confidence in Posvar's ability. Ultimately the airline went bankrupt, but not before Posvar managed to put his imprint on it. Until the actual collapse, Posvar must have been as happy with his appointment as the fox in the proverbial hen house, because directors, wives, and dependent family members traveled free on the airline. This perk afforded numerous opportunities that Posvar gleefully exploited.

Once the chancellor was on the board, Eastern announced that it was opening a branch office in the Oakland section of Pittsburgh, at the corner of Forbes Avenue and Semple Street. Since no other airline had ever established an Oakland office, does this suggest a Posvar influence?

Surprise! Surprise! Eastern captured the Pitt sports business, both charter flights and individual ticket sales. Did Eastern suddenly become the lowest bidder or was this a Posvar fiat? After a trial period Eastern concluded that business was not adequate to keep its Oakland office open, and it folded.

While that office was open, I arranged a Caribbean vacation through one of its agents. In the process I came to know the branch's young female manager. Realizing that I was associated with the University, she remarked: "I'm trying to arrange a meeting with your boss. I have to explain a few details to him."

Being interested in all potential Posvar machinations, I asked about the specifics. Apparently when Posvar and/or his wife traveled, he could never decide exactly when he wanted either to leave or return. As a result he would order three sets of tickets (all free): one for an early flight and two for later in the day with the same pattern applying to return flights. This meant that for one round-trip he could tie up twelve seats, but planned to use a maximum of four. The office manager wanted to explain that, potentially, planes departed with eight seats unsold because of his travel indecisions.

Eager to perform her job effectively, the manager believed that she could explain the basic logic of efficient requisitioning of tickets to the chancellor and he would be pleased to comply. Unaware of the egocentric personality that she was dealing with, she was certain that he would cooperate because the airline was experiencing financial difficulty. I warned her that she would never get an appointment, especially if she stated her purpose. After our discussion on that topic, when I would walk by the Eastern office, I would frequently stick my head in the door and ask if she had procured her appointment yet. The answer was always some variation of "No, but I'm working on it." Her office closed while she was still waiting.

Viewing the ticket episode as another evidence of Posvar's self-importance, I filed my skimpy airline notes in a drawer, not to be dusted off for years. Then, while my wife and I were shopping for a new car, we encountered a personable salesman who was new to that assignment. Wanting to answer questions honestly and fully, he checked information thoroughly and apologized for not having answers at his fingertips. On the assumption that he may have been downsized, I asked about his former employer. "Eastern Airlines," he proudly replied, "Until it went bankrupt."

I asked: "What did you expect with Posvar as one of the directors?" Thinking that he wouldn't know the name, I was surprised to learn that it had a jarring ring to it. My comment had made it clear that I was not one of his sycophants, and with that signal, the salesman realized that he could talk frankly.

In time he provided names, addresses, and phone numbers of those who could verify and add to his storehouse of Posvar tales. I followed up on those leads. Except for one woman who would not comment to me, a stranger to her, others spoke freely; I gathered that Posvar would never win a popularity contest that depended on their votes.

Apparently the Eastern staff had a good grapevine of its own through which its members could exchange information about both the company's financial condition and management's upper echelon. As faithful employees they worked to see the airline succeed not only for the sake of their livelihoods but also for the sake of a valued employer. The Posvar incident that they most resented occurred in Charlotte where most of Eastern's ticketing was done. A vast majority of the 24 staffers there knew the Posvar name because of his ticketing maneuvers of frequently claiming twelve for the price of none.

Their resentment ultimately coalesced around a specific incident in which the chancellor and his wife were returning to Pittsburgh from Florida on an overbooked flight with a stopover in Charlotte. There the airline had two passengers who desperately needed that flight to make connections in Pittsburgh. With the Posvars traveling free and with their knowledge of the airline's financial status, a member of the Charlotte staff incorrectly concluded that the Posvars would be pleased to cooperate, explained the problem to the chancellor, and asked that he and his wife consider a 30-minute layover to accommodate the couple.

In reply to this request, the haughty director responded with all the grace and decorum of a budding buffoon. Pulling himself up to his full but limited stature, Posvar uttered those infamous words: "Get yourself another patsy, sonny!" and then slumped back into his seat where he found a cocktail at his elbow.

To Eastern employees bustling to keep the airline financially afloat, this insensitive and tactless reply had the resonance of a traitorous rebuke. Beamed via the airline's grapevine to all of Eastern's service areas, the comment was interpreted as an elaboration of character. Thereafter the appearance of the Posvar name on a manifest signaled employees to be on the alert for more aberrant behavior.

One Eastern sales representative whom I interviewed referred to Posvar as the "King of Mooch," not an endearing title, but one accurately descriptive. It conveyed the image of a chancellor repeatedly trying—unlawfully, according to the airline's interpretation—to con the flight attendants into providing him with free liquor.

This quarrel with Eastern employees centered on the miniature bottles of liquor served to passengers during a charter flight. Because the University booked travel on football weekends and Posvar was the University's Mr. Big, he concluded that he was entitled "to mooch a little hooch" at the end of the flight so that he could party free before the game.

Grudgingly on some flights attendants had given him a few bottles, but the showdown came when one young woman, head of the cabin crew, refused to bend the law requiring that the miniature bottles to be served only in flight. When she remained obdurate, Posvar's anger showed, and he commented: "I'm always suspicious when flight attendants won't allow liquor to be removed from the plane." This and subsequent comments caused the crew to conclude that the chancellor was implying that they were keeping the liquor for a party of their own. He insisted that he would check the liquor kits when the flight returned to Pittsburgh to determine if the attendants were imbibing illegally themselves.

After that incident an Eastern executive ordered that, on future Pitt charters, the airline routinely purchase a few fifths from a liquor store and deliver them to Walt Cummins, the Assistant Athletic Director, so that they might be passed on to Posvar's traveling secretary. Problem solved, at least until the chancellor could forge another.

Thus this airline fiasco remained neatly tucked away until now. Perhaps the destiny of Eastern would have been the same with or without Posvar's meddling, but it does illustrate much about his character. At that particular time the company could not afford the additional liabilities that this "talented" director provided.

DR. TOUCHDOWN, LTD.

Wesley Posvar achieved a distinction that eluded Chancellor Edward Litchfield throughout his career—a national football championship. In 1976 the community applauded this feat and hailed Posvar as a miracle worker, but the fall-out from that success was devastating; fiscal overindulgence and irresponsible management eventually brought the football program to its knees.

When Posvar arrived on the campus in 1967, the University was in the midst of a decade of disastrous football seasons. Within his first five years, he discovered the source of the problem and moved to correct it. The culprit turned out to be the Big Four pact with Penn State, Syracuse, and West Virginia universities, an agreement that was the brainchild of Milton Eisenhower, then president at Penn State. Coming as it did in the postwar period when many major universities were beginning all-out football recruitment, the pact maintained that the four institutions would take the high road and not admit players whose academic qualifications fell below those of regularly admitted students at their respective campuses.

In 1972 Posvar, with the smokescreen of a blue-ribbon committee, announced that Pitt was leaving the Big Four but downplayed the underlying reasons for the withdrawal. He piously explained that under the pact Pitt was bound to restrictions to which the others were not adhering (Alberts, p. 422), but he failed to add that he too didn't want to adhere; he secretly yearned for freedom to recruit.

And recruit he did! With reckless abandon during the first year after divesting Pitt of its ties to the pact, the chancellor authorized an unlimited number of football scholarships. Ultimately 78 recruits were corralled that year, thereby registering more than a slight deviation from the Big Four rule; it had permitted a university some flexibility in the number of football scholarships, but maintained that the number was expected to average 25 per year. Thus this departure from the Big Four stipulations marked the opening salvo of Posvar football, but such extravagance lasted only one year because the NCAA promptly ruled against casting the football net so broadly. (Alberts, p. 423) In the meantime Pitt coaches were given the signal to seek out top-notch players under the Posvar version of the 3Rs—recruitment without regard to Race, Religion, or Reading Ability. This winning combination, culminating in the 1976 championship, caused Posvar to conclude that he personally was qualified to assume the management of football operations. (*Press*, 06-05-81)

Within weeks after abrogating the Big Four pact, Pitt had appointed Johnny Majors as the new football coach, a position that he would not have accepted if Pitt had remained a member of the Big Four and the 78 scholarships had not been granted. (Alberts, p. 422) The new coach promptly provided the first winning season in almost a decade; the ten years that followed were as glorious on the gridiron as the previous ones had been ignominious, with the most egregious losses concentrated in Coach Dave Hart's three 1-9 seasons.

In addition to the acquisition of a winning coach and the application of the Posvar 3Rs, Pitt football fortunes were aided by the dramatic rise of the Black athlete. When admission policies were liberalized to encourage the enrollment of Black students generally, football benefited. Under the Pitt program minority students with academic deficiencies were not required to meet College of Arts and Sciences standards fully during their first two years; that provided many Black athletes, who previously were deemed academically ineligible, with an opportunity to enroll and compete. (Alberts, p. 423) This new provision was a boon to the Pitt football program, as well as to the game at institutions across the nation.

After four victorious years (1973-76), Majors returned to his alma mater, the University of Tennessee, and Jackie Sherrill became the head coach. Over the next five campaigns

(1977-1981), he compiled a phenomenal record. In his final years Sherrill posted three consecutive 11-1 seasons to establish himself as a premier coach. With his last bowl appearance in 1981, he left no doubt that he was the master of his football team, but that attitude challenged the Posvar ego.

Immediately following that Sugar Bowl victory, Sherrill, young, proud, and successful, expected to have the customary 5-10 minute closed-door session to savor victory in private with his players. But he was overruled by Assistant Chancellor Edward Bozik, who was speaking for Posvar. Before that players' meeting could take place, the doors of the locker room were immediately flung open against Sherrill's expressed wishes. "Suddenly the clubhouse was awash with the press, glad-handing well-wishers, and a swarm of deliriously cheering Golden Panthers." In his hour of triumph the coach felt as though he had been "stripped of his dignity by University administrators." In this instance Bozik relegated the coach's feelings to a secondary level in his callous effort to bag a few brownie points that were shortly converted into his appointment as Director of Athletics. (*Press*, 01-20-82, 01-21-82)

Before leaving New Orleans that very night to coach in the East-West game, Sherrill, livid over the defiance of his wishes, requested an immediate meeting with Posvar who told him: "Men don't do business that way." Sherrill promptly demonstrated for Posvar's edification how men do "do business." By the time he returned from the West Coast, he had resigned and accepted the head coaching position at Texas A&M University.

A second person, privy to the Posvar-Sherrill flare-up in New Orleans, stated that Posvar was so angry with the coach that he "ordered University administrators not to talk with Sherrill that night." (*Press*, 01-21-82) That's not unlike Posvar telling his administrators not to talk with me after I had voiced a few critical, but true, words about his conduct. Thus it might be concluded that the silent treatment was Posvar's preferred punishment; it also contained an admonition to his staff to stay in line or face similar ostracism.

After the Majors-Sherrill era, Pitt football headed for the dumpster, masterminded by Posvar and Bozik. Before half-time at games, the chancellor, conspicuous in his gold blazer, could regularly be seen wending his way from his private box down through the stands in order to arrive at the locker room as the players came off the field. This ritual underscored the fact that Posvar was close to his team.

Normally the athletic director administers his department, but under Posvar his AD was an assistant who controlled only what Posvar designated as his area of responsibility. To obtain ADs who would permit their departments to be run by remote control, the chancellor forced Frank Carver to resign so that his West Point classmate, Casimir Myslinski, could hold the position. When Myslinski revealed his independence, Posvar eased him into retirement in favor of Ed Bozik, who incidentally had been with the chancellor at the Air Force Academy.

Intellectually as well wrapped as a six-pack minus the plastic band holding the cans together, Bozik was inordinately useful to Posvar, because he was probably unaware of his errand-boy status. In time Bozik too was eased out, but to make leaving more palatable over the first six months, he was paid a $52,000 consultant (or should we say "consolation") fee. Obviously the University funds would have been better spent if he were paid $52,000 not to consult. (*Press,* 06-10-91) Later Ron Cook of the *Post-Gazette* (06-14-02) concluded that, when Steve Pederson took over as Athletic Director, "the Pitt athletic department was a joke," thanks largely to Posvar and Bozik; without their ineptness such depths could not have been reached.

Pitt athletic fortunes seemed to be dropping faster than the stock market in the dark days of 2008. Issues with coaches, players, and athletic staff all created embarrassments and alerted the press and the NCAA that the department was out of control. Coaching problems seemed endless. Posvar hired one coach who brought a scandal with him, another who had been suspended from his alma mater, and a third who had been given a "lifetime" contract.

He also demanded that one prospective coach promise to name a Black assistant as his first "hire." The prospect declared that he would have to prioritize Pitt's coaching needs and determine what Black coaches in the area of that need were available in the market before committing himself. Posvar told him that it didn't matter if a Black coach were qualified, "just hire him." The candidate promptly withdrew his name, knowing that race relations at the University could be further eroded if he brought in an assistant coach to an undefined position and set him up for almost certain failure. Thoughtful African-Americans and other minority activists should salute the candidate for expressing a judgment far superior to Posvar's recognition of Black pressure.

In 1989 the dynamic duo of Posvar and Bozik acted out their version of the "Saturday Night Massacre"—the execution of Mike Gottfried's coaching career at Pitt. That year the coach had enjoyed a successful season, and his team was invited to play in the John Hancock Bowl at El Paso. Literally hours before kickoff, Gottfried was fired. Several weeks earlier he had been ordered to resign or be dismissed. He obviously opted for the latter.

This course of events must have caused Gottfried to feel disbelief beyond description, because on several public occasions Posvar had stated that he had a "lifetime" contract. No matter what definition of "lifetime" Gottfried understood, he certainly did not expect the chancellor to thrust a pink slip in his hand on the eve of a bowl game.

This Gottfried episode represents one of the strangest chapters not only in the bizarre football saga of Wesley Posvar but also in the history of collegiate athletics. The dismissal was based on the coach's alleged objection to the establishment of new and higher academic standards governing the admission of freshman athletes. Adopted on December 15, 1989, the exact date that Gottfried was handed his resign-or-be-fired ultimatum, the new rules instituted only modest change.

This scenario defied logic from all perspectives. The new standards could affect no student, athlete or any other, during those last days of December. No faculty, athletic, or administrative purpose could be served at that precise point in time by dismissing the coach on the eve of the bowl game. Obviously once the new admissions guidelines were promulgated, the ball was effectively lobbed into the coach's court. If he had felt keenly on the subject, he could have resigned. Gottfried, under contract for the following year, had the option of submitting to the regulations and retaining his job or resigning and forfeiting his salary. But, why dismiss him and be responsible for a year's salary if he might be inclined to leave voluntarily?

The senseless firing was rendered even more absurd by the fact that another major university was rumored to be seeking the coach's services. Even if the chancellor were intent on ending the contract, why didn't he pause to see if the other university would make an offer and assume the salary responsibility? That could have saved the $450,000 that the University paid Gottfried for not coaching. (*Press*, 03-20-92) Furthermore, for Pitt to deliberately expose its internal dissension at a bowl game before the national media and hundreds of thousands of TV viewers scarred the University image in the face of an opportunity to enrich it.

Because the root cause of the dismissal cannot be found among these logical considerations, it must be sought among the illogical, illegal, and diabolical activity of which there was no scarcity during the Gottfried years. Ultimately an in-house University investigation uncovered 12 NCAA infractions, as well as nine other possible violations not fully supported even by Pitt's interpretation of the evidence.

The wrongdoing centered on recruiting and improper benefits doled out to Pitt athletes. No published evidence suggested that Coach Gottfried ever committed or authorized any violations. Aside from Bozik, he was the head of football operations under which assistant coaches, athletic staff, and student athletes did disregard NCAA rules. That clearly indicated that he couldn't escape culpability.

The College and Pro Football News Weekly captured the essence of the impasse with Gottfried when it reported: "Gottfried led the troops, but he never would become part of the administration's 'good ole boy network.' In actuality his failure to cater to Posvar was his downfall." John Hadley, the reporter who reached this conclusion, did so after an exhaustive series of interviews with Gottfried, alumni, school officials, and others familiar with the Pitt program. (*Press*, 09-30-91) Perceived as a challenge to Posvar's ego, Gottfried's conduct was interpreted as insubordination that had to be punished.

These Sherrill/Gottfried embarrassments, at New Orleans and El Paso, respectively, do not represent the limits of Posvar's questionable behavior. Out-of-town football games seemed to create an atmosphere conducive to non-football antics as well. Because the chancellor's entourage at away games always included non-University guests, as well as a liberal quota of subordinates, he understandably accepted responsibility for their comfort and enjoyment. Out of courtesy to their host, guests responded with a reluctance to publicize indiscretions observed in the process of being entertained.

Bits and pieces of the chancellor's behavior have been filtered to the general public, but none as shocking as the performance before a football game in Waco against Baylor University in September 1970. On the Friday evening prior to the game, Posvar took his contingent of guests to a pizza shop, where he proceeded to throw one of his ego-fits.

When the service at his table of 10-12 guests was slower than the chancellor expected, he charged into the kitchen and sought a confrontation with the manager, thereby setting up a potential clash of minds. With a little burlesque the situation possessed the ingredients to become a genuine laugher, and it didn't disappoint. Only seconds were needed to gain the manager's undivided attention. Although the dialogue remains a mystery, the two agreed immediately to disagree. The manager at once concluded that the battle line was not going to be set up in the kitchen and promptly forced Posvar to beat a one-man retreat.

With tapping toes and gyrating legs, the chancellor suddenly decided that the heat in the kitchen was too great and that there was merit in returning to the dining area. At first glance some thought that he had seized the moment to introduce a new dance step while others believed that he was merely expressing an urgent need to find a Men's Room. Both assumptions were dashed almost immediately.

To the consternation of the Pitt group, the manager was in close pursuit with a large carving knife pointed menacingly at the chancellor's midsection. Then suddenly changing positions, he raised the "kitchen machete" over his head, a position that lowered the chancellor's anxiety quotient, but not by much. The irate manager continued shouting "Out! Out! Out!" until the shocked and befuddled Pitt delegation was ushered, un-served, from the pizzeria. What a heart-rending scene! The chancellor was faced with the indignity of being on the street.

What a *volte-face!* The chancellor had entered the kitchen to hasten the feeding of the flock only to be thrust into the cruel night air and denied his pizza. The incident did, however, teach him a valuable lesson: In a volatile situation it's better to be behind a knife than before.

Unfortunately the lesson wasn't learned. In another year at an elegant North Miami restaurant after a Pitt football loss, the chancellor repeated his obnoxious conduct. When attempting to fete his football guests, he again encountered a waiter who failed to perform up to his standards. Of course, the waiter could not be expected to know that he was being called upon to serve a man poised to reenact his wacky Waco performance. "Fidgeting about the delay in service," as one of the guests described the scene, "he [Posvar] said he was going to kick some butts and invaded the kitchen. Moments later his wife Millie decided to rescue him." Apparently she had learned more in Waco than he had.

In these erratic years of Posvar football, the University caught the NCAA off guard with a few trick plays for major gainers. For example, one of my students, who served as the night clerk at the Webster Hall Hotel, informed me that a Pitt football player had taken up residence at the hotel because he was being hounded by his pregnant girlfriend. The coaches had thought that this distraction created too much pressure on his young mind and spirited him away to the seclusion of the hotel where the girlfriend nevertheless found him. This special "care and feeding" denoted another no-no that unfortunately was low enough to fly under the NCAA radar.

On the more humorous side, another football player, registered in one of my fall term classes, reported for the first time after six weeks of the term had already elapsed. He presented me with a simple note that he asked me to sign; it read: "This is to certify that [Mr. Special] was in class today." I honored the request, but drew a large asterisk after my name and wrote on the following line: "Present for the first time this semester." While I was affixing my signature, a broad grin crossed his face, but his expression changed when I continued to write. After he read my addendum, we engaged in a brief, enlightening exchange:

Mr. Special: I guess that means I flunk the course?

Kehl: No! I'll give you a W [withdrawal]; that means that you have no record as far as this course is concerned.

Mr. Special: Please give me an F. [He actually begged for it.]

Kehl: I do this [the W grade] for all students who never attend my course; it's no special favor.

This exchange proved that the football player was temporarily more alert than the instructor; that may explain why he ultimately signed a pro-football contract for more money than I earned in a lifetime. If I had withdrawn him from the course, he would have been registered for nine credits (most students register for 15-16), and NCAA regulations stipulate that athletes must be registered for a minimum of 12 credits in order to be eligible to compete. My W grade meant that every game in which Mr. Special had participated was subject to forfeiture, but the situation was not as dire as it sounds.

The University had changed the regulation; a student who registered for a course was entitled to receive a quality grade (A-F) unless he took an official step to withdraw. Thus Mr. Special was legally correct in asking to receive a failing grade.

After that term ended and I doled out the W as I had promised, I received numerous phone calls: two from Support Services for Athletes and two from the chancellor's office, all questioning the W grade. To all I replied that this was my custom for those who never attended. Then the CAS dean called and reminded me that technically Mr. Special was entitled to the F. The salient point is that over the preceding five years, I had assigned the W grade 12 times and never received a single call from any office, including the chancellor's, stating that the W grade was inappropriate. It's truly amazing that the chancellor's office could be so alert to one athlete while ignoring the un-athletic dozen.

With players feasting on a lax application of NCAA rules, coaches did likewise. I don't know with what regularity it happened, but I do know that one assistant coach whose contract was not renewed latched onto a similar post in Oklahoma. Before taking off on that trek, he wisely decided to have an auto tune-up and general maintenance check. Stuckert's Service Station estimated the work at $375, but by the time the car was pronounced ready for the highway, the cost had soared to $650. Ellsie Stuckert was personally alarmed at the discrepancy and was anxious to explain the added expense, but was not prepared for the coach's retort. As Ellsie proceeded to detail what mechanical work had been required, the coach, with a blasé wave of the hand, interrupted with the comment: "I don't care what it costs; Uncle Wes is paying for it." With that he slapped down a University charge card; case closed!

Having overheard the conversation, I was instantly so furious that I had to walk out of the station. Of course, I should have recognized that the coach was doing what the Posvar system permitted. Why was the system so skewed as to extend such a privilege to coaches? Basically the University's business is education, but no academic was ever treated so royally.

This same football presence prevailed to the very end of Posvar's career. According to a source who was present during the chancellor's final report to the Board of Trustees before retiring, his parting comment was: "See you at the next bowl game!"

AN ALMOST IMMACULATE DECEPTION

Although perilous times create great opportunities for those who find themselves in leadership roles, not all leaders are able to convert a crisis into a ringing triumph. Perhaps the Pitt scene did not lend itself to a positive solution; but, for whatever reason, Wesley Posvar failed to harness the discontent and gain the confidence of either the disrupters or the rank-and-file.

At both national and local levels, unrest in the late '60s and early '70s focused on dissatisfaction with the conduct of the Vietnam War, and for university administrators this disruption was transformed into a bifurcated albatross after the assassination of Dr. Martin Luther King, Jr. in the spring of 1968.

Aside from demanding a halt to the fighting and a curtailment of ROTC, the general student protest at Pitt demanded revisions in the College program. These causes came to the forefront simultaneously with the development of the Black protest movement that added a few issues of its own.

Limited justification for the general student sit-ins and demonstrations existed, and after much huffing and puffing, that movement faded into the background. On the other hand, issues (both on and off the campus) raised by the Black Action Society (BAS), as the organized Black student movement became known, had merit, but merit does not translate into license to take charge of any aspect of University life. Part of the chancellor's response to these demonstrations was to have bullet-proof windows quietly installed in his first-floor office.

A Building and Grounds person related this window caper to me but refused to supply details. That was my fault; I appeared too eager with my questions for one merely engaging in chitchat; that, in turn, caused him to resort to his clam imitation.

I wanted to know if all windows, or only the most exposed at ground level, had been so covered and, of course, knowing the cost was a high priority. I struck out on these requests, but I did learn a few facts. First, the window fortification was a second alternative. Originally the chancellor preferred to transfer his inner-sanctum to the Twelfth Floor of the Cathedral, but the logistics proved insurmountable. Second, the actual cost of the window protection never appeared as an expense item because it was subsumed under the allocation to protect the stained glass windows of the Nationality Rooms.

Although the protesting students, like the University family as a whole, never heard about the windows, the general atmosphere emboldened their demands. In fact, when the University trustees consented to meet with the students in a question-and-answer session, one student radical had the audacity to lecture the trustees via a memo on the proper conduct when engaging the students: "They should be careful not to filibuster the students' time away. In the eyes of many students the chancellor and his staff are experts at this...." To establish a meaningful dialogue, he instructed the trustees that, in addition to themselves, "student leaders should be at the podium."

Despite this arrogance the students raised many pertinent questions in their exchanges with the trustees and administrators. The latter were openly flustered by the substance of the queries. Recognition of that fact caused the protesters to push too far too fast in demanding solutions. Theirs was a costly but necessary gambit, because they realized that only an assertive approach could capture and hold the interest of the student body throughout the entire University. They had gained the initiative and wanted to retain it, because delay played into the hands of the administration. Within months a certain percentage of the student leadership would graduate and disrupt the momentum; regrouping would be necessary, and the initiative could be lost. Time demonstrated that the students were correct in these assessments.

A dean who had frequent contacts with Posvar throughout his tenure offered an explanation for both student and faculty disappointment in their relationships with the chancellor. He declared to me on two separate occasions that Posvar had the shortest attention span of any professional he ever knew. Given Posvar's intelligence, I am reluctant to give credence to that assessment. His impatience, coupled with a disregard for the mundane, may have triggered his disdain for lengthy periods devoted to a particular topic. But comments from two widely separate faculty sources cause me to pause.

One pointed out that, while chairing a meeting, Posvar wrote a note to one of the attendees who was sitting down the table from him, folded it, placed the individual's name on the outside, and passed it to the person next to him with the thought that it would ultimately reach the intended recipient. Like notes in grade school, something always went awry; not seeing the name on the outside, an individual for whom it was not intended opened it and read: "Are you available for tennis this afternoon?"

In the second incident another faculty member recalled Posvar going to a meeting carrying an impressive-looking folder; when the man stole a peak inside, he discovered that the chancellor was loaded only with the most recent edition of *Sports Illustrated;* he apparently planned to be a non-contributor at the meeting. Perhaps the dean's evaluation was on the mark.

On one occasion students entered the chancellor's office with five demands, and before they left he had agreed to six of them. On another, one of my students asked me how his group might overcome the chancellor's repeated denials for an extension of the hours during which men might visit in women's dormitory rooms. I informed him that I had no sympathy with any aspect of his proposal, but recognized that he had not sought my moral or social judgment. Therefore, I answered his question by recommending that the announcement of an organized sit-in at the chancellor's office the following Friday at high noon, with the media invited, would cause him to capitulate because Posvar dreaded any publicity that might prove negative. Before that weekend, I am sorry to say, the students received 80 percent of their demands.

One of the controversial issues during his early years in office was the war in Vietnam. At that time many faculty and students were disturbed by the course of events. Unable to turn the government from its pursuit of military victory, the more emotional Vietniks on the faculty and in the student body decided that they would seek their vengeance against the ROTC unit on campus.

The most radical protesters wanted to abolish the local unit immediately, whereas the less irrational wanted to abolish all credit for ROTC courses. Those most interested in drastic change were also the most vocal and appeared to have the majority of the faculty cowed into keeping silent while they

harangued. Posvar sat through two hours of their ROTC vili-
fication and never once said a word in defense of the military
that had paid for his total education and livelihood before he
arrived at Pitt. This silence didn't go unnoticed, and in later
years he must have come to understand why his yearning for
a high military position fell on deaf ears in Washington.

Posvar and his minions were so intimidated by these
Vietniks that they never defended the ROTC program that
the University had made available to its students for many
years. In fact, they were afraid to attend such programs as
ROTC Recognition Night in which they had participated
during previous years.

Because ROTC was a legitimate appendage of the College
of Arts and Sciences, I attended its functions as I did those
of any other department. For that loyalty, I was declared "not
a member of the team." The administration's attitude was
understood by Colonel David Clagett, the commander of the
campus ROTC unit. In a letter to me, he wrote:

> You have further gained the respect and high regard
> of the cadets and ROTC staff by your willingness to
> appear publicly at ROTC functions at a time when
> many members of the administration and faculty made
> every effort to dissociate themselves from the military
> for fear of criticism on the part of some academics and
> vocal student groups.

About the same time that Posvar and his merry men were
abandoning ROTC, they were coming to the defense of a
politician over a single student. This academically unquali-
fied applicant was originally rejected partly because he was in

the lower 25 percent of his high school class, a position veri-fied by equally abysmal SAT scores. The Admissions Office rejected the application and advised him to demonstrate improved performance at a local junior college or elsewhere and then reapply. Instead he turned to his aggressive father, who asked State Senator Robert Fleming to write directly to the chancellor.

The letter threw down the gauntlet, and the chancellor failed to do likewise; his assistant, who had been a student of mine, was assigned to contact me regarding the case. He explained: "Fleming wants an admission, not an explana-tion." I agreed to review the student's credentials and assured him that he would be given every reasonable consideration. In the meantime Posvar had written confidentially to the provost asking him "to review this decision in your academic capacity." His memo continued: "We will not corrupt our standards." But, like Fleming, he simply wanted the student admitted; standards had no role in his expectation.

I had the record thoroughly reviewed, and the result was unanimous: Reject the application. The kid's father was almost violent, because in his words: "You're sending my son to Vietnam." I didn't see myself as a draft board substitute, only an arbiter of College policy.

The father appealed again to the chancellor, who called me and told me that he was going to admit the student; (so much for the standards that he prated about to the provost). I replied that that was his prerogative, but that I would be no part of the decision.

Perhaps I should have taken the issue to the faculty. If I had, I would have exposed a major rift within the adminis-tration to the delight of the public press. In fact, I overlooked principle in this instance because I didn't think that one student, particularly this student, was worth a public fight at a time when student power, Black power, and football power, more crucial by far, were already ripping at the University's unity.

Until near the end of his 24-year career at Pitt, Wesley Posvar was the primary conduit through which students, faculty, alumni, state legislators, and the general public were informed about developments at the University. Despite some opposition to his policies, Posvar's image, superficially at least, seemed unruffled. Controversial issues were easily quashed for various reasons: Critics generally had comparatively limited access to documents and statistics; their complaints were usually not University-wide, and the chancellor possessed the resources to muzzle most criticisms.

The danger of this type of administration was succinctly outlined in a *Post-Gazette* op-ed piece (06-09-91) by Rudolph Weingartner, who resigned as Pitt provost in a dispute with Posvar over the provost's role in formulating the University budget. Professor Weingartner cautioned us that:

> Satisfying a boss... can become a more important motive than performing a task; avoiding blame can come to take precedence over fulfilling a goal. A management scheme that is heavily dependent on personal relation-ships crowds out concern with common objectives.

Although Weingartner described Pitt administration accurately, the Posvarites trumpeted the chancellor's pedestrian tenure as though it were a masterpiece of administration.

Posvar and his cohorts have also explained ad nauseam how he pulled the University from the brink of financial ruin by retiring a $19 million debt. In 1976 the chancellor dramatically put a match to the mortgage held on Pitt properties by its insurance companies; he thereby visually masterminded the return to solvency. This is the version of the debt problem that diehard Posvarites harped on, mostly to each other, on the assumption that somehow validity will emerge from repetition.

On the other hand, objective analysts realize that the University's financial status was altered for the better in 1966 by the action of the Pennsylvania Legislature that converted Pitt to a state-related institution. Chancellors Stanton Crawford and David Kurtzman accepted this help and charted a financial course that led to retirement of the debt in 1976 when Posvar happened to be the chancellor.

The Posvar period was also marked by two proclaimed successes through prevention. With the use of every legal, financial, and public relations resource available, the chancellor fought off two serious attempts to unionize the faculty. At the same time he navigated the treacherous football waters without NCAA censure. Waves of ugly publicity were churned up by both player- and coach-related scandals, but he steered the University ship through it all and escaped sanctions. This sanctified him in the eyes of the Posvarites, because few of the nation's major football programs were able to do so over two decades.

At one point this purity record stood on the brink of being besmirched when the NCAA found probable cause to examine practices in the Athletic Department. A team of investigators was sent to the Pitt campus to collect information and report their findings, but the group left without either exonerating or sanctioning the University program. More than a year later the NCAA announced that it was not fully satisfied with the information garnered and was returning to gather more evidence in the hope of resolving the issue.

One of those who had provided testimony to the NCAA on its first visit went to Posvar and confessed that he could not lie again if confronted with the same questions that he had answered before. In the interim he had become a born-again Christian and was committed to tell the truth even if it was to his detriment or to that of the University he loved.

For the chancellor this was a revolting development, but the second NCAA visit was mostly perfunctory. The crucial questions were never asked, and the case was subsequently closed. At that point the immaculate deception worked for Posvar, but not for the staffer who stood ready to be truthful. To show his undying gratitude and to make certain that the staffer was never again placed in a position of having to tell the truth on the subject of Pitt football, Posvar fired him without provocation or cause. This good news was conveyed by an underling three months after the NCAA announced that the investigation would not go forward.

These years were also distinguished by Posvar's annual pilgrimages to Harrisburg to ask the legislature and governor for more money than they were willing to appropriate. This result never proved to be a deterrent because he simply increased tuition and assured the undergraduates that their programs would be improved, a pledge that never kept pace with the tuition increases.

By a left-handed confession, after his tenure expired, Posvar admitted that undergraduate programs continued to lag. His advice to his successor included making undergraduate education a high priority, a goal that he had failed to achieve in 24 years. In fact, when he became a faculty member after his retirement as chancellor, he declared:

> What I have discovered as a faculty member... is that the administrative information system for teaching at this university is very inefficient and antiquated. I'm speaking of student registration, scheduling, and so on.... If I had only known when I had the authority to do something about it, I would have done it. (*Univ. Times*, 04-13-95)

If he didn't know after 24 years, something must have been radically wrong with his reporting system.

On one occasion before resorting to the tax-the-students syndrome, Posvar called a special meeting of the deans in the Bruce Hall penthouse to discuss the shortfall. Before the group addressed this need for financial austerity, they dined at a lunch that included two wines and lobster. A dean pointed out this incongruity and believed that Posvar never forgave him for that observation.

The inconsistency between the lunch menu and the deficit was vintage Posvar. He undoubtedly felt secure behind the public relations barrage that his staff could put down on a moment's notice in response to such an extravagant proposition as this menu/topic incongruity.

THE DEFLATED PARACHUTE

The term "golden parachute" conjures up visions of monetary sugarplums dangled before a high-ranking executive as he approaches retirement. Strangely these awards are more lucrative than those received at any time during his most productive employment.

In a few instances the organization is so anxious to "give him the boot" that it is willing to pay an exorbitant price to send him on his way. But, on most occasions the retiree feels justified in plotting his own journey into inactivity. Being in charge, he can bestow his choice of blessings on himself; and as a general rule, he awards himself more loot than his predecessor carried off. By this means he is able to demonstrate his superior achievements. At the same time he must be mindful not to plunder the organization so extensively that there is little left when his successor undertakes the same maneuver; that would not be prudent; the whole absurd system could collapse. Designed as corporate welfare, this retirement ritual passes the financial burden to the stockholders and consuming public to provide for the individual who needs it the least.

The bag of expensive trinkets doled out to these welfare recipients may include such items as: handsome pensions, country club memberships, stock options, no-interest mortgages, lump sum settlements, lucrative bonuses, and family health care coverage that will assure the best medical care available, short of immortality. Collectively these financial resources could provide generously for a dozen or more junior executives but are lavished on one individual.

Wesley Posvar was the recipient of numerous samplings from this corporate storehouse, but he wasn't the first to be shocked into realizing that a golden parachute isn't achieved without a few bumps into opulent retirement. He discovered that the embarrassing way. Neither word in the term "golden parachute" suggests a 100 percent guarantee of total fulfillment, and he didn't get it. Literally speaking, both words promise something less than certainty. Only when they are in juxtaposition do they become a booty to behold.

First, a parachute isn't a thoroughly predictable item. When associated with a jump from an aircraft, it is fraught with numerous impending dangers even if it opens perfectly. The wind may carry it off target; it may become entangled in trees or high-tension wires on its way down; it may hit the ground with a thud and jar the chutest senseless; and he, in turn, may be ensnared in the chute's cords and canvas. Thus the parachute itself always proffers an element of uncertainty.

Second, the word "golden" is often interpreted as a synonym for gold. When combined with "parachute," that's true; it connotes the sum total of the benefits bestowed on a retiring executive. In reality, a golden substance may have the color of gold, may shine like gold, may be as malleable as gold, may serve the same purpose as gold, and may be accepted as gold, but it is something other than gold. On occasion, that technical distinction makes itself known.

Pensions, insurance policies, bonuses, and such are only gold-like but are generally convertible to gold, although there is always an element of doubt. For Posvar that doubt became a moment of terror, but after a rough landing it jarred only a few prime benefits from the package; he still walked away with an excess of luxury items beyond all reasonable expectations.

As details of Posvar's golden parachute floated across the front pages of newspapers, the University community was at first shocked and then angered. Hundreds of letters to editors came from the pens of students, their parents, alumni, faculty, and the public at large. The breadth and depth of these writers' emotions contributed to the rough landing that can only be grasped by surveying excerpts from their responses:

(a) Posvar "has become a nuisance to the Pitt Community." –*Pitt News* editorial, 10-10-91

(b) Of Posvar "good riddance to your arrogant, double-talking, self-serving, opportunistic ways." –David L. Brock, Pitt '82, *University Times*, 10-10-91

(c) "Having two children in college at the same time is difficult enough without the help of people like Wesley Posvar." –*Pittsburgh Press*, 06-12-91

(d) "The level of arrogance of his [Posvar's] statements knows no bounds. I find his patronizing excuses sorely lacking in content, truth and remorse for misappropriating hard-earned tax money." –Nicholas M. Husok, *Pittsburgh Press*, 05-22-91

(e) "Last summer my son, then an incoming Pitt freshman, put a bumper sticker on my car which proclaimed: 'Proud Pitt Parent.' I was embarrassed... and removed it." –Sara Schneider, *Pittsburgh Press*, 06-09-91

(f) The faculty at the Titusville campus held a meeting "to express their indignation at the inappropriate and unethical behavior of Wesley Posvar and other Pitt administrators and the irresponsibility of the Board of Trustees." –*University Times*, 07-11-91

(g) An open letter signed by 60 faculty members stated that Posvar "systematically looted the University of Pittsburgh during his tenure" and added that he and the Board of Trustees "have brought shame and dishonor upon the University in violation of the spirit, if not the letter of the Board's trust." –*Post-Gazette*, 06-08-91

(h) "To me it just shows a kind of crassness that's simply inappropriate at a university." –Professor Donald McBurney, Budget Policies Committee, *Pitt News*, 05-29-91

(i) Letter from the School of Library and Information Science, with 20 signatures, declared that Posvar's actions "aimed at amassing personal wealth at the expense of the faculty, staff, students, and educational programs of the University." –*University Times*, 06-27-91

(j) "He [Posvar] sought to enrich himself beyond any decent academician's proper hope and to the long-lasting embarrassment and detriment of Pitt." –Professor Robert L. Gale, *Post-Gazette*, 07-02-93

(k) "In my 21 years as a faculty member at Pitt, I have never known morale to be so low and have never heard anger expressed so openly and forcefully toward the past leadership." –Professor Don Martin, *Pittsburgh Press*, 07-21-91

(l) In evaluating one of Posvar's deans, a faculty committee gave the chancellor a left-footed boot in the ass by remarking that the dean "was tainted with the corruption of Posvar's quasi-Stalinist regime." –*University Times*, 08-29-96

(m) Believing that Pitt stood on a solid foundation of its own, separate from that of any individual, I joined the letter writing brigade and concluded: "Posvar bashing should continue until every faculty and staff member, every student, and all alumni feel that their anger and disappointment have been avenged. After all, Dr. Posvar gained more with his conniving than John Dillinger did with a gun." –James A. Kehl, *Pittsburgh Press*, 07-25-91

Most of these vituperative remarks were "offered in evidence" during 1991, the year of the chancellor's resignation. Even within those 12 months, the information reached the public in boomlets. The *Post-Gazette* initiated one such outburst on May 23 assisted, a few days later, by a Sally Kalson news feature.

Writing on Memorial Day, Ms. Kalson, in her column entitled "THE PREXY WHO ATE PITT," was particularly helpful in suggesting ways to commemorate Posvar's deeds. Among her proposals were: (a) the establishment of a Posvar Memorial Library Wing replete with empty shelves "in honor of the book bequest that was diverted to his benefit package," (b) a collection of irate letters from students, parents, and alumni, bound in volumes of fine Corinthian leather, and (c) an extra large solid gold pork chop in honor of the free groceries provided for the Posvars. Although no details were given, I presume that the pork chop would be stored in a security vault within the Memorial Library Wing when it is not on display with the cherished letters from the adoring University community.

The combination of these two items generated a flood of letters to the *P-G*. The responses were so numerous that, on June 1, 1991, the paper's entire Letters-to-the-Editor page was devoted to those who wished to comment on the Pitt crisis. Excerpts from the best-of-the-best follow:

(a) "That he [Posvar] intends to provide for his children and grandchildren are noble goals. But at public expense!!" –Michael Lucarelli, Monroeville

(b) "The retirement benefits of Dr. Posvar should be subject to exhaustive scrutiny; if necessary, legal action should be taken." –Walter J. Vogel, Squirrel Hill

(c) "If more than a half million dollars of student tuition fees was spent on groceries for his [Posvar's] personal residence, I think he should refund the money." –Jean King, Clairton

(d) "This is to notify those who solicit funds for Pitt to save their postage and time as I do not intend to buy any more groceries for Wesley." –Robert C. Conti, O'Hara

(e) "Dr. Posvar's statement concerning his reduction in estate size if he is to provide for his offspring clearly shows a misplaced set of priorities that has been evident throughout his tenure." –David Fabrizio, Bethel Park

(f) "[Posvar], Get out of town, perhaps to Washington, D.C., where you might get a job." –Robert L. Gale, Oakland

Despite this avalanche of anti-Posvar sentiment, the chancellor continuously remained in denial. He elected to ignore the fact that his personal financial grab, plus scandals in the food service, medical research, sports recruiting, and sports fund-raising had sent the University and the region reeling. In late June 1991, he declared: "I have taken pride in a record of personal and professional integrity." (*Press,* 06-07-91) And almost two years later he was singing the same refrain when he told the *Pitt News* (03-31-93) that: "The information about me was to a great extent false and misrepresented.... Ninety percent of my retirement funds were my own savings and investments from over a quarter century."

Attempts to find corresponding pro-Posvar rebuttal letters were fruitless except for ones that seem to be Posvar-inspired. The first pop-gun salute came from a son-in-law who spilled his sour grapes in the *Press* (05-15-91). He claimed to be "embarrassed by the lack of appreciation we show to someone [guess who?] who has contributed to the city for so long." He too is in denial because he fails to consider how embarrassed many Pittsburghers were at Posvar's calculated steps "to loot" the University as 60 professors so quaintly charged.

In convoluted logic the son-in-law argues that Posvar should be rewarded for not using Pitt "as a stepping stone to a bigger, brighter career" that he could have enjoyed if he hadn't "paid the price and passed on many opportunities for lofty positions in the State Department, business, and Defense Department." Posvar made a personal decision to remain at Pitt, unfortunately to the University's detriment, not his, but that did not give him license to loot it. Although Posvar had at times alluded to vague positions in Washington and elsewhere in the cosmos, this marked the first written and specific designation of the State and Defense departments.

Although colleagues from his military days turned up in these departments, logic does not suggest that he was destined to do likewise. That was a Posvar delusion. These former associates may have enjoyed friendly lunches with him and talked generally about jobs that were opening up, but they knew his reputation.

In an obviously orchestrated letter four days later, C. Holmes Wolfe, who occupied a chair at the Board of Trustees' meetings, wrote a follow-up letter to that of the son-in-law. In a nothing statement he (a) expressed his gratitude to the son-in-law for writing, (b) felt that by writing he [Wolfe] had "the opportunity of placing his [Posvar's] presidency in some perspective," but never clarified that perspective, and (c) agreed that "successes of Dr. Posvar's leadership are everywhere," but admitted that "probably no two people will agree on their ranking" [whatever that means]. He expressed a desire to see the chancellor receive a "rousing vote of appreciation" because he viewed the golden parachute criticism as "petty" and "carping." (*Press*, 05-19-91)

Gradually Posvar and the trustees recognized that criticism of the retirement package, both within the University and in the public at large, was a relentless barrage that could not be overcome by a few anemic responses in the press. Thus they set about reluctantly to restructure the golden parachute to make it more palatable to the public, but the amounts surrendered were not as generous as they superficially appeared. In the revision:

(a) Posvar's retirement salary was reduced from $201,000 annually to $141,000 (or $11,800 per month), but the $60,000 reduction represented a substantial tax break because it was regarded as an annual donation to the University.

(b) The $3.3 million in annuities remained unchanged, thus granting him a $108,000 annual pension for the remainder of his life.

(c) The $740,000 mortgage loan under KEMP was canceled but had accrued $93,000 in interest. Posvar agreed to donate [read tax deduction] this amount to the Ridgway Center in the School of Public and International Affairs.

(d) The life insurance policy valued at $424,000 was kept in force and payable at death.

Both the faculty and the community took some consolation in this restructuring. They had been heard; some concessions to their concerns had been achieved; and they accepted the trustee promise that such a secretive arrangement would not be repeated. It was agreed that in the future the Trustee Compensation Committee, the Executive Committee, the chairman, and the trustees in general would be kept on the same page; no future chancellor would be able to pit one of these groups against another by not revealing the full extent of his retirement package or by showing one part here and another there.

Personally I was not that forgiving. I did not think that the trustees demonstrated sufficient remorse for their duplicity. The University trustees and administration didn't see it that way. In May 2000 they decided to ignore my preference and rename the Forbes Quadrangle as Wesley Posvar Hall.

The University faculty was invited to the renaming ceremony, and they registered their enthusiasm by staying away in droves. The occasion was reminiscent of the 1936 Liberty Party conclave known as the convention held in a telephone booth. With an audience that swelled to more than two dozen die-hard Posvarites, including those whose positions required their presence, the renaming would have been a rededication held in a phone booth if they could have located such a vintage item.

That dedication was the final tribute to Posvar until his death in July of the following year. Generally an individual's positive character traits are highlighted in eulogies and obituaries, but the reader does not expect to find a vita wildly distorted in such statements. The *Post Gazette's* obituary referred to Posvar's "50 combat missions in Vietnam." This was the first public mention of such heroics, and it is difficult to comprehend because he was only briefly in Vietnam during one summer. If the combat missions occurred, they should have been reported in Alberts' history of the University, written two decades after Posvar had temporarily been in the battle zone. With a hundred pages devoted to Posvar and his first 19 years at Pitt, surely there was enough space to squeeze in those five significant words: "50 combat missions in Vietnam."

It's no quantum leap to conclude that Posvar was more adept in leading an assault on the Officers' Club at happy hour than in charging hostile air space at any hour. In a second obituary the editor of *Pitt Magazine* continued this overstatement and described Posvar's alleged participation in the Berlin Airlift as "combat" duty. Without a war how could this be called combat even if it did occur? This writer, as well as the one from the *P-G*, portrayed Posvar as a more accomplished warrior after death (obituaries) than in life, but at my request for information, neither could identify the source of his material.

The obituary also refers to Posvar as a brigadier-general. Because it is not mentioned in Alberts' volume, it must be concluded that this title was bestowed some years after his retirement from the Air Force. Thus it deserves a word of explanation because it was an honorary award. Posvar never served a day as a brigadier-general and never received a dime in pay at that rank. In Air Force parlance his brand of general is unofficially called a "tombstone general," a term likely to appear only on tombstones and in obituaries.

On the day that the former chancellor's death was reported in the newspapers, I received two phone calls pertaining to the subject. One came from a Pitt professor who wanted to know if I would discontinue writing my sketch of Posvar because of his passing. My answer expressed disappointment that he had died without an opportunity to read what I was assembling; I wanted to challenge him to attempt to rebut every idea set forth, but I stated that I would overcome my disappointment and write on.

The second call was from a former Eastern Airlines staffer who said that learning of Posvar's death reminded him that he had long intended to give me a call. He admitted that the death of anyone he had known saddened him, but pensively added: "But he wasn't a nice man."

PART THREE

THE EDUCATIONAL CORE

(1969-1992)

President Truman's expression concerning the temperature in the kitchen is adaptable to the teaching profession, with only a slight re-phrasing necessary: If you can't stand the heat, get out of the classroom. That's excellent advice to any teacher or would-be teacher who is unhappy and uncomfortable when called upon to display his/her talents publicly on a daily basis. I can't imagine a more ego-deflating punishment than being trapped day in and week out, month in and year out, with students whom you are attempting to inspire when you yourself are not inspired.

I always viewed each class session as a serious undertaking and attempted to convey the attitude: "Today I have something constructive to say, and all of you should want to hear it." The few teachers who are unwilling to achieve that standard disturb me. One of them, Reggie Shortstraw, was never driven by the excitement of the classroom.

When I was in high school, I was already aware that my future lay in the teaching profession. From that point forward, sometimes subconsciously, I studied not only my academic subjects but also my teachers' techniques and student reaction to classroom situations.

During most years of my involvement in administration, I taught one course, but that was not the pattern during the final four. Thus in 1969 I welcomed my return to being a full-time professor. That opened the second half of my career encompassing another 23 years.

I was blessed with a plethora of superior students, but they, as well as the less well prepared, at times deviated from normal channels. Some of these bizarre antics are remembered more clearly than the accomplishments. As a result I have devoted a chapter to student *faux pas,* because those deeds brought hilarity to an otherwise serious academic scene.

Another chapter in this section is focused on a faculty wife and a student's parent whose exploits were both outrageous and memorable. I'm not sure whether my personality attracted these strange characters or if I were drawn to them. Perhaps by the time you have concluded this volume, you will have arrived at your own answer.

CHAPTER 8

Return to My First Love

In 1969 my return to full-time teaching was greeted with inordinate anticipation. Every working day for a decade, I had observed the unexplored collection of source materials that filled the shelves behind my desk. Certain that this cache represented the raw material for a political biography, I looked forward to the day when I could delve into the secrets hidden within. Now that day had come. Teaching provides, even demands, that time be allocated to research. I was grateful for the dual opportunity that awaited me.

Over time this research collection had developed a history of its own, begun long before my involvement. In the mid-1930s, Professor John Oliver had announced to the historical profession that he was about to write the definitive biography of the late controversial US Senator, Matthew Stanley Quay of Beaver, Pennsylvania. Once he had procured verbal permission to study the senator's papers, Oliver proceeded with extensive research into the secondary materials before asking to examine the senator's actual records.

At that point Coral Quay, the senator's spinster daughter and self-appointed guardian of family secrets, became agitated and highly emotional about Oliver's request. She believed that he, and possibly other historians, were "out to destroy papa." Disappointed at this rebuff to his overtures and fearful that insistence might cause Coral to suffer a heart attack, Oliver, a truly gentle man, dropped the project completely.

In the mid-1950s Miss Quay was still living; Oliver had retired; and I was zeroing in on a research topic. I identi-fied this as an opportunity to face the senator's daughter and "make my pitch" to utilize her father's papers in writing a serious, objective biography. Eschewing the conventional approach of sending a letter of introduction and declaring my purpose, I drove to her Edgeworth residence and, unan-nounced, rang the doorbell.

A nurse answered my ring and informed me that Miss Quay was seriously ill. She asked for my name and phone number so that Coral's nephew, who had been designated to take charge of his aunt's affairs, could contact me when he arrived at her home in the next few days. That I interpreted as evidence that my ploy had failed and that the Quay Papers, highlighting his years in the US Senate (1881-1904), were permanently beyond my reach.

Coral Quay died the following week, and to my surprise the nephew called to invite me to come to her residence to pick up, not to study but to keep, any of the papers considered useful. I went that day. Some of the senator's papers were already at the curb, either for me or for the trash pickup. I seized everything in sight and thanked him profusely.

Several days later the nephew called again to say that he had just cleaned out the basement and had uncovered other materials that might interest me. This turned out to be a significant historical collection, unfortunately disguised—hidden in suit and hatboxes and crumpled folders. The nephew's attitude was opposite that of his aunt. When I thanked him the second time, with the papers' worth yet to be determined, he replied: "Grandfather belongs to history; make of him devil, saint, or what you will." This was an expression of the enlightenment that historians welcome from those entrusted with valuable research materials.

The senator's papers proved to be a great find, nonetheless hopelessly incomplete in terms of his total career. There was a gap of ten years for which no known record existed. The collection did contain 15 letters signed by Theodore Roosevelt, with several others from presidents Benjamin Harrison and William McKinley, as well as scattered letters from such Republican bosses as Mark Hanna, Tom Platt, George Hoar, and James G. Blaine. If I had elected to sell the Roosevelt letters piecemeal to New York autograph dealers, they would probably have netted $200,000, but that was never part of my plan. The papers had cost me nothing; why should I make a profit from them? After extracting my scholarly needs from these documents, I donated them to the Library of Congress, where they were catalogued with a miscellany of the senator's papers already there.

This collection had been tempting me every day when I walked into my office. Now that I was teaching, I organized these materials, and they became the basis for a volume entitled: *Boss Rule in the Gilded Age: Matt Quay of Pennsylvania,* published in 1981. The collection also served as the springboard for a major article in the Pennsylvania Historical Studies Series entitled: *Pennsylvania Kingmakers,* as well as for a speech before the Southern Historical Association.

Upon returning to teaching, I was struck by the contrast between teaching conditions as they were in the 1946-1958 era and those present in the 1970s. The most dramatic change occurred in the number of hours per week that an instructor was expected to be in the classroom. In the earlier period, 12 to 15 hours represented the norm, but by the later period, the number had been reduced to nine. If an instructor could demonstrate that he was engaged in active research, that number was dropped to six.

Likewise, the student load was much less in the more recent period. At Ellsworth Center in the late '40s, I taught approximately 260 students in six separate sections per term; in my second teaching stint, the average load was 100 students in two or three courses. Although the latter sounds like a limited assignment, evaluating 100 research papers, plus time allotted to research, carries far beyond the 40-hour week yardstick.

In this second teaching career, I discovered a method, new at least to me, for evaluating student performance. Almost a week before a scheduled examination, I would give all students a list of six questions and assure them that the test would consist of two of those questions. Unless a student opted to play Kehl roulette by developing answers to only a few of them, he was forced to study all six questions, which were indeed comprehensive. I encouraged students to study in groups if they preferred that to the individual approach. The material was in the text, the lecture notes, and the readings collectively.

With this system, no question was a surprise to anyone, but in return for my "generosity" in providing the questions, I expected well-reasoned, well-written responses—writing skills as well as knowledge. Because information retained long-term is derived more from preparation time than from the test itself, my questions were merely providing a general organization for the study period. Of course, the student who had not diligently kept abreast of the course material during the term could not organize and present a coherent paper based solely on the week in which he/she possessed the questions.

This technique produced one of the finest pieces of evidence of learning that I can recall, and I had only an indirect role in it. Without my knowledge, three of the students in one class decided that they would pull out all stops to garner A grades on the test. They agreed to meet on a Saturday morning in a vacant Cathedral classroom with a blackboard on which they proposed to assemble a compilation of their separate bits of information pertaining to each question and then devise integrated answers. Each arrived with both text and class notes, plus individual notes from the readings. Accompanied with brown bag lunches, they proposed to work all day, if necessary, until the questions were all dissected and cogent answers developed.

Part way through the process, they discovered that they had different interpretations regarding one question. As a result their designated spokesman called me at home that Saturday asking for verification. I was overjoyed to hear about their collective study session. Real learning was taking place while I was sitting at home sipping a Coke. For those three, whether they realized it or not, the test was incidental.

Whatever learning from that course that they would retain far beyond the end of the term had taken place on that Saturday.

In order for a teaching experience to be both successful and satisfying, the instructor must enjoy such challenges of interaction with students. Exchanges may take the form of humorous or deadly serious encounters, political or economic differences, personality-oriented crises or philosophical discussions.

Despite a teacher's best intentions to be thorough and clear, his/her remarks can often be twisted or misconstrued. For example, once while trying to bring a discussion to closure at the end of a class period, I offered a few salient comments, at which point a student blurted out: "That proves that you're a communist." The whole class roared in laughter, and to the volatile student I said simply: "I think that the class has supplied you with my answer."

Not all student remarks can be so easily turned aside. Another student apologized profusely because he thought that he had disappointed me. Despite my efforts to dissuade him, I don't think that he ever accepted my assurances. A brilliant young man who had completed all requirements for a doctorate except the dissertation, he withdrew from the program. Of course, I was immediately concerned lest he be acting in haste; when it was fully evident that he had thought his decision through to a logical conclusion, I was pleased because it spelled happiness and fulfillment for him.

Because he was a highly skilled computer expert, as well as a good historian, he was offered a job that he thoroughly enjoyed and paid him, as he said, "beyond all expectations." For me not to accept the fact that he had identified his intended role in society would have been disrespectful and unprofessional. My basic assumption has always been: Help the student achieve his/her goals; let history or any other discipline assume second place in such situations.

Some ten years later at the time of my retirement, this student, who had joined the land of computers, wrote: "You are a rare teacher, one who motivated and brought out the best in your students. You will never know your positive influence on me. Thanks."

Another superior student saw it differently. She was disappointed about what she had learned in my course. She claimed that I hadn't pushed her hard enough because, when she enrolled in an Ivy League MA program, she felt in her mind that she was ill prepared to compete with her class-mates. Hers was a difficult comment for an instructor to rebut; I was certainly at a loss. When all masters' candidates in her field were given a common examination at the conclu-sion of the program, she scored first among the 28 examined. At that point I felt relieved, and she did admit that she had overreacted.

The most complex aspect of interacting with students, however, pertains to examinations. When there is uncer-tainty about an answer, the problem is generally one of inter-pretation. One student, for example, wrote: "William Penn seduced a large number of Germans to come to America." After acknowledging the humor, I asked myself: "In the haste of writing the examination did the student simply misspell the word or was he confused about the difference between "seduce" and "induce?" In either event the inaccuracy was minor unless, of course, he did mean that Penn had seduced many Germans.

On an even more humorous note, one student supplied a unique twist to a question about Alexander Hamilton. First, she recalled two facts gleaned from my lecture: Hamilton was an illegitimate child, and he developed into a self-made man. On the exam she combined these bits of information with a little learning that came either from her home or from the street culture that referred to an illegitimate child as one without a father. Thus she wrote: "Alexander Hamilton was a self-made man—being illegitimate." I decided not to comment.

The incidents are endless concerning how far an instructor should go in interpreting a student's exam paper. The difficulty rests between giving too much credit and underestimating the meaning of his/her words. Once when I asked for a description of the Fourteenth Amendment to the US Constitution, a student wrote that the amendment "made Negroes citizens of the South." Possibly he wrote "South" when he meant "United States." On the other hand, he may have been sarcastic—meaning that in the South, Negroes were citizens subject to southern interpretation of the amendment. In reality that reading of the student's statement has merit, but was that what he intended to convey? Unknowingly, his intent created a dilemma concerning the amount of credit to assign.

From these few illustrations, it's obvious that a funny or flip side is often prevalent in teaching and learning situations. The intensity and zest with which students explore life create gaffes, some of which are worthy of elaboration; such recognition is chronicled in the remainder of this volume.

CHAPTER 9

Student Capers

College students are adults with limited experience. The changes and challenges that they face are normally taken in stride. For a few, however, the intensified campus atmosphere converts their foibles into major problems that are, in turn, manifested in bizarre behavior. Whether caused by social blunders or an inability to adapt, such maladjustments are more responsible for college dropouts than is academic failure or financial hardship.

When these social breakdowns occur, the classroom instructor is generally the last to know. He may observe poor student participation or demonstrations of outrageous conduct, but seldom does he have a clue concerning what is below the tip of that social iceberg. The instructor's role shields him from prying into the facts that would provide a broad understanding of the situation. Unless a student volunteers details, the instructor is often left with an absurdity that, because of its uniqueness, becomes riveted in his memory.

With clarity I can personally recall aberrant behavior of many such students. Their peccadilloes twisted their personalities, at least temporarily, and in the process presented me with a distorted view of their problems. Although I had only a superficial knowledge of what was transpiring in their lives, those limited visions yielded a lighter, more eccentric side of their conduct.

A LATE NINE O'CLOCK SCHOLAR

Regardless of the number of years I had taught, the outset of every term intrigued me, and the prospects were always exhilarating. That first glimpse of a class's personality seemed important: How many students had enrolled? How many were eager to delve into the course content? Would they respond enthusiastically to the stated requirements? How inclined toward discussion would they be?

In the fall of 1958, as I first surveyed the group of seniors and first-year graduate students who had elected my course in the history of American Political Parties, nothing special stood out except the enrollment. With only 21 students the class was abnormally small, but the numbers were deceiving. Although the class lacked quantity, it excelled in scholarship.

Years later I reviewed a few statistics pertaining to this group and discovered that eight had become college professors, five of whom matured into authors contributing (by the last account) 17 monographs in the field of history. That fall, one held a Woodrow Wilson scholarship, and three others acceded to the same honor the following year. In addition, other class members received prestigious awards. As a result they represented the most academically productive class of my career.

Despite these remarkable achievements, the class was not without some blemishes. One of them was recalled by Professor Art Barbeau at a meeting of historians. At that moment I didn't remember that Art had been a member of the 1958 group, but when he asked me for an update on Horace Borus, I promptly made the connection. In our discussion Art chuckled as he recalled, for a third party in the group, his version of what he called my "famous put-down" of Horace. I clearly remember the incident but would not characterize it as he did.

Horace Borus was a first-year graduate student from Huntington, West Virginia. Anyone who engaged him in a philosophical discussion never doubted his mental acuity, but his social skills and physical appearance were cause to pause. Horace was a big man; his six-foot two-inch frame lugged 260 pounds from class to class. With short, brown, unkempt hair, round, baby-like face, and sallow complexion, he was an imposing presence, but certainly not that new face for which Hollywood was searching.

Horace's clothes, perhaps even his under shorts, were all too small, which may account for his constant squirming in his seat. If two people had an opportunity to examine his shirt, they would have been tempted to wager on which button would pop first. He had a thick neck, accentuated by the fact that he always buttoned his shirt at the top. That created the illusion that the top button was in the process of strangling him; a necktie might have disguised the chokehold, but that was never tested because Horace had an aversion to such a formal appearance. The shirt created a convincing impression that it held him in a death grip until one looked at his eyes;

they weren't bulging. On the contrary, they were deep-set slits that never seemed to open.

Seldom was his placid face graced with a smile, but he could readily muster a grin when he exposed someone else's limitations. His constant companion was a battered leather briefcase; either it had been handed down through generations of Boruses or he had started carrying it at age six and scuffed it badly before he was tall enough to keep it from dragging on the ground. One or both straps were invariably unbuckled, and as he carried the bag by the handle, the front tilted forward, thereby exposing books and papers—perilously close to falling out.

In cold weather Horace truly embodied the needy scholar making a heroic sacrifice to gain an education. He wore an undersized overcoat with several buttons missing, but that didn't seem to matter; with his 54-inch girth, the two sides of the coat could be brought together at only one point. Thus one button carried the full burden and showed the strain.

This depicts a man who was forced to endure untold hardship to attend school, but the facts do not merit that conclusion. Horace was the only son of affluent parents who were willing to underwrite his education. Simply a slob, he wanted to be walking evidence that "clothes do not make the man." His appearance belied his ability to humble most individuals in any discussion.

After several years of Horace bumming around the University in this garb, a senior professor who admired his talents took him aside and ridiculed his slovenly appearance. Eager to see Horace fulfill his ambition to become a college faculty member, the professor suggested that his dress conform to his goal. This castigation was accepted, primarily because Horace had greater respect for that professor than for anyone else. Still change came ever so slowly; refinements were not apparent when he first appeared in my classroom.

With a capacity of 45, our room provided ample space for 21 students to roam in search of a satisfactory seat. Some jockeyed for the few window seats from which they could observe center-of-the-campus activity if the class became dull; others coveted the back row; friends sought seats together, while those with vision problems elected to sit with a close-up view of the blackboard, because I was known as an inveterate scribbler.

Horace was the only student who confounded the do-it-yourself seating arrangement. The door from the hallway was at the front left, and Horace, for reasons known only to him and to God, insisted on sitting in the seat on the right front corner. That in itself created no problem, but he repeatedly came to class five minutes late. Apparently Horace was born five minutes late and never adjusted. In contrast, I insisted on starting the class on the hour, promptly at 9:00 A. M.

When he did arrive, he would fling the door open with a flourish, stand motionless for a second as though he was stunned that the class had begun without him. As he proceeded to his seat, he was always confronted with the same dilemma: to pass in front of me as I stood at the lectern (a choice that he must have considered a little impolite) or to go behind my back where he challenged the limited space between the blackboard and me.

To reach his chosen spot, although numerous empty seats existed inside the door, he ignored them and debated with himself concerning the less hazardous route to the front corner. Sometimes he would start one way and then opt for the other. The space between the lectern and the blackboard was not adequate to accommodate Horace and me simultaneously. Several times I stepped away from the lectern to ease his advance when he headed in that direction; I did not want to create the spectacle of the two of us wedged between the two immovable objects. In any such contest, I was destined to lose.

The second phase of his arrival involved squeezing all of that avoirdupois into a regular student desk/chair. With effort he always completed the maneuver, but in the process of getting his legs situated, he invariably captured everyone's attention. Frequently he kicked the tall, free standing metal cabinet that had been placed in that corner. Because the classroom was also assigned to geographers, the cabinet held maps that precluded the need to transport them to every geography class. When Borus accidentally kicked the cabinet, his action rattled the maps, and he would lunge forward to grab the cabinet with both hands in order to steady it and stop the noise. In the process his reaction would cause additional disruption before he was settled.

Horace's dramatic and frequent late arrivals escaped the attention of no one in the class. After he made the crucial decision to pass in front or behind me, I maneuvered accordingly and raised my eyebrows, rolled my eyes, or feigned a smile during the exercise. The class generally responded with a collective snicker or an occasional smile, but Borus was oblivious to our body language. Members of the class, I'm sure, wondered how long his antics would continue before I reacted publicly or privately. Fortunately happenstance absolved me of that choice.

During each session I would propose one or more hypothetical or thought questions to the group, not only to break the monotony of the lecture but also to stimulate their thinking. The questions were designed to elicit options (other than those actually taken) available to political leaders at a given juncture: What were Jefferson's alternatives to an Embargo Act? What would have been John Adams' fate if he had not signed the Alien and Sedition Acts? How do you account for Jackson's reaction to Calhoun? I encouraged students to try to deduce the answers from material already presented.

This technique worked well, but at times the responses were, as expected, off the proverbial wall. Because this was an exceptionally well-motivated class, two or more students offered plausible explanations to each of my queries. Sometimes half the class participated; anyone who wanted to weigh in on an issue was heard, but with this particular group, a flaw became apparent.

Despite the superior quality of the class, Horace consistently offered the most thoughtful responses. After a week or two, I decided to call on him only after all others who wished to contribute had been heard, because his comments were so cogently crafted that he stifled further discussion.

Electing this procedure was a mistake, because Horace focused not only on the question but also on the quality of the answers already expressed by his classmates. Laced with sharp and piercing adjectives, his remarks were not appreciated by his colleagues; "simplistic," "biased," "irrelevant," and "without foundation" were a few of his descriptive terms. In vintage Borus his responses always provided a formal moment that required added time to unfold.

With his seat in the front row that was otherwise unoccupied, all other students were behind him. Thus it didn't seem appropriate to him to face only me and the blackboard when delivering his *bons mots*. To rectify that situation, he stood and faced the class every time he spoke. That effort required considerable time to twist his oversized body out from the standard-sized chair and then turn toward his audience. In addition to being both pompous and awkward, he elevated this procedure to a unique level: the distinction of being the only student throughout my career who felt compelled to stand when reciting.

As a result of this behavior, Horace was quickly transforming himself into a persona non grata with his classmates, and his conduct threatened to curtail the dialogue I was trying to foster. After class one morning I spoke to him as delicately as I could, reminding him that he was usurping my prerogative to evaluate the quality of the responses and humorously adding: "I get paid for that; you're not after my money, are you?" I explained that, in the interest of camaraderie with his fellow students, his remarks should be tempered and not personalized because he was making students reticent to enter the dialogue. I was not convincing, but shortly the point was driven home by a fortuitous incident.

Harvey Hooper, one of the students who had not participated in the discussions, obviously felt intimidated by the abnormally high percentage of superior classmates around him and was understandably uncomfortable. He seized on a brief reference I had made to dueling as a means of resolving political quarrels in early 19th Century America, identifying it as a subject by which he could compensate for his routine silence in the classroom.

Because Harvey was aware that dueling had developed an etiquette and protocol of its own and that I had skipped over it, he saw this as an opportunity to bring that information dramatically to his fellow students. He arrived at class one Friday morning with a set of dueling pistols neatly encased in a polished cedar box as was characteristic of the Jacksonian era.

According to the protocol the one challenged to a duel had the right to determine the weapons, and generally the choice was "pistols at dawn" [except, for the notable exception of Davy Crockett who, when challenged, selected bows and arrows]. When the two pistols were presented at the duel, the challenger had the choice of pistols. Harvey opened the case as he stood before me at the lectern and explained that he would like to demonstrate dueling etiquette to the class.

Suddenly my mind was thrown into confusion with three ideas jumbled together. Harvey's proposal set off the most uncomfortable minutes I ever experienced before a class. Earlier a woman had suffered a fatal heart attack during a lecture, but that didn't unnerve me as much as the presence of guns. Here was a serious young man proposing to make what he considered an edifying contribution. I did not want to dampen his spirit; but on the other hand, I was instantly aware that numerous individuals had been killed by the supposedly "empty" gun.

Harvey was oblivious to my concern, assuring me that there were no shells in either the chamber or the barrel. Trying not to strain his psyche, I agreed that he could take the first five minutes of the class for his presentation. To provide an added safeguard, I instructed him not to point a gun toward the class and not to place his finger on the trigger while he was handling either gun.

The day had begun normally enough but suddenly was in a shambles. I was prepared for the lecture, was on time, and no black cats had crossed my path until Harvey Hooper popped up with his pistols. I was also agonizing over a third thought: What had happened to my brilliant class? Had it degenerated into a Friday morning Show-and-Tell?

With these ideas uppermost in my thinking, I forgot an important factor in the equation: Borus's regular late arrival. Adhering accurately to his schedule, he charged through the door while Harvey was still in the midst of his presentation. This time Horace's normal expression of surprise turned to shock. Instead of seeing me checking to determine if he were going to pass in front or behind me in the dash for his seat, he was suddenly aware of a student, whom he did not recognize as a classmate, brandishing a firearm—pointed in his direction, partly because I had limited how Hooper could exhibit it. For a moment with a .45 caliber aimed at his head, Horace stood traumatized, not knowing whether to turn and run, drop prostrate to the floor, or say a quick prayer.

Realizing that he was without a clue, I was able to seize the moment. "Sorry, Horace," I deadpanned, "Harvey took exception to your remarks last Wednesday." Then for a second, complete silence reigned before the students grasped the humor in my statement and burst into laughter. Without a word Borus took his seat and never spoke to me again for a year. Afterward we became good friends until he suddenly died in a college library while fulfilling his role as teacher and scholar.

A Major's Squelch

As Harvey Hooper's figurative gunning down of Horace Borus demonstrated, students can be adept at controlling classroom conduct. Although Harvey succeeded by happenstance, another student who will forever remain nameless (because he actually was) took charge and solved a similar problem before I could find a propitious opportunity to act. His target was a newly appointed member of the ROTC faculty.

Major Daniel O'Leary registered for my evening course that focused on American Foreign Relations since 1890. Army officers assigned to campus billets were always alert to opportunities for personal fulfillment. They could advance their careers with graduate courses and perhaps earn master's degrees or PhDs while concurrently complying with their military assignments. That accounted for the major's presence.

Having just returned from a training experience at an Army "Command School," O'Leary arrived at my first class session full of information that he was anxious to impart. No one who heard him could ever doubt that he was highly motivated, even inspired, by the Command School program, but his almost ceaseless determination to convey his learning to my class at its first meeting was inexcusable, more obnoxious than I had ever encountered.

As a standard procedure at the first class session, I planned to devote a half-hour to the course requirements and to an overview of the topics to be discussed during the term. I tossed out a number of controversial generalizations that would be explored and noted that these topics had the added complexity of clashing with each other.

First, I stated that, from the 1890s forward, the United States would be examined as the world's greatest economic imperialist. Before I could proceed to the next point, Major Dan interrupted to explain that at Command School he had been taught otherwise. In a tone that removed all doubt, he let it be known that the Command School version was the definitive word on the subject.

I patiently explained that there was no desire to minimize the significance of his information and that, when that aspect of American policy was studied in depth, he would be afforded ample opportunity to express his views. I skirted the idea of a discussion at the time, because this was simply a course overview, but he refused to accept my version of what was taking place. Eager to impart what he deemed relevant material, he persisted in rambling on.

To his chagrin I tactfully moved to my second point: namely, that the course would trace the evolution of the nation's policy from one of isolationism to that of responsible world power. Again O'Leary broke into the presentation. Prefacing his remarks with "at Command School we learned," he launched into a monologue, decrying isolationism. I attempted to reemphasize that this was only illustrative of the topics that would be covered in the student readings, and at the proper time he would be welcome to comment on that topic as well.

Believing that I had reaffirmed the purpose of this half-hour that was gradually being elongated into Major Dan's show time, I stressed that there were a few intriguing and debatable topics, controversial as the major's comments attested, that the course would examine. I knew from the expression on his face that he was not buying any part of my explanation. I also sensed that the other students were more interested in the overall perspective on the ensuing 15 weeks than on his editorializing, and again I abruptly short-circuited his remarks.

Concluding that he possessed enough common sense to recognize that this was my course, even if he disagreed with much that was being said, I assumed too much. But on that assumption I turned to the idea that American foreign relations faced monumental complications that, comparatively speaking, were nonexistent in most other nations. I stressed that our diverse ethnicity and a commitment to democratic decision-making hindered the task of formulating prompt, clear-cut, and decisive policy responses. Unwilling for a third time to accept my generalization, the major asked to be recognized; he again introduced his comments with the "at Command School" litany.

Anxious not to convey a negative message in this first session, I eschewed the doctrinaire approach. Not desirous of creating the impression that I characteristically stifled student exuberance or curtailed class participation, I, in retrospect, was allowing Major Dan too much latitude but was temporarily at a loss on how to rein him in.

I couldn't comprehend his aggressive attitude. Perhaps he concluded that his Army rank, buttressed by his Command School exposure, entitled him to inject his bits of knowledge at will. On the other hand, he may have decided to psyche me out with his major's uniform. If the latter were his ploy, he succeeded, at least in part, because I was most reluctant to censure his outbursts in public; the uniform did deserve that much respect.

Because of that decision, this marked the only time in my career that I had difficulty in presenting a course overview. Through a total of five or six interruptions, the major began by reciting the "at Command School" phrase. The class was obviously becoming exasperated and restless, shifting from one side of their chairs to the other and audibly dropping their pencils to their desks every time I recognized O'Leary. Through it all, the major remained oblivious to these signs of annoyance. Later when I attempted to rationalize his behavior, I surmised that he may have imbibed two too many beers with his dinner or two beers and no dinner, but that was only conjecture. At the time I was more concerned lest students become impatient with me for permitting his display of marginally useful knowledge.

When I finally finished the overview, I opened the class to questions and comments. Several students responded with requests for clarifications; one raised a particularly cogent question, and I answered at length, in part by drawing a diagram on the blackboard. As I turned back to face the class after adding my last line, a well modulated, male voice from near the back of the crowded classroom blurted out: "Did you learn that in Command School?"

For a moment a deafening silence prevailed, but quickly I recovered my composure to announce that it was time for our ten-minute break. When the group reassembled, the major was missing from classroom action and officially resigned from the course.

A year later, when I taught that course again, Major Dan O'Leary registered and performed like a model student without one mention of Command School. Neither he nor I went down that road. He gave no recognition of the incident in the previous year when an unknown student had placed the issue squarely in perspective with his seven defining little words.

TRAGEDY IN, TRAGEDY OUT

Because not all wide-eyed college recruits emerge as happy, mature graduates, it is only appropriate that a few of the maladjusted should pass through my classroom. I expected that but was ill prepared for pathetic Magnesia Murphy, who was burdened with more than her name. Even her problems had problems, but she could muster only disdain for the basic rule governing those who find themselves in a hole: Stop digging!! She couldn't.

In analyzing such student behavior, an instructor learns to accept the unexpected as normal. To their detriment, students frequently have a faith that major problems will vanish if their existence is denied long enough, and minor ones are presumed never to have occurred in the first place. Too often these patterns of neglect are permitted to grow until they fester and assume major proportions. As a result an instructor is unaware of such issues until they reach a crisis stage and the facts defy a happy solution.

After years of teaching I was convinced that no student was ever going to handle with aplomb the simple task of reporting an anticipated absence from class, but finally a postal note suggested that I was wrong. About ten days before the beginning of a winter semester, I received a letter from Magnesia Murphy not only outlining her plight but also providing a thoughtful solution.

Prior to that correspondence, I had no idea who Magnesia was; intrigued by that moniker, I wondered if she had been named for an ancient Turkish city or for a respected family member or for a trusted family remedy. It was a relief to learn in time that she preferred to be called Maggie or M & M, but for the present I was elated with her foresight, not her name, although it possessed a distinctive ring.

Maggie's note explained that she had enrolled in my course but regrettably would be absent from the first three one-hour sessions due to surgery. Fearful that she might be dropped from the course as a "no show," she wanted to proclaim her commitment and requested that I send her a copy of the course syllabus and the title of the text, along with the specific material to be covered during the period of her convalescence.

On that flimsy but positive evidence, I jumped to the conclusion that I was about to meet a truly independent problem-solver who would be a genuine classroom asset. Her inquiry suggested that she understood how to confront a special situation, and I was impressed. In contrast, many students knowingly missed the first sessions of a term and provided no explanation. As a result Maggie's requested information was dispatched with an accompanying note offering to assist in her late adjustment to the course. Anticipating a mature student, I continued in this delusional state for more than a month.

The course moved into its second week, and Maggie had not yet reported. Thinking that the surgery or the recovery had gone awry, I wondered, vaguely at least, about a student I had not yet met. Her thoughtful preplanning and her name both made it easy to remember, but the weeks passed and my anticipation waned. Then one day after class during the fourth week, a smartly dressed, debonair young woman in her early twenties approached me and announced that she was the long awaited Magnesia Murphy.

I expressed the hope that she was in good health. Speaking excitedly and rapidly in response, she gave the impression that she was on drugs, perhaps for medication. With no other detectable evidence that she had been ill, I later concluded that her hospitalization was not for surgery, but for psychiatric help.

Now nervous but articulate, she explained that she had left the hospital on schedule but became bogged down with undefined personal problems. Because more than the projected week's delay had passed, she provided the lame excuse that she was afraid to come to class lest I embarrass her in front of other students. Fond of my record in keeping student problems confidential, I was mystified and asked if she had any reason to conclude that I would publicly question her conduct. Her reply was negative, except for suggesting that her action warranted such a response.

Maggie insisted that she still wanted to attend the class. When I pointed out that 25 per cent of the course had already elapsed, she countered by referring to an old student ploy that "history has always been my favorite subject," and she was certain that she could catch up. Aware that something more than enthusiasm was needed, I was less certain. That prompted her to figuratively pull out the proverbial violin and strike up a sad tune that was new to my ear. She described how she suffered from a terminal case of fallen arches that had required numerous trips to the Mayo Clinic.

Unable to confirm or deny the accuracy of her statement, I stood silent for a moment. That hesitation caused her to swing into the second verse and elaborate on her anticipated surgery in more vivid detail than I cared to hear. I quickly brought the discussion back to the course. Reluctant to give her a green light to remain in the class, I nevertheless was sympathetic enough to gamble on a second chance, partly because I had originally pictured in my mind a student with great potential.

Maggie explained that she had opted out of two courses in order to salvage three others including mine. I was aware that a good student could step in under those circumstances and do well; but from the conversation I gleaned no substantive clue that her work fell in that category. Agreeing that she could come to class for two weeks while also working on the materials she had missed, I suggested that together we review her status at that point.

This was proposed on the assumption that she would then know in her own mind if she were capable of achieving what had to be done to complete the term's work. Elated with this decision, she was more firmly convinced than I was that I had decided wisely. She pledged that I would see her beaming face every day for the remainder of the term.

For the next few sessions, she sat in the front row with her motorcycle headgear stowed beneath her chair and seemed to hang on my every word. Then she missed a class and concluded that an explanation was in order. Declaring that her absence was unavoidable, she stated that she had to appear in court. Being slightly suspicious, I asked if she were a litigant or a witness. Proudly she announced that she was a litigant— suing her mother "because the bitch had refused to continue to pay my tuition." That outburst was evidence enough that I was being confronted by a troubled woman whose maladjustments far exceeded the realm of my history course.

Clearly Maggie's problems were not academic, but personal and social. Prior to enrolling at Pitt, she had attended Death Valley State (DVS), where failure was almost impossible. As an embarrassed member of that school's board of trustees had confessed to me, it's "another high school in town." Aware that DVS was not one of academe's pillars of excellence, Mrs. Murphy knew that her daughter did not leave DVS because of a lack of ability. By her calculation she had paid enough tuition for Maggie to have a college diploma, instead of an autographed Grateful Dead poster hanging on her wall. Unfortunately she had progressed only to sophomore status and was on probation with dismissal lurking on the horizon.

By refusing to continue to "shell out" tuition money, the mother, a tough-minded Philadelphia lawyer, was trying to shock her daughter into reality. Her college program had lost all semblance of serious intent, a drift that Maggie refused to admit. Mrs. Murphy wanted her to refocus her goals; thus her monetary decision was supported by more than unsatisfactory academic achievement. She was painfully aware that Maggie had diluted her scholarly pursuits with an abnormal passion for the Grateful Dead. Joining the Dead Heads, as the group's followers were called, she relegated her education to second place while she accompanied this musical troupe as it toured from city to city throughout the Mid-Atlantic region.

Cut off at a most inappropriate time, the tuition money provoked a family crisis that found its way to court. With Maggie in the throes of health, money, and academic woes, she needed support and looked to her mother; but her failure to provide it was interpreted as a lack of love at a time when she desperately needed reassurance. That realization aroused her to anger. Thus tragically she was suing her mother not only for tuition but also in a strange and pathetic way for her love.

In this time of need, Maggie's father exacerbated her emotional crisis. Unexpectedly she received a phone call announcing that he was dying of cancer in a Philadelphia hospital. As any young person might react to such a jolt, she took off for home—hopefully not on her motorcycle. About to enter her father's hospital room, she encountered another young woman about her age. Almost in unison they asked: "Who are you?" The similar answers, however, detonated a bombshell: "I've come to see my father. Do you know him from the office?"

Thus Maggie made the shocking discovery that, for 20 years, her father led a double life as the head of two households. She now had to assimilate the awareness of a half-sister and attending implications, as well as the myriad of problems based in Pittsburgh. I do not know, nor did I ask, how truly critical her father was or how imaginary her half-sister was, but this account provided another excuse for an absence from class.

Not wanting to learn more about her personal life, I advised Magnesia that, if she were serious about the course, it was to her advantage to be present and do all the work. Despite this gentle warning, she missed the next lecture. When she appeared at the following session, she again felt obligated to explain her conduct. This time she was unavoidably absent because "my boy friend's brother escaped from the insane asylum, and I felt compelled to join in the search for him." (It immediately struck me as strange that someone from her generation would employ that term to identify a mental institution, but Maggie was never without surprises.)

Without stopping to catch her breath, she gave me a sincere look and asked: "What did I miss?" Not accepting the boyfriend's-brother nonsense, I replied: "You didn't miss a thing because the class was canceled. I too experienced an emergency. My pet monkey escaped from its cage, and I was compelled to spend the day rounding it up." Pouting, she exclaimed: "You're angry with me."

Assuming that she would drop the course after my sarcastic reply, I was wrong again. She continued to come to class sporadically, and after every absence she reported her reason; some were plausible; others were off-the-wall. Once a "degenerate son-of-a-bitch stole the carburetor off my motorcycle" while parked outside her apartment building. That required her to make a report to the police at precisely the hour of my class.

I gave no response, but through our numerous conversations, I was able to piece together a few characteristics of her life, principally that she lived alone with a pet python named Henrietta and other assorted snakes. After a subsequent absence she explained that someone had broken into her apartment by shattering a window. It's equally plausible that the incident occurred when someone was attempting to break out with undue haste, perhaps one of Maggie's boyfriends who on a first-nighter informally met Henrietta or one of her pals and instantly identified the window as the superhighway to his future.

As the term wound down, Maggie wrote me a letter "because I am to [sic] embarrassed to speak to you in person." She recounted the catastrophes of the term and added a new factor: A bout with mono was a contributor to her difficulties. She concluded: "The point being, I've been a real asshole. I lost sight of all of the goals I set for myself." In desperation she pleaded for an opportunity to do extra work in order to pass the course; because she had not yet faced up to the regular assignments, her suggestion was that of a failing student grasping for a straw that didn't exist.

Obviously the term spelled tragedy for Magnesia—one that ranged beyond my control. I do not know if she ultimately salvaged her college career, but success, I am certain, depended on parting company with Henrietta, or learning to survive without the boyfriend, or both.

ANGER AND PREJUDICE

After reflecting on Magnesia's record, I'm not sure that she stands unrivaled atop the list of my students with social dysfunctions. In contrast, Lulu LaFarge repeatedly and with glee trespassed on the time of others; Magnesia never disrupted a single class. Comparatively speaking, LaFarge's technique was unforgivable; she was more like Major Dan but refused to go away after one session as he did.

Lulu enrolled in the second half of my American Political Parties course before taking the first half. Although not uncommon for students to do so, Lulu converted her presence into a classroom weapon. She thought that it was immature of America to have its politics played according to American rules rather than according to 19th Century European standards. At the outset of the term, I explained that, unlike European politics, the American brand was more pragmatic and less ideological. The first half of the course had explored this aspect of the nation's political character in detail, whereas the second half emphasized other attributes, with the assumption that the non-ideological factor was generally accepted.

One of the more exciting times for me during a term was reading the first examination papers in a lecture course. By that point four to six weeks had elapsed, and I had compiled a few general clues about individual student abilities by watching how they took notes, who initiated discussion, and who responded insightfully to questions raised by others.

With more than a few years of experience as a guide, I was accustomed to the unexpected, academically as well as socially. Students who had uttered not a word during class often wrote the most cogent examination papers, and those who participated in class discussion with their questions and comments frequently proved to be partial or complete failures with pen in hand. Either they possessed limited ability to communicate in writing or lacked an ability to be analytical when confronted with a broad topic.

Aware that a few of these extreme results surfaced with the first exam every term, I still did not anticipate LaFarge's resounding F. She had commented a few times during those first weeks, but I had not detected anything either brilliant or inane in her remarks. Her written answers were a diatribe; basically unprepared, she attempted to "snow" me with mere words.

At first I suspected that she had overlooked the pragmatic nature of American politics; that, in turn, caused me to assume that I was partly responsible for her failure. Because of her accent I concluded that I did not properly assess her background and compensate for her being an immigrant. Perhaps in those first weeks, I should have taken her aside and explained in great detail the non-ideological factor. My overture to compromise the F and salvage her standing in the course was to suggest a reexamination, an offer that she immediately rejected. She knew better than I did at the moment that her grade was largely the result of her lack of preparation; a reexamination would have only verified the obvious.

I then realized that Lulu was simply a student who believed that she could bluff her way through a course with blather as a substitute for hard work. The F grade became a springboard to an expression of her deep-rooted anger, a cause celebre in her mind that would permit her to lash out frequently at the American political system as the course unfolded. I tried to convince her that she did not have to accept the system, only to evaluate its functioning in the American context. She couldn't do that; periodically she attempted to belittle American political practice with a scintilla of information.

Once, with a little of her buffoonery, she tried to challenge a remark that I had made at the opening session of the class. I had indicated that I did not wish to discourage "way-out" assertions about parties, politics, or the system, as long as an attempt at a viable proof was advanced. This occurred during the 1970s, when many students believed that they had a constitutional right to thrust on society any cockamamie thought that popped into their heads. I wanted them to know that my classroom was not a forum for that kind of irresponsible expression, but if they offered some logic for their statements, they could speak out. Either Lulu did not remember the "viable proof" part of the statement or decided to test my resolve to uphold it; in time I knew that she was inspired by the latter.

Her little offensive began one day when she appeared at my office and abruptly announced: "Abraham Lincoln was a fraud, you know." I asked for her supporting evidence, and she answered by repeating the assertion. With a bemused smile I said: "no support, no discussion." She again repeated that Lincoln was a fraud, and I asked her not to let the door-knob strike her on her way out. Apparently surprised, she left without another word—only to consider, I'm sure, her next insulting approach.

Older than most students, Lulu seemed to assume that age bestowed a special status on her—a right to speak on any subject without information. Her fellow students were unwilling to accept her half-baked wisdom, which was delivered in a whiny voice that could be modulated to a slow frequency when attempting to emphasize one of her questionable points. That voice would have hopelessly diminished even a lucid argument. When coupled with her slender build, drab clothing, and a hairdo scrambled by an eggbeater, those screeching sounds created the image of a tortured soul.

Like me, her classmates resented her determination to launch into inane outbursts in response to legitimate questions, but she was hard to ignore. Sitting in the front row, she waved her hand every time a question was asked, as well as on other occasions when something that had been said simply sparked a stray thought to emerge from deep in the recesses of her mind. Never wanting to give the impression that I intended to discourage discussion, I found it difficult to overlook her upraised hand; to keep her distracting hand from waving incessantly, I generally permitted her to volunteer her unsophisticated answers, which I, in turn, tried to short-circuit once she demonstrated their lack of merit.

On one occasion when she set forth a superficial argument, a classmate systematically rebutted her points and offered a reasoned resolution of the issue. Because other students added supplemental comments to buttress his argument, Lulu took offense—believing that the class was deliberately conspiring against her. When I had recognized the first student, the sound of his name suggested to Lulu that he was probably of Polish extraction. Thereafter during that session she referred to the class as her "Polish cousins," whom she was trying to denigrate for disagreeing with her. After class I spoke to her privately about her choice of words; that prompted her to refer to me as "the other German."

Realizing that the comment was intended to bait me, I decided to play her game and asked: "If I'm the other German, I guess that there must be a first German. Who is he?" Suspecting by this time that she was a racist, I expected her answer to be "Adolf Hitler," but she surprised me. Without hesitation she responded: "That's my husband, and I don't like him either." By innuendo her statements in class had indicated a strong aversion for African-Americans, Jews, and men in general; when she wasn't attacking the US government, any combination of these registered as suitable targets. Bringing such attitudes into a course on American politics required more than a modicum of verbal absurdity, a quality that Lulu exuded with the slightest provocation.

She didn't believe that anyone should object to her lemon juice remarks because they represented the essence of truth—a realization with which all serious-minded students should be prepared to cope. Her presence in class was based less on a desire to learn than on a determination to use the classroom as a private soapbox to impart her warped beliefs. I never took her barbs personally, because I was one of many in the University who had become the object of her "afflictions."

A colleague in the department who was also subjected to Lulu supplied his own answer to her outbursts. After several exposures and after he had presented a lecture on the causes of the French Revolution, LaFarge had the audacity to assert that he was improperly informed on the subject and proposed to enlighten the class with her version. He quickly interrupted her by saying: "Let's do this democratically! Let's have the class vote on whether they want to hear your 15-minute diatribe or whether they want me to continue!" After a brief pause the class chorused "Continue," and she was shut down for a day.

Even when LaFarge was not registered as a student, she was intent upon not permitting those of us at the University to forget her. She would select certain days, by what means I have no clue, to come to the campus to blind-side someone with her nasty comments just to let us know that she hadn't surrendered to the establishment. On a warm afternoon in spring, I must have been the first individual whom she identified as worthy of harassment as she sauntered by. A student of mine was sitting on a wall eating his brownbag lunch and had beckoned me to stop as I was returning from class. He wanted to discuss his future plans.

A senior who had just received an offer as a teaching assistant in communications, he was undecided about accepting the award, because a law degree was his ultimate educational goal. As we exchanged ideas on the pros and cons of a year's detour from the study of law, Lulu approached from behind me and addressed the munching student whom she had never met: "Young man, do you realize that at this very moment you are being misled?" Adding nothing more, the incorrigible Lulu walked on. With his jaw sagging, the student sat wide-eyed and waited for me to explain what that was all about. I pointed out that her elevator didn't always run to the top.

On another occasion, during a student conference with my office door closed, I answered a knock. There stood the indomitable Lulu, silent for a moment because she immediately realized that she couldn't come in. Shifting gears, she announced that she only wanted to hand me a paperback, extremist of course, and suggested that I read it "to get smart." Nothing more was said; the paperback went on a shelf and remained there until she again thought that it was my turn to be honored with one of her impromptu and enlightening visits. When she stuck her head in my open door, I jumped up, grabbed the paperback, and said: "This is yours," and excused myself by saying that I had to make an emergency phone call.

On a succeeding appearance in my office, she solicited my advice. That in itself was not only novel but also equally ludicrous. On that particular occasion she was flirting with the unthinkable idea of becoming a teacher. She had already attempted to major in French and History and had alienated the faculties of both departments. Now she was toying with this incomprehensible thought of teaching these subjects to unsuspecting high school students. Without being formally accepted into an education program, she had enrolled in several such courses, making enemies of both instructors as she had done with all of her previous ones. Outwardly unperturbed by these failed encounters, she may have been a masochist who wanted to fail every program she attempted so that faculty members might be accused of conniving to subvert her talents.

I would have been pleased to sanction the thought that she run, not walk, away from this teaching whim, but that was not the issue on which she sought my opinion. Wanting me to help erase part of her record, she explained that state policy prevented anyone with a psychiatric background from being issued a teaching certificate. Lulu confided that she had spent time in Western Psychiatric Institute and Clinic (WPIC). That came as no surprise to me, but she wanted to have that part of her record expunged. Arguing that I had no knowledge of the institution's policy, I begged off.

In doing so, I made the fatal mistake of asking who had committed her to the facility. Because her estranged husband, like me, was on her list of unsavory people, I thought that he probably had been the "culprit" who perpetrated the deed. That assumption was wrong; in one of her wiser judgments, Lulu had signed herself in. By her reasoning, because she had initiated the action, she had the right to revoke it. This she had done physically by departing without a formal release. By the same logic she believed that she had the right to destroy the document acknowledging her presence in WPIC and wanted me to tell her how to do it.

As these contradictions indicate, LaFarge rendered difficult the task of ignoring her. Being rude was interpreted as encouragement. During the term in which she was enrolled in my evening class, she would inevitably begin a conversation with me immediately after the session ended at 7:50 PM. As she began her discourse, I would methodically place my folder in the briefcase, pull on my topcoat, and head for the door with Lulu still babbling, interspersed with a few grunts of recognition from me. There was little opportunity to utter more; in a sense I was grateful to escape with such noncommittal responses, because I didn't want to say anything that would prolong the conversation. Despite my indifference toward her monologue, it kept flowing—accompanying me down three flights of stairs, out of the building, and along six blocks of Forbes Avenue to Stuckert's Service Station, where I regularly parked.

As a plum to a regular customer, the attendants always pulled my car in front of the building so that I could jump in for an immediate getaway and dinner at home. As I approached the car, Lulu was still matching my stride. I tossed the briefcase across to the passenger's side, got in, and said: "Good night, Lulu." On at least three occasions, she was still standing there as I drove off.

I had always advised students with questions about term papers, exam preparation, or other related issues that they could call me any time in the office or at home before the 11:00 evening news, except never on Sundays during Steeler football season. They always laughed, because I added that "anyone who disrupts me during the game is destined to flunk." Lulu never challenged the game dictum, but otherwise interpreted the statement liberally—believing that she could call anytime she was so moved. She apparently worked evenings as a switchboard operator at a residential hotel, and when bored on the job because the phone lines were not busy, she would dial my number with absolutely nothing to say. Other faculty members admitted that they too suffered from the same strange Lulu interruptions.

In the process of being eliminated from a teaching career, LaFarge met in conference with a professor of education, who politely tried to explain that she lacked the attitude and temperament for the classroom. When she protested the obvious, he tried diplomacy to suggest that perhaps she was finding it difficult to grasp concepts in the English language. This prompted one of her little temper tantrums that he was trying to avoid. She haughtily proclaimed that her understanding of English was as good as that of any student. In frustration the professor leaned back in his chair and blurted out: "Then hear this: Get the hell out of my office and never come back."

His sentiments simply encapsulated the attitude of many who had been forced to deal with LaFarge. Her conduct was so irritating to many who had offices in the Cathedral of Learning that drastic action became necessary. She was informed that the first three floors of the Cathedral, where classes were conducted, represented the public domain, but the offices on the higher floors were considered private property and that, because she was no longer a student, she was not welcome there. Assured that her presence would trigger a call for security officers to escort her out, her University visits came to an end. Only by a combination of the good intentions of so many and the obtuseness of one individual could the education system be reduced to such a bizarre interlude. Long live Lulu!—now that she has stopped haunting the campus.

You Be The Judge

Although they may alter their decisions in the process, most students attend college with a clear set of academic objectives: procedures to be mastered, a creative talent to be honed, a body of information to be explored. Only those at the extremities of the grading curve give as much emphasis to course grades as to the objectives to be achieved.

Of necessity those at the bottom of the grading scale recognize that course grades are determinants for probation, failure, and dismissal. In contrast the brightest students view grades as stepping stones to graduate and professional school admissions and, coincidentally, to fellowships, scholarships, assistantships, and other attending awards.

But all undergraduates expect fairness and objectivity in the grading system. No faculty member disagrees, but application of such a system is at times elusive. In subjects where materials can be quantified, grading is comparatively simple; with a 60 per cent cut-off, passing and failure are automatically determined; a student with a score of 58 fails and one with 61 passes—end of story. In fields where essays, critiques, artistic works, and analyses defy easy quantification and require interpretation, grading is both difficult and subjective.

With my teaching always concentrated in the latter category, I was at times unsure of the grade to assign. When, for example, doubt caused me to hesitate between awarding a C+ or a B-, I seldom delayed long before giving the student the benefit of the alternatives. On a few occasions, however, I wavered in my decision even after it had been finalized. Those cases are reviewed here so that, with the facts in hand, the reader can second-guess my judgments.

ONE

Despite the general assumption, F does not always denote failure. For two of my students, moral character trumped the grade itself. Both asked to be failed (as had Mr. Special, noted in Chapter 7); another's arrogance provoked an F. He represented one of the few times I angrily concluded that no extenuating circumstances could stave off a failing grade.

The first of the honorable students demonstrated her high standards when she came to my office for a make-up examination. After placing her books and papers on a chair, she and I went over the questions to be answered. Then I escorted her to the departmental library where she spent an hour writing her responses. Following routine procedure for make-ups, she returned the examination booklet on schedule and thanked me for providing the opportunity for her to complete the work. Retrieving her possessions, she departed.

Fifteen minutes later she returned and asked if I had graded her paper. Surprised that she seemed to expect such instant service, I nevertheless gave her a polite negative in a somewhat indignant tone. Oblivious to my demeanor, she was relieved by my answer. "I'm glad," she sighed, "I don't want any credit for question three." Curious, I requested an explanation. Visibly shaken and to the point of tears, she hesitated to answer. Then she volunteered that the response was not her own work. Unsatisfied, I pressed for an elaboration, and in a low voice she recounted what had transpired in the library.

While sitting quietly pondering the third question, she was interrupted by a well-dressed, handsome, part-time instructor who could never pass up an opportunity to flirt with a young pretty face, and my student qualified. In an elevator, in the hallway, or in the cafeteria, he spoke to every beautiful girl whose eye he could catch. I think that he was a harmless jerk motivated partly by a desire to be noticed and partly by a need for the gratification that came from attracting the attention of young women.

Observing my student staring at her exam booklet for a few minutes, he asked if she had a problem. She indicated that she was uncertain in how to approach the question. Helpful Henry leaned over her shoulder, read the question, and gratuitously provided an answer. The question was asking the student to differentiate the attitudes toward slavery in the western territories as expressed by the Kansas-Nebraska

Bill, the Republican Platform of 1856, and the Dred Scott Decision. Having formulated no response of her own, the young lady wrote out the wisdom that she had just received.

In the fifteen minutes after returning her booklet, she reflected on what had transpired. I don't think that the time was spent in determining right from wrong, but in deciding how to explain it to me. When she insisted on receiving a zero for that question, I immediately picked up her paper, read the suspect answer, and informed her that she would be graded only on the other two questions. I thanked her for her honesty but wasn't totally candid myself, because I did not reveal that the information provided to her was completely erroneous; the interrupter missed the subtle distinctions that I wanted the student to supply. Was I fair to the student? Was I fair to all other students who answered three questions on that exam?

TWO

The second incident represented a delayed reaction by comparison; not fifteen minutes but two years elapsed before the student returned to seek an F on his final examination. To consider changing a grade, particularly after that length of time, the registrar would demand a clear and concise reason. That did not concern the student, but I was aware of the process. The student was about to graduate, but vowed that, if the change in my opinion resulted in his failing the course and that, in turn, meant that he didn't graduate, he was prepared to accept that verdict.

He explained that he had been standing in front of a departmental secretary's desk when he happened to overhear her phone my office, alerting me that my final examination questions had been photocopied and were ready for pick up. Overcome by the temptation of the moment, when the secretary was distracted by a second phone call, he pilfered the top copy from the pile. This provided him with three or four days to formulate answers to the questions, an advantage shared by no other student in the class.

Sometime over the two years following this incident, he had become a born-again Christian. This obligated him to atone for all possible wrongs in his past because he was expecting to become a ministerial student. With that as the basis for his F request, he stood before me calm and resolutely resigned to accept my decision.

The windfall of knowledge that was potentially his by swiping the questions did not translate into the blockbuster exam that one would expect. He had received only a C on the test. I empathized with his newly acquired sense of duty but was unsure of how it could be incorporated into the grading system. At the same time I mentally calculated what a change to an F for the exam would have meant in terms of his final grade and concluded that the change would be too slight to open the issue with the registrar.

The change would have resulted in a D for a final grade, not the C that was originally recorded, but that grade had little relevance to his graduation status. I decided that the burden of carrying the misdeed on his conscience for two years was sufficient punishment for a person of his temperament. I didn't change the course grade, thanked him for his delayed honesty, and wished him well in the ministry. Did I err? Did I have an obligation to all other students to make the record as accurate as possible?

THREE

From my standpoint both of these decisions were merited. But in another case I had no doubt that an F was warranted, mainly because no lower grade was available in the system. Assigning a failing grade is generally an agonizing decision, because there is always so much of a student's life that one does not know. Many instructors like it that way, because the only topic being evaluated is the course content. That's truly objective, and I too strive for that standard. But, if mitigating circumstances contribute to a student's performance, I would like to know that information when making the ultimate decision.

This student to whom I awarded an F with gusto was a member of a class with 176 others. To me attendance in my class is beneficial to a student in varying degrees, because I assume that some learning, not available in the textbook, always takes place in the classroom. Checking on the presence of 177 during each class period was a challenge without redeeming benefits. One of Pitt's large lecture halls, 324 Cathedral of Learning, is an amphitheater style, with its rows of seats slanted downward toward the lectern, screen, and side tables.

During the first three weeks of the course, I detected that the same 25 students were habitually absent. I had never had to contend with such numbers before and concluded that these 25 were the most likely to follow the same absentee pattern throughout the term.

To forestall this trend, I announced that, following every class period for the remainder of the term, a dated signature sheet bearing the names of the infamous 25 would appear at the lectern to be signed each day. The purpose was to assure that, if anyone of the group missed more than two additional classes, he/she was perilously close to failure for the term on that basis alone. I had never resorted to this technique before and never heard of anyone else adopting it. As a result I had no forewarning concerning how the affected students would react to my ultimatum.

The first day I closely observed the reactions. Everything went as I planned, except at one point I looked up and out of the corner of one eye detected something too bizarre to be true. Realizing my probable mistake, I said nothing at the time.

At the end of the next class period, I observed a repeat of what I believed I had seen the previous day. A student came through the door, down the steps to the lectern, and signed his name on the signature sheet. I asked: "Why are you signing the sheet? You just came to class!"

His response: "You didn't say that I had to be in class; you said that I had to sign the roll" unnerved me. Caught off guard, I swore at a student for the only time in my career. I blurted out: "Get the hell out of my classroom, and never come back."

As he turned and headed for the steps, he mumbled in a low but distinct voice "racist." Now really angry, I wouldn't let the issue drop and asked: "What was that? I'm not sure of what you said. Please repeat it." Without a word he continued up the steps, and I followed him, asking him several times to repeat his remark. He never did, and I dogged him until he reached the corridor.

His grade in the course was immediately determined. When I returned to my office, the teaching assistant in the course who had witnessed the scene came in and suggested that I give the student a second chance. My reply was unswerving: "One more word from you on that subject, and you're relieved from all course responsibility." I'm sure that the signing bonus that the student received in the NFL mollified his attitude and let him forget the F if he ever really cared, but I hope that he learned that, when the subject is attendance, racism is not an acceptable substitute. Did I overreact to both the student and the assistant?

FOUR

After a student misses excessive class time during a term (e.g., three weeks or 20 per cent of a course) due to illness or other personal problem, a discussion with an adviser is critical. Should that student attempt to complete the requirements of all his/her courses? What is best for both the student and the integrity of the total course load?

Generally the student wants to continue in all subjects without considering the consequences. If his/her schedule includes five courses and he elects to play "catch-up" in all five, success may be achieved in one or none. On the other hand, a decision to pursue only the three in which the course record is the most encouraging and write off the other two may provide the best chance to salvage part of the term. Proceeding with the full course load may place the student on probation or facing dismissal.

Thus a serious review of alternatives is an essential strategy, one that I proposed to any student who approached me after missing an abnormal amount of class time. When a student would not consider this plan of attack with either an adviser or me, I preferred not to have him continue in my course.

One of my students came to this crossroads and did not want to drop any courses. He was determined to remain in my class and tried to win my endorsement with a detailed description of his prolonged absence. I listened, politely refraining from laughter.

His rendition was a page out of his love life. According to his chronicle, his steady girlfriend and expected fiancée announced one day that she had acquired a significant other. My student was crushed emotionally—couldn't eat, sleep, or focus. A psychological wreck who couldn't study, he was unable to meet his university obligations, so he brooded at home.

One night during this troubled period, he dreamed of meeting his ex and her new love interest on the street, and the two men physically fought. While still dreaming, he rose from his bed, sleepwalking and shadowboxing as he wandered into the family's living room. Hearing an unidentified noise, his father charged into the darkened room.

At this point, if the tale had recounted how the father had clobbered his son over the head with a baseball bat and awakened him from his tortuous dream with a mighty swat, I would have viewed the incident as a plausible tragedy, but dreams often diverge sharply from reality. This one certainly did, taking a bizarre twist. The father wielded a less formidable weapon, a light switch. When he flicked it on, the brightness was so glaring that his startled son fell backward through a picture window onto a pile of cinders behind the house,—thus accounting for the cuts and bruises still visible on his face.

Unable to accept this version of the love triangle, I conjured up a more acceptable account, although it did not include a dream. According to my scenario, the three (my student, his ex, and her newly found love) did meet on the street, and the student's bumps and lumps represented the result of an altercation between the two young men.

I did not permit the conversation to expand beyond his revelation of the dream or suggest the validity of my assumption. I had to make a judgment concerning the student's continuation in the class. All of us can empathize with his disquieting love life. Would you believe his explanation for a three-week absence? Would you endorse his continuation in the course? Would you consider his account an adequate demonstration of creativity to entitle him to continue in the class? I did not accept any part of it.

FIVE

A weird student often makes weird requests, and I had one who never disappointed in that regard. Late one Friday afternoon, as I prepared to leave the office, the phone rang. I hesitated to answer, made the wrong decision, picked up the receiver, and heard an agitated voice. It was the weirdo. He could reach no one in the University's School of Medicine, so he expected me to help him contact the research office that, according to him, paid eighty dollars for a cadaver.

By suggesting that he wait until Monday and call the Medical School's information number, I tried to end the conversation without delving into the reason for such a request. Instinctively I knew that it was something that I didn't want to hear, but my ploy failed. He thought that I had on my desk a special phone directory containing such information and was now withholding it from someone in need. He insisted;

it was imperative that he receive the number NOW. Annoyed by his demanding tone, I asked: "How sick are you?"

"Nothing's wrong with me. I need the dough to party this weekend." He was naïve enough and desperate enough to think that, if he signed on the dotted line that day to will his body to science, the School of Medicine would hand him eighty dollars and be prepared to wait for his body, perhaps for 50 years, until he died of natural causes.

Although I knew none of the facts concerning the procurement of cadavers for research, I assured him that no sane person was about to give him money on such a cockamamie basis. I suggested the scenario that he might die across the country years later and that shipping the body back would be prohibitive in cost. On that note I asked: "Are you nuts?" and hung up. Too harsh?

CHAPTER 10

One Man, One Woman: Planets Apart

On every campus the basic interactions are between students and faculty. But, because all students have parents and many faculty members have spouses, it is inevitable that some members of these groups will impact a university scene. The two sketched below are my nominees for the most improbable characters representing these categories.

NATE'S WORLD

Nate, stamping on each step harder than on the one before and mumbling incoherent phrases, stormed up from his basement workshop. Still ranting as he reached the living room, he blurted out: "Those damned cats! I'm gonna kill 'em all." Desirous of halting him in mid-rant, his wife, Alma, abruptly interjected: "Dear, this is Jim Kehl, Dick's instructor, whom we invited to spend the evening."

That was my introduction to Nate. For me the exchange of greetings was awkward, because I felt embarrassed for all of us, particularly Nate. At that moment I assumed that, when he uttered his intemperate remarks, he believed that he was alone at home with only his wife and son. Later I suspected that his call for cat annihilation was staged to elicit my reaction.

Without knowing anything about my personality, he wanted to make a statement: "I'm who I am; I'm an incorrigible gadfly; accept me or reject me without hours of chitchat." By the end of the evening, he had erased all doubt that he was the consummate showman, enjoyed the role, and was anxious to demonstrate a mental acuity that always possessed a diabolical twist.

I had met Alma only minutes before Nate's declaring war on cats, and she had offered no hint of family dysfunction. Tall, slender, and friendly, she made me welcome immediately. Her salt-and-pepper hair gave the appearance of an older woman than I had imagined, but I hadn't had much time to reflect on her age before Nate's dramatic entrance. By the time of my departure, he gave me some clue to the graying of her hair.

Nate and Alma were proud parents of an 18-year-old son who, during the previous year, had been a history student of mine at the University of Pittsburgh. That was the extent of my connection with the couple before this fateful August evening in 1948.

One day during the preceding spring term, a student had pointedly asked if I would be teaching in the summer session because he wanted to consider scheduling one of my courses.

I said that I would not be teaching because of my plans to begin doctoral study at the University of Pennsylvania.

After that class period, another student, who had done little to erase his anonymity during the term and who had never initiated any informal discussion with me, came up and invited me to visit at this parents' home in Norristown while I was in Philadelphia that summer. Although nonplussed, I thanked him for the invitation, but added the caveat that I would be in touch if my schedule permitted.

Because I possessed no information with which to conjure up an image or understanding of what such a visit would entail, his proposal slipped from my mind. How large a family was it? Did they live in a house or an apartment? Would a total stranger be welcome if invited by a spur of the moment action? How formal and sociable was the family? Although I realized that it would be inappropriate to voice these questions, the answers would have prodded me to ponder the invitation seriously.

With no such knowledge available, I had no mental picture and was totally neutral on a visit; but on the final day of the term, Dick Pharoff reiterated his original invitation by presenting me with a card bearing his home address and phone number. At that moment I realized how seriously he viewed the invitation, especially when he added that his parents wanted me to know I would be most welcome. Thus I reaffirmed my conditional acceptance.

I had no idea how lonely and isolated that 18-year-old was when making that overture to me. The University of Pittsburgh at the time was primarily a commuter school with few dormitory accommodations; hence Dick's out-of-town status placed him at a disadvantage at the outset. Furthermore, he was assigned to an off-campus campus, where the enrollment was 100 percent male, of which 99 percent went home at night rather than to off-campus housing; also a majority were older World War II veterans who heard the beat of a different drummer than did a teenage freshman.

Without a burning passion for college, Dick had come to Pitt largely through the initiative of his roommate, a high school classmate and family friend. With a pharmacy degree as his goal, he was more sharply focused, and his science course requirements dictated that they be fulfilled on the main campus, where he met a more diverse group of students, including the coed who became his wife.

Although I don't think that Dick ever diagnosed his own dilemma, it was at the time a combination of homesickness, career confusion, and unintentional social ostracism. My comment to him concerning graduate study in Philadelphia struck a chord to which he could readily relate. I was going to be away from my home base, which caused him to conclude that I would welcome a friendly face. Apparently he wanted to be helpful because I had awakened his interest in learning; although he had not distinguished himself with a sterling performance, I assume that the invitation was his way of expressing empathy and appreciation.

One evening during my first summer in Philadelphia, feeling that I needed a change of pace from a study routine, I called the Pharoff residence and was encouraged to visit at my convenience. I accepted and was briefed on travel instructions: Take the westbound trolley to the 69th Street terminal and transfer to an interurban car programmed to express me to Norristown at the end of the line. On the appointed evening I followed the instructions and experienced an exhilarating ride in which the trolley had two speeds: 50-60 miles per hour or sudden stops, the latter to accommodate passengers at intermediate stations. Dick met me at the Norristown terminal, and we walked to the family's Stanbridge townhouse.

During the evening's conversation Dick's father returned to the incident that had brought him blustering up the stairs. Apparently neighborhood cats had interrupted his sleep the night before, and he was determined to confront the annoyance by simultaneously electrocuting all cats in the immediate area.

His strategy was to place a large bowl of milk on a steel sheet and charge it with electricity, but his cat-trap malfunctioned, shorted out, and left him with a superabundance of cats meowing their approval as they lapped heartily from the dish. Dick seemed undaunted by his father's revelation; Alma, who day-lighted as an industrial nurse in nearby Phoenixville, also took the announcement of the failed mass execution in stride. To them it was simply another of "the crazy inventor's" schemes gone awry.

At first I thought that I was being spoofed by all three, having never heard of this method of eliminating cat noises. That was overly suspicious, I'll admit, but I had no way of knowing that both mother and son were fully reconciled to Nate's unstoppable antics. They simply relaxed, joined the charade from time to time, and adopted a constructive attitude in helping him analyze what must be corrected to make the scheme workable. I was intrigued by Nate's vagary, but felt uncomfortable throughout that first encounter because neither Alma nor Dick had clued me in; I was left to interpret for myself.

I didn't comprehend the "crazy inventor" label that night, but over the next 25 years I came to understand that Nate's cynical attitude toward most people and issues prompted his skewed conduct. The most daring ploy that he pulled from his arsenal concerned Clem Phleym, an associate in an all-male club, who constantly bragged about his sexual prowess. Like Nate, most members were convinced that Clem exaggerated beyond the realm of possibility, but naturally no one could confront him with *prima facie* evidence to the contrary. Nate concocted a scheme to provide such incontrovertible proof and to place the issue of Clem's sexual performance at rest for all time.

He of the perverse mind proposed that, at the club's annual banquet, they should award a super door prize to a lucky individual: namely, a night with a hooker in a room at the motel where the banquet took place. The drawing was rigged so that Phleym would be the winner. To expose Clem thoroughly, Nate planned to wire the motel room in order to televise all that went on therein back to the banquet room, where the other members were still reveling and could receive a private viewing of Nate's X-rated production.

A room was rented for two days, because it took Nate that long to set up the surveillance equipment needed to telecast live coverage via remote control. There was much eating and drinking before the fateful drawing at which Clem became the "pigeon." He toasted his good fortune on winning with another Jack Daniels and set off for his date with the hired lady. All went as planned during the first stage; the picture, beamed into the banquet hall with perfect clarity, captured Clem entering the room. But he was so inebriated that he collapsed on the bed and slept into the night. The revelers watched with waning anticipation as the prostitute sat stoically knitting in a chair for her contracted two hours before walking out.

Nate's well-conceived scheme netted only catcalls from fellow club members for months to come. As he relayed the scam to me, Alma rejoiced over his fiasco and told him that he well deserved being the butt of club comments for the audacious undertaking.

Alma laughed with him as he recounted such tales, even when she disapproved. She accepted the fact that he was incorrigible and meant no harm, but sometimes his uproarious fun provided no redeeming quality. At times Dick stood askance at these actions, because he knew that his father's sense of humor would appall many outside the family. For some reason known only to Dick, he thought that I might relate to Nate's buffoonery.

Years later I remained as perplexed as ever. Why did this young man want me to meet his father? Although I was intrigued by the way Nate's mind seemed to work, chances were good that I would have been turned off by such antics. After all, Dick didn't know that my temperament possessed a flair for the unconventional, but he did know that his father had an ability to charm almost everyone he met. He apparently gambled that we were reasonably compatible, but in that situation I would have steered a more traditional course. If my father's mental elevator ran sideways, I wouldn't have invited one of my college instructors into the family circle for a demonstration. I'd be inclined to follow Lyndon Johnson's advice: If your mother-in-law has one eye in the middle of her forehead, you don't keep her in the living room.

Before I departed that first evening, Nate insisted that Alma snap a few pictures to mark the occasion. Being the family cinematographer, he directed her to take only action photos. Having a camera limited to still pictures, she inquired how that might be achieved. Nate grabbed the camera, directed Alma to pick up the teapot from the silver service on the coffee table and to place its spout in the breast pocket of my jacket. When she had fulfilled this assignment, he snapped the picture and declared it an action shot [pouring tea in pocket].

That demonstration ended my first visit to Stanbridge Street, but my impression of Nate was truly clouded. He talked much but revealed little of an intimate nature; in fact, he remained elusive throughout our acquaintance. A man of mystery, he was never straightforward about where he worked regularly or what he did. I gradually concluded that he was an assembly line/efficiency expert, particularly in regard to paper products with an emphasis on boxes. I also gathered that his day-to-day employment allowed enough flexibility for him to go on consulting junkets in his specialty whenever asked. This expertise commanded $500.00 or more per day when the average American worker was pleased to take home that amount in a month.

Nate's political thoughts were also an enigma. I have no idea whether he was a Republican or a Democrat, liberal or conservative. Probably he was turned off by politics in any form. As a youth in the late 1920s, he had served with the Marine occupation forces in Latin America, but he refused to be pinned down to Cuba, Haiti, or Nicaragua. Like Alma, he was of Russian-American extraction, but there was no trace of foreign culture anywhere around the house, except the occasional presence of Alma's bearded father, who spoke no English. In the few brief instances when he was present, Nate and Alma made a point of speaking to him in English while directing him with hand signals.

My second excursion to Norristown was scheduled for an afternoon when Dick proposed to take me on an aerial tour of Philadelphia. Both he and his dad held pilot licenses, and for a time they owned a plane based at the nearby PATCO airport that has since succumbed to progress. My low-level view of the City of Brotherly Love was informative—a panoramic impression that put my few prior reference points in context. After circling the city several times, we landed on a New Jersey airstrip, sipped a Coke, and flew back to PATCO.

In flying the plane, as in other situations, Nate was a Tom Sawyer show-off. When he would be arriving home from a trip, he would swoop down over their Stanbridge home and clang a cowbell kept aboard to alert Alma to have dinner on the table by the time he arrived from the airport.

Tending to give advice gratuitously, Nate was disappointed when it was not accepted. Once he warned a friend who operated the local hardware store that his security was being breached regularly by young thieves, who were stealing him blind. The friend ignored the comment, minimized the problem, and took no steps to prevent thefts. Nate then proceeded to demonstrate the wisdom in his admonition. Every time he was in the hardware store, he "lifted" something, took it home, and carefully placed it in his basement. When the total value of the "heists" reached $1,000.00, he invited his hardware friend to view his basement loot—proof to him that his warning was justified and that the enterprise needed stricter monitoring.

My visits tapered off to about two per year, until I graduated in 1954, and became even more irregular thereafter. Nate made certain that each visit provided live action or a graphic report or two of hijinks. As my graduation approached, Nate announced that he was going to take a day off to attend the ceremony. As he said somewhat dejectedly: "It may be the only graduation I'll ever attend." Dick had dropped out of school when he was within a year of completing requirements for a baccalaureate degree, because he hadn't settled on a career goal. Without that incentive he found college a waste. Because he held a pilot's license, the Air Force welcomed his decision to volunteer; and by 1954 he was flying for the Strategic Air Command and loving the challenge, because he understood the purpose behind what he was doing.

I stayed at the Pharoffs the night before graduation, and because of Nate's tardiness, we almost arrived late for the ceremony. He advised me not to fret; he would park my car and meet me after the exercises. With no alternative available, I acted on his suggestion, but before I could find my group of graduates, Nate had caught up with me. Surprised that he had been able to locate a parking spot so quickly, I inquired about his surprising good luck. Acknowledging his success, he explained that one had opened up on the street within a block of Philadelphia's Convention Hall, the site of the proceedings.

Not until after the ceremony did I realize that Nate had parked in front of a fire hydrant. Even though no ticket adorned the windshield when we returned, I was disturbed at his bold and illegal action. Nonchalant, Nate reminded me that special events are occasions for parking lots to charge higher rates, which would have been higher than the price of a parking ticket. Thus to him it was a clever move, and the price was right.

I was concerned about the principle of violating a city ordinance, whereas Nate saw it as a practical solution. I would have gladly paid the five-dollar parking charge while Nate enjoyed the excitement of living beyond the letter of the law. From a practical standpoint he considered it stupid to pass up the more convenient fire hydrant spot when the worst-case scenario equaled a fine of a similar amount. He thought it appropriate to ignore the law if he was prepared to pay the consequences for this or any other violation if he were called for an infraction.

Once back at the Pharoff residence, Nate insisted that dinner was his treat; he proposed to take Alma and me out in his new car. I accepted the invitation, but mentioning his car caused Alma to relate her first encounter with the purchase. She explained that, when she had attended her club meeting several weeks before, someone asked: "What's new?" Knowing nothing exciting, she replied "Nate bought a truck today." The Ford dealer's wife, sitting in the group, responded to that remark: "Alma, I was in the dealership today when your husband drove off in a new Lincoln Continental, not a truck."

Chagrined, Alma replied: "We didn't need a truck, but there's no anticipating what Nate might do. When he told me he had bought a truck, I accepted it and figured I'd learn more later." That night at home Alma questioned Nate about his purchase and why he had reported the Continental as a truck. He deferred to duck logic and explained: "It's as big as a truck; it can haul as much as a truck; it costs as much as a truck; it's a truck."

Agreed that we would drive Nate's truck to dinner, I insisted that we select a restaurant within a half hour's drive, because I wanted to return to Pittsburgh that night. Nate proclaimed that he had identified an exclusive hideaway that I had to try. We drove off with me describing the morning's ceremony to Alma.

When I looked up, Nate had just turned onto the newly opened Northeast Extension of the Pennsylvania Turnpike. Agitated, I asked where we were headed. "Allentown" was his response. I reminded him: "That's 50 miles away, certainly more than a half hour." Nate was ready with the answer: "It's only 45 miles, and that's a half hour." With that revelation he accelerated until the speedometer registered 90 MPH, and true to his word, within 30 minutes he slammed on the brakes before his chosen eatery.

The meal took longer than anticipated, and I agreed to stay over until the next morning if the return from Allentown were at a more leisurely pace. Back in the Pharoff living room, Nate looked at me and said: "By the way that's a God-awful necktie you're wearing. Did you cut a piece off the end of the tablecloth and drape it around your neck? I bought a gross of beauties the other day. Go upstairs and pick out a dozen from those in the top drawer of my dresser."

That was his way of telling me he wanted to give me a dozen ties. I protested against accepting his generosity but agreed to go up and look. After I was about five steps up, he yelled: "Don't take 13; I have other friends, you know." I couldn't resist and shot back: "Name one." Of course, he and Alma loved the exchange because most individuals never challenged him. Perhaps that was the key to our strange attraction; Nate's pranks and my sometime wit played off each other.

The next morning as I was about to leave, Nate advised me that, because of construction on the approach ramp at the King of Prussia entrance to the Pennsylvania Turnpike, he would direct me to an alternate approach. Because both his car and mine needed gas, we agreed to drive to the station he regularly patronized. I knew where it was located, so he went ahead while I thanked Alma for her hospitality. When I reached the service station, I saw Nate chasing a kid through an adjoining meadow where the grass was 15-18 inches high.

Nate returned without the kid, his trousers soaked up to the knees from the morning dew; out-of-breath and red-faced, he was in a foul mood. I asked for an explanation and received what I considered a laughable response, although Nate had a totally different "read." Apparently the kid began pumping the gas and thoughtlessly looked up and asked: "What's an old man like you doing with twin tailpipes?"

Still out of breath and angry, Nate said, so that all bystanders at the station could hear: "I don't take that 'old man shit' from anyone." I roared in laughter, and Nate smiled sheepishly, but his ego had been wounded. I always knew that he was proud of his youthful appearance; never was his vanity more vividly on display.

At one time I had remarked that he could pass for Dick's brother. That must have endeared me to him, but it was a fact. Anyone who did not know the Pharoffs might have assumed at first meeting that they represented three generations, with Dick, who had a pallid face and receding hairline, to be the father and Nate the chubby son. Alma readily admitted that she looked the oldest, because she had grown that way from living with Nate and his antics. Buying a gross of neckties or socks, or telling tall tales, or walking through a grocery store clandestinely placing unwanted items in unsuspecting customers' carts represented only the tip of the iceberg in his repertoire of atypical conduct.

One day the unthinkable happened; Nate didn't feel up to his normal abnormality. Upon examination Alma suggested that he go to the hospital for a check-up. Because they both knew many of the doctors and nurses, he consented to go so that he might kibitz with them since he hadn't enjoyed that pleasure for a while. In the face of Nate's youthful, healthy appearance, he was shocked by the findings; the doctors diagnosed his condition as a mild heart attack. This he was not prepared to accept. As soon as he heard the report, he declared himself cured and angrily proclaimed that "the damned doctors are quacks;" someone as physically fit as he thought he was couldn't possibly have had a heart attack.

Nate demanded an immediate release, but his plea was rejected; thereupon he set out to make everyone in the hospital miserable. He proceeded to get the elevator stuck between floors, poured apple juice in the specimen bottle, gratuitously diagnosed other patients, and when advised that he needed a laxative, protested. After considerable negotiation, he relented, provided that he could select "his own poison." The staff concurred, and he ordered sauerkraut juice. The hospital reported: "None on hand," so he refused further compromise, and negotiations were back to square one. In due course the doctors asked Alma to take him home because he was upsetting the whole hospital; out of consideration for her fellow nurses, she complied.

Nate was happy but still contemptible. Upon arriving home Alma went into the house expecting him to follow. Instead he walked around the house; placed a 24-foot extension ladder against the structure, and climbed to the top. From there he yelled: "Alma, I told you those damned doctors were quacks. If I suffered a heart attack, how the hell can I be up here?" To coax him down, she agreed that the doctors had made a mistake. Fortunately there were no repercussions from the whole ordeal, and life returned to normal—as normal as Nate would permit it to become.

His pranks, however, necessitated a second visit to the hospital, but the nurses experienced no repeat harassment. This second visit came about suddenly when a neighbor girl several houses up in their complex was going out on a date. As she and her escort strolled down the walk, Nate decided to embarrass her by shouting: "That's not the guy you went out with last night, is it?" Concentrating so intently on observing her reactions, he didn't see a kid's skate that was left on his own sidewalk. He tripped over it, broke his ankle, and agonized over another clever idea that had misfired.

At the ridiculous end of the scam chart was Nate's most unforgettable encounter with another neighbor, Frank Pruitt, who lacked any appreciation for Nate's twisted sense of humor. When a second neighbor placed the sale of his house in the hands of a realtor, Nate decided that the colors on the For Sale sign clashed with the color scheme of the house and concluded that it would be more artistically displayed on Frank's lawn.

The sign was held in place by a stiff wire at each side; the ends were jammed into the ground and could be easily removed by a sudden thrust upward. In keeping with his artistic whimsy, Nate went out late at night on several occasions and relocated the sign to Frank's yard. Humorous only to Nate, the transfer angered Frank, who had no intention of selling his house.

One evening as the neighbors gathered informally for a chat, Frank expressed his displeasure. Everyone agreed that the sign-transfer was a despicable deed and that, when caught, the guilty neighborhood kids should be punished. No one was more vociferous in condemning the action than Nate. Frank had alerted the police several times, but no culprit was apprehended. He declared that he was going to sit behind his living room drapery with a shotgun and pepper the instigator personally if the sign were transferred to his yard one more time.

Nate interpreted this as a challenge. Several evenings later, just at twilight, he and Alma were seated on their front porch swing when they realized that Frank was true to his word. His drapery moved ever so slightly several times to indicate that he was in place to trap the sign snatcher. Nate remarked to his wife that Frank really didn't know how to enjoy life and that this was probably the most excitement he had ever experienced and couldn't handle it.

With Alma's "Yes, dear," the subject was dropped, but a few minutes later Nate suggested that they should host a Fourth of July party for the neighbors. Always up for a party, she agreed. Nate slyly suggested that Frank should be invited, adding that he was probably the most difficult to pin down on a holiday.

To check the social pulse of the neighbors, he suggested that Alma begin by calling Frank to ask if he could attend. Nate knew that Frank's phone was in the rear of the house (this predated portables) and that he would have to leave his guard post to answer it. When he heard Alma inside their house talking on the phone, Nate knew that contact with Frank had been made, sprinted full speed to capture the For Sale sign, pull it up, run across the street, and jam it into Frank's lawn.

Frank never suspected the source of his grief. It certainly could not have come from the husband of the woman inviting him to a festive celebration; in fact, Nate was so convincing that Alma didn't realize that she was an unwitting part of the deception until Nate laughed about it afterwards.

Unfortunately devastating tragedies struck Nate's world of foolhardy showmanship. Although Dick's withdrawal from college was a major disappointment, his success in the Air Force softened the blow. While on active duty in the Seattle area, Dick met Jean, the girl he hoped to marry. He wrote to me for advice, confiding that he had tried to explain his father to her. He suspected that she failed to grasp the full impact of Nate's lack of conformity to social norms. Cognizant that his father was one of a kind, Dick wanted to know if I thought he should marry Jean before he introduced her to his parents or if it was safe to take a chance on a transcontinental visit before tying the knot.

I provided no direct answer and stressed that neither choice was more likely to be fatal than the other. Dick ultimately decided to marry first, but all the Pharoffs came to love Jean, who reciprocated their affection. Dick announced that he planned to finish college and enroll in medical school if accepted. In due course he was admitted to the Pennsylvania College of Osteopathy. To minimize expenses they lived with his parents. All seemed serene. Jean was expecting, and as a nurse Alma was ready to assist if needed. Then the first major calamity struck; the baby was born with Down's syndrome. The Pharoffs assumed all costs and placed the baby in a suitable health care facility.

With his medical studies completed, Dick elected to practice in California where, unlike Pennsylvania at that time, osteopathic graduates were accepted on a par with medical school doctors. He and his wife selected Los Angeles, where Dick happily threw himself into his practice, which provided the long sought channel for his talents—one that not only delighted his parents but also offered self-satisfaction.

In time Jean became the mother of two more boys whom, the grandparents admired, mostly from a distance. Overworked by the Watts Riots, Dick came home on the afternoon of his 34th birthday and stretched out on the couch, before a planned dinner with Jean to celebrate. After thirty minutes she checked to see how soon he would be ready to leave only to discover that he had died of a heart attack. The Pharoffs never fully recovered.

With Dick's death, Nate lost all enthusiasm not only for his pranks but also for life itself. In time Jean remarried; unfortunately both Pharoffs considered this an affront to Dick's memory. That estrangement meant that contact with the two California grandsons was almost lost.

One day at work Nate was fatally injured in a truck accident. I was in Pittsburgh at the time and could not go to Norristown. Alma was so broken in spirit that she could give no details. Although I talked with her by phone regularly, she could only sob when she touched on the circumstances surrounding the accident. To no avail, she was seeking rational answers to her losses; unable to eat or sleep on a regular basis, she sobbed until her last breath was gone. Nate's world too was gone, survived only in memory and shared by those with the stamina to endure it.

DISABLED MABEL

A strange invitation often heralds a strange party. Sixty years ago as a fledgling history instructor, I first experienced this ominous combination.

Invited to my first social event by a senior faculty member, I assumed that he was showing appreciation for a favor extended that summer. After a second reading of the "invite," I realized that I had no clue to the nature of the event to which I had been politely summoned.

The stated arrival time, 6:00 PM, was a little late for a tea or punch party (a cocktail party seemed beyond the realm of possibility for the Jamisons), but there was no hint that dinner would be served. Always a chowhound, I knew that arriving on an empty stomach could mean hours of discomfort if no food was offered. On the other hand, eating in advance would not enable me to do justice to any repast the Jamisons had in mind. I compromised, with a large snack at home before departing for this ill-defined party.

I parked on their quiet, secluded street at the rim of Schenley Park Golf Course at 5:57 PM. Waiting three minutes, I punched the doorbell at the designated hour. After a reasonable pause, Mrs. Jamison answered and welcomed me with a polite smile.

Because I was the first guest to arrive, the appearance of the living room triggered a mental alarm. Was I at least an hour or two early? After more careful surveillance, I surmised that maybe I had appeared on the wrong day. Nothing about the room suggested that a festive event was about to unfold: no peanuts, pretzels, or potato chips scattered about in little dishes; no napkins or coasters present; in short, no hors d'oeuvres of any type were in sight.

Politely, even apologetically, I asked if I were early and was assured that I was "right on time," a comment that belied all physical evidence. Obviously Mrs. J. was no party animal. Their living room could only be described as an untidy Early American work in progress. The rug was rolled up against one wall, a custom outdated by more than a half century practiced to prevent the sun's rays from fading the carpet during the summer months. By observation I concluded that Mabel was continuing to observe this outmoded practice.

To keep the rolled rug in place, a rectangular walnut table with an open front and a bookshelf on each side, was strategically lodged against it. A cardboard box, now filled with history books but originally home to 48 cans of Carnation Condensed Milk, graced the area beneath the table with the milk company's Carnation logo and familiar slogan, "from contented cows" clearly visible on the side of the box. I recognized the box immediately, because our family regularly substituted Carnation for fresh milk. As a kid I had jokingly needled my parents with two questions on the subject: Did all other milk come from discontented cows? How could animal psychologists determine the degree of cow anxiety?

At the moment my own anxiety was running a bit high, because the books and rolled-up rug suggested a family about to move. The windows gave off the same vibes: no draperies or curtains, only empty curtain rods and window blinds pulled below half-mast. I was convinced that the family was at least in the midst of a thorough housecleaning—not on the verge of merrymaking.

The minutes dragged aimlessly, with Mrs. Jamison divulging nothing to clarify the reason for any gathering. I tried to fill the dead air with a mundane monologue about the weather, the view from the picture window, and the serenity of the golf course surroundings.

Out of ideas and a little panicky, I decided to be direct. I had assumed that her husband was in the upstairs study and did not realize that the first guest had arrived and that, in her usual befuddled state, Mabel had failed to alert him. Not confident that that was correct, my mind wandered and speculated that perhaps he was ill and she didn't know how to convey that message. Although indiscreet, I blurted out: "Do you think that Dr. Jamison will be down soon?" To that she was direct, and I became the one who was speechless: "Oh! He's in Washington this week, at the Library of Congress." Thus ended that line of speculation.

[Readers: Do not assume that you can write the next paragraphs. I was not about to be seduced by my own Mrs. Robinson. This encounter was unfolding almost 20 years before the filming of *The Graduate*, and my hostess was no Mrs. Robinson. I stood absolutely clueless concerning what was about to transpire.]

The background to my role in this supposed soiree had been brief, occurring during the first two weeks of that August when I taught an evening course in recent American history. Without benefit of air conditioning, the schedule was grueling, because I was behind the lectern from 6:00 to 9:00 PM for two weeks, Monday through Friday.

Although evening students' ages varied over a broader range of years than did full time day students, 45 generally represented the top of the age scale. Before the start of the first session of this particular course, I casually looked around the classroom. My eye was quickly drawn to an older woman in the back row; her appearance suggested that she could have been the mother of the next oldest student in the group. Crowded to capacity, the room was nevertheless not congested enough to obscure her presence.

Clad in a black ensemble with a matching pillbox on her head and a clutch purse on her lap, she appeared to have stopped by on her way home from a funeral or high tea. Sitting erect, head straight forward revealing a sad face with pursed lips and granny-glasses, she gave the impression that she had come to mourn rather than to learn. Her body language shouted: "I don't want to be here."

She appeared to be 80 and dressed in clothes that required carbon-dating to authenticate, but I knew that she was in her mid-60s and reluctant to embrace the present. The notepad on her desk, although larger than a postage stamp, could record a small grocery list but little more. No typical student, she had obviously left her link to reality at home in the dresser drawer.

I couldn't believe the spectacle: The wife of a senior member of the History faculty had enrolled in my course. What could I teach her that she hadn't heard from her husband expressed with deeper insights than anything I could add.

After the first hour and a half of lecture, I gave the class a ten-minute break. At that juncture, the woman from the back row came to the lectern to introduce herself (her identity was no mystery to me) and to announce that she was just auditing.

That was a relief. Although I felt confident with my class procedures, she made it clear that she would take no tests; that, in turn, meant that I would not have to evaluate her performance and have my grading system critiqued by one of my superiors. She added that her husband had assured her that the course would be enjoyable. At that moment, I didn't know if "enjoyable" meant that I was an engaging lecturer or a charming entertainer. In time I realized that it meant that my course was scheduled at the proper time to occupy the wife for 30 hours during those two weeks while the professor worked.

Gradually the pieces began to assume an intelligible focus. Professor AP Jamison was encountering a little difficulty in meeting a publisher's deadline on a manuscript and thought that three additional hours of peace and quiet each evening for that fortnight would return his writing to the established schedule. That could be achieved if someone could "baby sit" his wife for that period; with that knowledge, I understood the reason for her presence in my classroom.

Because the Jamisons regularly spent their evenings together, Mabel was reluctant to surrender her husband's company for that two-week period without a satisfying alternative, and I had become the designated substitute. Unfortunately the television set had not yet become a household fixture in Pittsburgh, but even if it had, the Jamisons probably would not have allowed this new technology to intrude in their lives. Before investing, they would have elected to wait to make certain that it was not a passing fad. In fact, five years elapsed before the professor's retirement, but no TV screen ever lit up their living room.

Although she was a shrew, a prude, and a helpless clinging vine, Mabel had mastered a technique that caused her to be the envy of many wives, a secret surpassing anything Victoria ever contemplated. She had convinced her husband, a justly proud Rhodes scholar who catered to his wife's every whim, that food preparation made her ill. Her argument was so compelling that the couple ate breakfast and dinner at restaurants seven days a week. At noon Professor Jamison dined at the University's Faculty Club, and Mabel munched on crackers at home. For the two weeks of my class, this routine was slightly altered; he took his wife to an early dinner, deposited her at my classroom door, and headed for his office and a few hours focused on his project.

After the course concluded, Mabel explained to the department chairman's wife that I was a "funny man." That didn't do much to erase the possible entertainer image that I thought AP might have painted for his wife, but it did mean that she was satisfied. Thus I guess that I didn't "strike out" in my assignment.

Within a week of the term's end, I received the infamous invitation to the six o'clock party to be held ten days hence. I incorrectly assumed that my inclusion in the Jamisons' gathering was the professor's expression of appreciation for accepting Mabel as an auditor. But the "He's in Washington" comment exploded that theory.

Almost down for the count, I was ultimately rescued by the bell—the doorbell. Mabel ushered in and introduced two of her "sorority sisters." The three of them may have belonged to the same sorority but not in the same generation. Our hostess had 40 years seniority on the arrivals. Much later I concluded that the sorority's local chapter sponsored a reception that included all members living in the area, regardless of age. Mabel had answered that call and met the girls there.

How this shy prude "engineered" the girls' invitations to our exclusive party will ever remain a mystery. Intimidated by the telephone (when someone other than her husband or son was on the line), she probably summoned them by note. Most likely each sorority sister was provided with a list of names and addresses of all who attended the reception in order to stimulate future social interactions without anyone anticipating my hostess's subsequent perversion of the intent.

Both of the new arrivals were about my age (mid-twenties), one a strawberry blonde and the other a striking brunette. They were nattily attired, pleasant, reserved, and—like me— perplexed because they had no hint concerning the reason for their presence. While Mabel sat idly by, we exchanged a little information about our backgrounds; in the process, I learned that both girls worked in the health care field at the University. As we were in the midst of self-discoveries, Mabel called upstairs for her son, William, to join the happy throng.

Dressed casually, Bill, in my opinion, had no more knowledge than we did about the "crew" being assembled. He descended to the living room, undoubtedly thinking that he was alone in the house with his mother. If he was aware that any guests had been invited, he was a superb actor. Obviously he had met neither sorority sister, but he and I were acquainted because he was taking graduate courses in the History Department at the time.

Bill's personality lacked a capacity to breathe life into this moribund party. A shy, slightly overweight man about my age with a round bespectacled face, he was cursed with a high-pitched voice. His chief claim to fame was an ability to recite railroad time schedules, including intermediate stops, for all "Pennsy" passenger runs between Philadelphia and Chicago. In those days, the trips were many because air travel had not yet surpassed the clickety-clack of rail cars, and Bill's recall was prodigious. Because none of us shared his special talent or was about to embark on a whistle-stop tour to any destination, Bill's input didn't jump-start the group's evening.

I anticipated the arrival of other guests who might bring clarification to this incongruous assembly, but unfortunately we represented the total guest list. Conversation again lagged hopelessly. When Mabel sensed that it had reached the point of all lag and no talk, she whipped open a photo album lying strategically on the walnut table. Capturing her youth in Wisconsin from her bicycling days to a 1912 picture of the touring car in which she had learned to drive, the volume became the conversation focal point for 45 minutes.

The evening turned into a clock-watcher. When two hours had elapsed from the moment I unsuspectingly entered the house of social horrors and we had reached the end of the first volume, I was still mystified. Apologizing insincerely for being a party pooper, I announced that it was time to depart. Because I had arrived first, it seemed logical that I take the first step to break up this unforgettable "bash." Not having been offered a glass of water or a peanut, I was grateful that I had the foresight to eat something before joining this happy gala.

Mabel stood aghast at my comment and exclaimed: "But you haven't had anything to eat yet! You can't go!" Short of peeking into the refrigerator, I saw no evidence that she expected to serve anyone anything. The possibility of food here seemed far more remote than the crisis faced by the Biblical multitude with only five loaves and two fishes.

Spurred by my impending departure, Mabel reached for her purse, pulled out several dollars, and instructed Bill to run down to the corner drugstore and bring back "some soda pops and potato chips." Like a dutiful son, he took off and shortly returned with his purchases. We all partook, and I soon acted on my original impulse to get the hell out of there. The girls followed my lead so closely that I had the privilege of holding the door for them.

Later I reflected on that evening and realized that I had been on a blind date without knowing it; in fact, it was so blind that I didn't know whether it was the strawberry blonde, the brunette, or neither. I concluded this only after learning that Bill had been dating a girl who worked at a restaurant, and his mother thought that he was socializing beneath the family dignity. To direct him to her concept of the high road, she contrived this little party to have him meet girls from the sorority circle. I was invited as window-dressing or a pawn.

I'll readily admit that Mabel demonstrated good taste in the choice of girls, but as a matchmaker, her technique was atrocious. If those girls are among us today, they are probably still wondering what that evening was all about. To them, it must have remained more of an enigma than it was to me. At least I had a background on which to hang my theories.

Even when we became better acquainted, I never mentioned the incident to Professor Jamison, a stately Virginian devoted to his wife. Afraid that the details would have been an embarrassment, his son probably adopted the same course and never brought up our common night of endless gaiety. Perhaps Bill never discussed the subject, because he remained as confused as the rest of us. To have had a microphone hidden in the living room after the two girls and I departed would have, I am sure, produced more excitement than we generated all evening. Mabel must have tripped over her tongue a few times attempting to explain to Bill what she thought she had maneuvered. It was undoubtedly a classic in double-speak.

My hostess was obviously a fragile person, and her husband went beyond the call of duty to preserve her stability. Stoic in every way, he always referred to her as Mrs. Jamison, never as Mabel, and never uttered a disparaging word. Almost everyone in the History Department, young and old alike, who understood the relationship, expressed empathy for him.

When one of the younger members of the staff planned to attend a national history conference in Madison, Wisconsin, he invited Professor Jamison to accompany him and his wife. Believing that this might be the old gentleman's last opportunity to associate with his colleagues throughout the profession, as he had done annually in earlier years, Jack was eager to assist in providing him with an enjoyable experience.

AP was overwhelmed by the invitation, because he was not accustomed to having others extend kindnesses or to extending them himself. Reluctantly he declined the offer but added that, if Mrs. Jamison were included, he might respond otherwise. With trepidation, Jack and his wife rephrased the invitation to make it inclusive, a concession not to be forgotten.

First, Mabel had to impose her touch of security before the house could safely be left unattended. This translated into having the gas lines to the hot water heater and to the furnace shut off. She had once heard that a faulty gas valve had caused a house fire while the residents were out of town; the moral she took from this incident was that she wanted no such calamity to befall her. AP accepted the fact that the temperature in the house could drop below freezing during their absence and that the water pipes could freeze and split open, resulting in a call to the plumber. He was resigned to the inevitable; it had happened several times before and had curtailed his desire to travel, especially during the winter months. Acceptance of these conditions was part of the price for living with Mabel.

As Jack was about to pull away from the curb for their Midwest jaunt, Mabel remembered that she had to return to the house to retrieve a family "strong box." Because she did not trust safe deposit boxes, important documents such as property deeds, marriage license, car title, and birth certificates were kept in this locked metal chest that always accompanied her when out of town. This cumbersome container could not be relegated to the trunk of the car, so space had to be allotted in the passenger compartment where Mabel could guard it with her eye. As a result, it became nestled on the back seat between the Jamisons.

A few hundred miles into the trip, Mabel became bored and began to reminisce about her early life in Wisconsin, including the story about her first experience with an automobile. In the course of her recitations, Jack learned that, as the car speed increased, her thought patterns were diminished. Thus speed became the most effective means to curtail her tales. If he drove fast enough, she lapsed into total silence and sat on the edge of the seat in trepidation. With mouth and eyes wide open, she attempted from the back seat to catch an undetected glimpse of the speedometer. Jack's speed technique proved successful both on the trip to the convention and on the way home. Mabel was a challenge, but AP uttered not a word.

On several occasions after that fated trip, Jack and I exchanged thoughts about the Jamisons' lifestyle. One of the numerous curiosities that intrigued us was the couple's decision to build a more modern house two miles from the one on Chesterfield Road. We couldn't understand their motivation for change, because neither one, particularly Mabel, exhibited modern tastes. Perhaps her reluctance to move from the first house explains why they retained it as a rental property.

This proved to be a poor investment of their funds because of the abnormal restrictions to which Mabel insisted that renters adhere (i.e., no parties with alcohol, no gas to the furnace when out of town). This meant that either the house stood vacant for long periods or the rent was ridiculously low in order to entice renters who would conform.

Ten years after her unforgettable appearance in my classroom, a young man joining the History staff was in desperate need of housing. At that time, the Jamisons' Chesterfield house was not rented. I mentioned its availability, adding that he and his wife would have to stand for Mrs. Jamison's personal inspection. They were interested, were instructed concerning adherence to the stringent rules, but surprisingly they were excused from having to shut off the gas when leaving the house overnight. By the late 1950s, Mabel apparently had come to accept the furnace as a non-lethal, even a non-hazardous piece of equipment.

One unstated and unthinkable part of the contractual negotiations provided the owners with the presumptive right to personal visits to the house at any time. Mabel at least assumed that was part of the pact. One day at noon, when the wife was upstairs preparing to leave for an appointment, she heard a key turn in the front door lock. She called down to inquire who was there and heard a frail, squeaky voice: "It's only Mrs. Jamison. I came over to have lunch with my old house. I'll be in the basement, in front of the furnace with my crackers." That "love affair" with the house was further evidence of Mabel's weird and wacky world and proof that, in Mabel's life, the past was never past.

EPILOGUE

Over the seven decades that I have been associated with the University, change has repeatedly worked and reworked its magic. By 1940 Pitt was firmly established as a streetcar school, an image that it retained for another 15 years. Since then it has dramatically evolved successively into a regional, state, and national institution with programs that have achieved international distinction.

The development of Pitt as a "school for locals" was a deliberate act. Not only Chancellor Bowman but also the region's industrial, financial, and philanthropic leaders of the early 20th Century joined in the project. The mills and mines that emerged along the Allegheny, Ohio, and Monongahela rivers lured thousands of immigrants from all parts of Europe. Pittsburgh became the nation's ninth largest city, and with Allegheny and surrounding counties, it was a mega-center of economic stability. The region's developers recognized that the mushrooming population that they had attracted required a higher education base to satisfy the needs of the area they sponsored.

Immigrant families, as well as longer established residents, were eager to push their children to a higher level of education than they themselves had enjoyed. Thus a plethora of students traveled daily by bus, trolley, and train from as far as McKeesport, Washington, Beaver, and other commuter points to attend University classes. Anyone who came from a greater distance generally required local living accommodations and was at the mercy of the Pittsburgh community to provide them. Several rooming houses existed, but a basic lack of University housing discouraged distant applications. This pattern demonstrates that University planners focused only on the needs of the immediate area.

Fraternities and sororities offered limited assistance to out-of-town students who had to live somewhere and became "Greeks" to simplify their problem. Furthermore, these organizations generally owned their own houses, sometimes with rooms to rent to non-members. This availability aided the fraternities/sororities financially and gave the University a broader appeal, limited though it was, to students in need of housing.

The aftermath of World War II was not enough to spur the University to develop dormitories. In fact, the University experienced a major difficulty in finding classroom space for students who lived within the "street car radius," and by then the increasing number of students arriving by auto, as well as by the traditional conveyances, complicated the education task. Not until Chancellor Litchfield purchased the Schenley Apartments and the Schenley Hotel could the University declare that it truly had residence halls for students.

At first Oakland businesses were pleased with his acquisitions, but as Litchfield continued to acquire property for University expansion, they became alarmed lest their district be recast and overshadowed by a sprawling campus. One group angrily identified Litchfield's approach as "Today, Oakland! Tomorrow, the world!"

Expansion of the University's physical facilities was accompanied by increased enrollments that, in turn, were joined by an upgrade in quality of students, faculty, and programs. All of this was achieved while the University was still a private institution, receiving minimal state funds. As a result of this rapid growth, University finances were strained until the state assumed part of the burden in 1966, when Pitt attained state-related status.

Publicly at least, Litchfield was opposed to state-relatedness, which did not come until his successor, Chancellor Crawford, negotiated the arrangement with the State Legislature. Primarily with private funds supplied by local philanthropists, Litchfield had transformed the University into an internationally recognized institution. The single most significant accomplishment on this road to academic prominence was the endowment of the Andrew W. Mellon Professorships and Fellowships.

The years of Chancellor Posvar (1967-1991) enlarged upon this beginning, but the most notable achievement for which Posvar is credited came in the area of civil rights. He directed the rapid expansion of the number of African-Americans both on the faculty and in the student body. University rules and regulations were adapted to civil rights laws, and rigorous enforcement was carried out. Although the observance of civil rights for all is an on-going process for both the University and society at large, the Posvar administration and those that followed have retained a sterling watch-dog attitude toward policy adherence.

In the 1990s the University hit a plateau; but with the appointment of Chancellor Mark Nordenberg, the institution resumed its march toward excellence, and in various ways offers the results of its classrooms and laboratories as gifts to the community and the world.

With regularity, tidbits of such information proclaiming the University's contributions to society cross my desk. Recently, for example, I learned that the *Princeton Review* (2011) listed Pitt as the only Pennsylvania public institution among the top 50 educational values available for students in the nation's public colleges and universities.

At approximately the same time, I learned that in research Pitt ranks fifth among all American universities in terms of National Institutes of Health grants awarded to individual faculty members. Perhaps this explains why *Saviors of Our Cities* (2009) ranked Pitt first among American public universities in university-city partnerships. Such facts bring our memories to the realization that our generation has played a distinct role in the ever-evolving change. The University meanwhile stands as an enduring synthesizer of change, melding our generation's contributions into those of the past, as well as into those still beyond the horizon.

ABOUT THE AUTHOR

James A. Kehl was educated in the schools of Pennsylvania, ultimately receiving a Ph.D. from the University of Pennsylvania. He served as a Navy officer during World War II (1944-46) and participated in the invasions of the Philippines (Luzon) and Okinawa. In 1997 he published a human interest account of his Navy experience in a volume titled, *When Civilians Manned the Ships: Life in the Amphibious Fleet during World War II.*

James Kehl, Author

Photo courtesy of Herb Ferguson, University of Pittsburgh

Following the war Jim was appointed to the staff of the History Department at the University of Pittsburgh and remained in that capacity for 46 years (1946-92) after which he was named Professor Emeritus. For 11 of those years he simultaneously served as a University administrator, culminating in his appointment as dean of the College of Arts and Sciences. He also taught briefly at the Carnegie Institute of Technology (now CMU) and at The Pennsylvania State University (Middletown Campus).

Dr. Kehl's field of expertise was the history of American Political Parties and during his tenure he authored two books: *Ill Feeling in the Era of Good Feeling* and *Boss Rule in the Gilded Age.* He also published numerous scholarly articles and received various honor society awards, plus a Meritorious Award from Phi Alpha Theta (History honorary) and a Distinguished Alumnus Award extended by the College of Arts and Sciences Alumni Association in 1969.

During retirement he volunteered as a Meals-on-Wheels driver for 18 years in the Pittsburgh area where he lives with his wife Barbara.

WA